# An *Extraordinary Tale of Travel*

**Steve Hannes**

An Extraordinary Tale of Travel

Copyright © 2019 by Steve Hannes

All rights reserved. No part of this book may be used or reproduced in any manner whatsoever without written permission from the author, except in the case of brief quotations embodied in articles and reviews.

Published by Bonfire Books Publishing House

ISBN: 978-0-578-50888-7

Cover and interior design by Deborah Perdue, Illumination Graphics

# TABLE OF CONTENTS

Introduction .................................................................... 1

Chapter One        A little road trip ................................... 3

Chapter Two        My circumstances and whereabouts
                   immediately preceding the journey ........ 61

Chapter Three      Home ...................................................... 65

Chapter Four       Crossing the Atlantic ............................... 71

Chapter Five       The Holy Land ........................................ 107

Chapter Six        Culture Shock ......................................... 133

Chapter Seven      South of the Border ............................... 139

Chapter Eight      North of the Border ............................... 175

Chapter Nine       The Belmont Hotel ................................. 179

Chapter Ten        A Wasted Winter .................................... 185

Chapter Eleven     India and Beyond ................................... 189

Chapter Twelve     Overland to India .................................. 255

# INTRODUCTION

I had always dreamed of travel. But how does one make it happen? Where does one begin?

And I had barely any money.

Why don't I hitchhike from Baltimore to California? Seemed as logical a plan as any for a guy who had reached the age of twenty-four and still had not a clue what he should do with his life.

Thus, the journey commenced. Nothing complicated. I simply walked out to the highway and stuck out my thumb. And my directionless existence would finally find purpose in a six year odyssey spent wandering the planet Earth with a backpack on my back.

The extraordinary tale of which is told within these pages.

## Chapter One

## A LITTLE ROAD TRIP

I had a crazy idea to hitchhike from Baltimore to California. On a mid-August morning in the summer of 1972, with a mere one hundred dollars in my pocket and a backpack on my back, I walked out to the highway and stuck out my thumb.

The first driver to pull over carried me a distance of four hundred miles, to the city of Cincinnati, and offered me a safe place to sleep in his home for the night. The following night I made my bed in a patch of woods on the side of the road somewhere in the state of Missouri, and on the third day of my journey across America, a young woman, the sole navigator of a Volkswagen van, delivered me to the Rocky Mountain state of Colorado.

Julie brought the vehicle to a stop at a narrow crossroads in the far reaches of a vast evergreen wilderness that saw no beginning and had no end.

"I turn off for my college here," she said. "I can't take you any further."

Under a dark and foreboding sky I stepped out to the winding mountain road. A driving rain began to fall.

Stranded in the eye of a hammering tempest, I stood at eight thousand feet, chilled to the bone and close to despair. I watched cars come rolling round the rain drenched misty mountain bend and pass me by. A vehicle finally slowed down and came to a stop.

Through the splashing windshield I could see two young guys sitting in the front seat. I jumped in, thanked them with overwhelming appreciation and apologized for the water dripping from my plastic poncho onto the back seat of their car.

"No problem," the driver replied. "We're glad to help. It's damn nasty out there."

A couple of guys in their early twenties from Peoria, Illinois, Bob and Jimmy were on their way to a Rocky Mountain resort. Their hometown friend Carol had spent the summer waitressing in the resort's dining room and had arranged for them to stay free of charge for a week. From there they would spend a few days at the Grand Canyon before returning to Peoria.

We rolled through the torrential downpour, over winding pine forested mountain roads. To my astonishment, Bob and Jimmy invited me to not only join them at the mountain resort, but all the way to the Grand Canyon as well.

By the time we arrived the storm had passed, dark clouds drifted away and a beautiful Colorado sky spread like a sparkling blue pearl across the Rocky Mountains.

Carol led us to a row of cabins where the resort's seasonal employees lived. Several had gone back to college, leaving empty beds for us to use.

"Dinner's ready," Carol announced a short time later.

We walked to the dining room, located in the main lodge, overlooking a lake and surrounded by pine trees.

*Chapter One*

In the afternoon I stood stranded, soaked, and shivering on a remote mountain road, and in the evening of the same day I found myself sitting in a wonderful dining room like a tourist on an expensive vacation, enjoying a delicious seafood dinner, including vegetables, salad, drinks of our choice, and dessert.

One week later we departed for the Grand Canyon, pulling into a campground in Albuquerque, New Mexico nearing day's end, falling asleep in our sleeping bags under a star-filled New Mexican sky.

The following day, rolling through the great state of Arizona, we caught the scenic road north from Flagstaff to Grand Canyon National Park.

Stopped dead in my tracks, I stood, my gaze fixed and frozen the moment the Grand Canyon appeared in my sight. Resplendence shaped, carved, and sculpted by the hand of God alone. I felt as if I were staring into the face of eternity.

"We still need to find a place to sleep tonight, the campground's full," Bob said, breaking the silence, his voice jolting me out from the spell I had been under since the instant my eyes and nature's undreamed of masterpiece first met.

We strolled through the park, hoping to find some kindred spirits in whose campsite we could crash, when a couple on a cross-country trip in a Volkswagen van invited us into theirs.

"Make yourselves at home," they said. "There's plenty of room here."

We dropped our packs on the dusty ground and helped our new friends build a campfire as the perfect Arizona day turned into a cool summer's night.

In the morning we took a hike into the canyon, spending about two hours on the trail. My companions seemed satisfied, but for me our short trek was only a preview.

Bob and Jimmy headed home to Peoria the following day. I couldn't thank them enough for all they had done for me. With hearty man hugs we bid each other farewell and my slow descent to the bottom of the Grand Canyon commenced, under a blissful blue sky on a beautiful Arizona morning. I had plenty of food and a full canteen. The view was spectacular, and the sun, as it moved throughout the day, created an ever-changing scheme of shadows, colors, and reflections.

I sat on a bench at the first rest area, ate a peanut butter sandwich, the staple of the journey, as per plan, topped off my canteen, and struck up a conversation with a twenty-one-year-old Texan named Ray. Ray was tall and thin, with straight blond hair pulled back into a long ponytail reaching to the center of his back. Ray traveled light. A rolled up blanket with a strap enabling him to carry it on his shoulder held almost all of his possessions. His canteen and hunting knife, both of which he wore on his belt were the only possessions not carried rolled up inside of the blanket. He said he had been living off the land for several years and especially enjoyed eating rattlesnakes.

"They're real tasty if you cook them right," he said.

Ray and I continued on the downhill hike together.

I offered to share my peanut butter sandwiches with my new friend. But not my energy mix of nuts and dried fruit, which I planned to save for the more strenuous uphill hike on the return trip. Like a spiral staircase without steps, the trail kept winding round and going down. I wasn't tiring at all. To the contrary, I found myself becoming more energized as the hike progressed. Several hours later we arrived at the halfway point. A cabin offering shelter and bathrooms welcomed us.

We took a short break, filled our canteens and continued along the trail, hiking at a smooth and steady pace until we found ourselves standing on the banks of the Colorado River.

## Chapter One

In the shadows of the setting sun we watched the river flow along its ancient path until the final glimmer of daylight disappeared. Slumber called. I crawled inside of my sleeping bag, Ray rolled himself up in his blanket, and upon the rocky earth on the floor of the Grand Canyon we slept.

In the morning I set off exploring the Canyon, climbing small rock formations and walking along the banks of the Colorado River. Satisfied with my short expedition, I returned to our campsite. Ray had gone off in a different direction. Figuring the uphill trek would take twice as much time, worried I might not make it back to the shelter at the halfway point before dark if I didn't head out soon, and having no idea when Ray would return, I began the arduous trek back to civilization without him.

I trudged on, all day, narrowly arriving at the halfway point shelter before darkness descended upon the Grand Canyon. I resumed my hike back to the top at first light, reaching my point of origin, the south rim, by day's end.

I strolled through the park and found another generous soul whose campsite I was invited to sleep in before hitchhiking back to Flagstaff in the morning.

In Flagstaff I stopped to replenish my supply of peanut butter, bread, and energy mix of nuts and dried fruit. Cheap, nourishing, easy to carry, and no refrigeration required. I finished my shopping, headed back to the highway, and by late afternoon I found myself passing through the Painted Desert and the Petrified Forest, where magnificent multi-colored hills and mesas decorate the arid landscape and fascinating crystallized logs, over two hundred million years old, lie scattered about the Arizona desert.

The sun, from where I stood on the desert highway, looked like a gigantic red ball of fire slowing sinking into the edge of the Earth. I was heading north, to Utah. A tractor-trailer slowed down and came to a stop.

"I can run you north a stretch, then I'm turning east," the trucker said. "I'd be dropping you off at night in the middle of the Navaho Indian reservation."

"That's fine with me," I replied.

The mammoth vehicle roared down the dark and narrow two-lane desert highway. The trucker reached his turnoff and brought the vehicle to a stop. I opened the door, thanked him, grabbed hold of my backpack and jumped to the ground.

A million stars filled the Arizona sky and as it does in the desert when the sun goes down, the night had turned cold. I rolled my sleeping bag out upon the desert floor and crawled inside. Unexpected sounds of laughter and conversation caught my ear, unnerving me. A bunch of young Indians from the reservation out drinking and having a good time, no doubt. I tried to determine their number. At least one car load, maybe two. I was alone, in the middle of the Navaho Nation in the pitch-black desert night, and I was spooked.

I commenced to having a brutal, how did I get here, what am I doing here, and what the hell have I gotten myself into moment with myself, leading me to only one conclusion: I was without a doubt completely insane. Stretched out on my back inside of my sleeping bag on the Arizona desert, I stared at the stars, praying they wouldn't see me and wondering what would happen if they did. At best, I figured, I would have to party with them. That alone would be a nightmare. I'm not sure what the worst would have been, but people can become pretty crazy when they're drunk. How I managed to fall asleep with the level of anxiety and paranoia racing through my brain eludes me to this day.

My eyes opened as dawn spread its early light across the desert. To my utmost relief, my uninvited guests were nowhere to be found. I climbed out of my sleeping bag, put

## Chapter One

it away, threw my pack on my back and rambled down the narrow two-lane desert blacktop, under a cloudless desert sky, embraced in all directions by an infinite landscape of arid sands and a never-ending blue horizon reaching out to the edge of the Earth, and beyond. The solitude of the moment, the intensity of which I had never before experienced, cut straight to the depth of my core.

Perhaps it picked up later in the day, but at this hour of the morning along this desert road the cars were few and far between. Several hours passed before a vehicle finally came to a halt. "Hop in," I heard a woman's voice say. To my surprise, a young couple with a child had stopped to give me a lift. Ed and Kathy and their two-year-old son were on a two week camping trip to Zion and Bryce Canyon National Parks in Utah.

We traveled through the Hopi and Navaho Indian reservations, every long dry dusty mile reminding us of what has become of the once great Indian Nation, a proud agricultural people reduced to small desert dwellings spread out upon the flat arid earth. We crossed the state line into Utah and entered Zion National Park. Ed and Kathy pulled into the campsite they had reserved for their vacation.

Both Zion and Bryce Canyon National Parks are stunning showcases for the State of Utah's spectacular landscape of majestic geological formations. Ed and I set up the tent and gathered wood for a campfire while Kathy tended to little Sam. Evening approached. We sat around the fire, talking and listening to Ed play guitar until our yawns and the dwindling campfire told us the time had come to call it a day. Ed and Kathy joined their little boy in the tent for the night. I crawled inside of my sleeping bag under the starry skies of Utah, amazed that a family had taken me along with them on their vacation.

Ed played guitar and sang folk songs. Some were contemporary, some were old and obscure, and some he had written himself. He also spoke at great length on a multitude of subjects, considering himself an expert in almost all areas of interest. His extensive rambling took the form of storytelling and teaching. It made no difference to Ed whether or not one showed interest, followed his line of speech, or even answered him. As long as he had someone to bounce his intellectual musings off of, he was happy. In other words, Ed loved to hear himself talk and in me he had found a captive audience. Kathy spent most of her time taking care of the toddler. Of what I had learned on the road so far, I would put the importance of blending in at the top of the list. And if I did a good enough job of it, I also learned, people might even take me on vacation with them.

Ed cooked a hearty breakfast every morning. I assisted in the clean up. After cleanup I would take off on my own for several hours exploring the canyons and cliffs. I made a daily routine of it. It kept me from wearing out my welcome. I also wanted to hike the more rugged trails Ed and Kathy couldn't do because of little Sam. We spent the first week of Ed and Kathy's vacation at Zion National Park, and the second week at Bryce Canyon, a few hours north, where more of Utah's magnificent geological wonders are on display.

Meeting Ed and Kathy had been nothing short of incredible. And meeting Bob and Jimmy had been no less incredible. First, a one week vacation in a beautiful Rocky Mountain resort, free of charge, meals included, and a ride to the Grand Canyon. And now, a two week vacation in two of the most beautiful national parks in America, also free of charge with meals included. Both made available to me by complete strangers as if I were a member of their own family.

The second week passed and with their holiday coming to an end, Ed and Kathy prepared to go home to Texas. We

## Chapter One

took down the tent, packed up and headed out. Ed made sure to drop me off at a good hitching spot on the highway, where a driver could easily pull over to the side of the road to pick me up. By midafternoon I found myself in Salt Lake City, Utah, pounding the pavement in the midday sun, surrounded by the hustle and bustle of city life.

I walked into a crowded bar, took a seat on a bar stool and asked the bartender for a Coca-Cola, giving myself a rare respite from the extreme austerity I had chosen to impose upon myself in return for the opportunity to travel.

"Hi, I'm Charles," the guy sitting next to me said. "Can I buy you a beer?"

"Thanks, but I don't drink," I replied.

I looked around. Two curious details jumped right out at me. First, I saw not one woman in the place, and second, I found myself catching lots of stares. I had walked into a gay bar and I stuck out like a sore thumb.

Charles initiated conversation, which soon turned into a seething, scorching rant, relating to me a saga of persecution he claimed to have suffered at the hands of the Mormon Church. And when he finished his tale of woe, he invited me to stay at his place for the night. I did give it a moment's thought, I will admit. After all, a place to sleep is a place to sleep. One simply needs to let these guys know one's preference from the onset. But with several hours of daylight remaining, I decided to take my chances and keep looking instead. I politely declined, but I took his phone number just in case.

"Call me if you change your mind," he said as I left the bar and walked back out to the streets of Salt Lake City, hoping I wouldn't have to, but prepared to if I did.

"Lookin' for a place to stay, brother?" A voice hollered from the rolled down window of an automobile stopped in traffic.

Having a backpack on one's back in the era in which these events take place was certain to bring a charitable offer from someone somewhere sooner or later. The driver was thin, pale, and disheveled. His clothes were old and worn and didn't fit him right. I would have to say he was more than questionable looking, but I hopped in anyway. After all, how many offers can a hitchhiker turn down in one day? We drove to a quiet, tree lined residential neighborhood and pulled into the driveway of a small single home where a muscular Hispanic fellow invited me to crash on his floor after a brief conversation in which he seemed satisfied with what I had to say.

It didn't take long for me to realize I had walked into a heroin house. Several people were sitting on the sofa, nodding off. A young woman stood in the kitchen obsessively chewing on ice cubes. People were in the bathroom, shooting up. I thought about calling Charles, the angry Mormon gay dude. Or maybe I should start all over again looking for another place to sleep. Even the biggest fool could see that to remain in this place would amount to an act of absolute lunacy, defying all logic, reason, and good judgment. But I went ahead and stayed anyway.

I took a seat on the sofa in the living room. A guy in his early twenties came in, sat in a chair across from me and proceeded to take off his shoes. But along with his shoes, his feet came off as well. Greg had lost both of his feet in Vietnam. He had decided to take a break from his prosthetics for a while.

Greg offered to drive me to the highway in the morning, and to my surprise, he showed up exactly as he said he would. The mightily built Hispanic fellow stood by the door as we prepared to leave. He seemed to have an odd Godfather type of status in the house. Charismatic, clearly in command, respected beyond question, and he gave advice, which every lost soul who walked through the door heeded. I couldn't recall ever having been in a stranger place.

## Chapter One

I gave thanks to my host for allowing me to sleep on his floor as I headed out, shuddering to think how my risky decision to spend the night could have ended me up in jail.

Greg drove me to the highway. He pulled over to the shoulder and stepped out of the car with me.

"Good luck brother," he said as we gave each other hearty man hugs.

I wanted to say more than simply thanks for the ride and good luck back to him, but I didn't know what to say. His country called, and straight out of high school he went, and he lost his feet. I couldn't imagine what he had been through and what he had to deal with at his young age, same age as myself.

A few hours later I stood on the side of the highway somewhere in the scenic state of Idaho. Little could I have imagined the grand slam of a ride about to come along. A car pulled over and came to a stop. I jogged over to the waiting vehicle and climbed aboard. A fellow in his early twenties named Robert sat behind the wheel.

My wish since the onset of the journey had been for my feet to first touch the Pacific Shore in the small coastal town of Seaside, Oregon, a couple of hours from Portland. I was born in Portland and I had memories of having been on vacation in Seaside with my parents before we relocated to Baltimore when I was seven years old. I filled Robert in on my personal aspiration.

"Must be your lucky day," Robert said. "You can ride with me all the way to Portland. We'll spend the night at my parents' house and the next day I'll drive you the remaining distance to the coast."

Robert asked if I could drive and I replied in the affirmative.

"Great!" he said. "I've been hoping someone like you would come along."

Robert displayed an excessive friendliness right off the bat, as if we had been best of friends for years, and he talked incessantly, with an odd, idiosyncratic pressured speech. I would arrive on the Oregon Coast having heard every minor detail of the guy's life, and he would know nothing of mine, because the length of time Robert was capable of showing interest in any subject other than himself bordered close to zero.

But I have to say, his kindness and generosity far outweighed his peculiarities and he couldn't have been happier to have me along for the ride. And as I had well discovered by now: The task of showing infinite patience while sitting through hours of endless rambling is a hitchhiker's obligation.

"We're going to spend the night in Boise at the home of old friends of my parents," Robert said.

We arrived in Boise, Idaho in the early evening and pulled into an upscale suburban neighborhood.

"There it is," Robert said, referring to a lovely two story red brick home.

We parked the car, walked up a short flight of steps, stood on the front porch and Robert rang the bell. A middle-aged woman soon appeared in the doorway.

"Frank!" she yelled to her husband. "Look who's here!"

Robert introduced me and explained the situation.

"Not a problem, we're more than happy to help," Mr. Miller said.

I wasn't entirely convinced, but what else could he say?

The house was immaculate. Everything shined. Mrs. Miller had dinner partially prepared already. They were expecting Robert. He had called in advance from a phone booth. The Miller's had known Robert since he came into this world. His visit overjoyed them.

We sat at the Miller's dining room table enjoying a mouthwatering home cooked meal. Steak, mine was well done, as I had told her beforehand when she kindly asked my preference, mashed potatoes with gravy, a fresh vegetable medley, and for dessert, apple pie with a scoop of vanilla ice cream on top. And for the first time in weeks I slept in a real bed with wonderful soft pillows and clean cool sheets. In the morning we chowed down on scrambled eggs, bacon, and homemade French toast with butter and maple syrup. Robert didn't want Mrs. Miller to trouble herself so early, but she insisted. After breakfast, our bellies bursting, we got back on the road, continued westward, traveled the remaining distance through Idaho and crossed the border into the great state of Oregon by noon.

"You're in timber country now," Robert said as we rolled along, hugging the border with Washington State and sharing the road with long diesel fueled flatbeds hauling freshly cut logs.

We pulled up to Robert's parents' house in the countryside outside of Portland by day's end and for the second night in a row, a real bed with wonderful soft pillows and clean cool sheets welcomed my arrival.

The following day Robert delivered me to Seaside, a four hour round trip from his parents' home. I had been humbled several times thus far on this journey by the overwhelming generosity of strangers, and I was humbled once again by Robert's tremendous act of kindness. To be humbled was a new experience for my limited but slowly expanding intellect. Everyone should be humbled once in a while. It's good for the ego. It keeps it in check, as I would so humbly discover.

A cool ocean breeze blew in on a clear and sunny autumn afternoon. I stood upon the shore, took off my shoes, rolled up my pants and let the surf of the Pacific Ocean roll over my feet. I had hitchhiked from coast to coast, from sea to shining sea. I had hitchhiked across America.

The town of Seaside, Oregon is the official end of the historic Lewis and Clark expedition, celebrated by a monument commemorating those legendary explorers and their remarkable feat of reaching the Pacific Ocean in 1804. The adventurous stories of those early pioneers and the wagon trains of the Oregon Trail had made a strong impression upon my imagination as a young boy living in Portland. Now, I too had ended my journey West in the same place where the courageous men led by Meriwether Lewis and William Clark, under the authority of President Thomas Jefferson, had ended theirs, as was my intention. My journey; however, had been over paved roads in comfortable motorized vehicles. Their journey, taking over two years to complete, from the Mississippi River to the Pacific Ocean, had taken them over uncharted waters and unknown wilderness trails, on horseback, in small boats, and on foot. Fraught with danger from nature, man, and beast, they set about facing the perilous unknown, bravely paving the way to the Great Northwest.

Couples and families made up the majority of the small resort's tourist population, not the best scenario to find a floor to crash on. But good fortune would rear its head once again, springing forth this time from a most unlikely source and at a most unexpected moment. I struck up a conversation with a burly salmon fisherman while standing by the Lewis and Clark monument.

"I've done some hitchhiking myself. I know what it's like. You can stay in my trailer," he said.

From the monument we walked to the trailer park. I dropped off my backpack and spent the remainder of the day wandering about the lovely Pacific coastal destination of Seaside, Oregon. In the morning I headed for Portland, backtracking away from the coast for a stretch so I could visit the city of my birth.

One of the great perils of hitchhiking is the occasional maniac driver. My final ride from Seaside into Portland would find

## Chapter One

me in high anxiety seated in a car driven by one such lunatic. Wouldn't it be ironic for my life to end on the road to the city of my birth? I asked myself while watching the speedometer reach one hundred miles per hour. I was terrified!

We couldn't have arrived in Portland soon enough. I stepped out of the car and took a deep breath. Never had the ground beneath my feet felt so good. I threw my backpack on my back, pulled myself together and commenced to walking the streets of Portland.

In the mid 1960s an exotic ancient Hindu Sect manifested itself upon American shores. And soon after, Hare Krishna temples began popping up all over the country.

I came upon the Portland Hare Krishna temple. Filled with curiosity, I peeked through the doorway. I could see several young guys clad in saffron robes with short ponytails dangling from the backs of their clean shaven heads milling about inside.

"Hare Krishna, come in," they said.

I slipped off my shoes and entered the unusual religious sanctuary, at one time a small store front on a busy downtown Portland street the followers of the blue skinned God of ancient India had transformed into a Hindu temple. The room had no furniture. Not sure what to do, I took my lead from the others and sat cross-legged on the floor.

"Would you like to take prasadam with us?" they asked.

I gave them a quizzical look.

"The food eaten by those who worship Lord Krishna is known as Prasadam," they explained.

An opulent altar formed the centerpiece of the room. Sitting upon the altar were mysterious doll-like representations of the Hindu deities, lavishly ornamented in colorful costumes and jewels, showered with flowers and peacock feathers. An alluring fragrance of incense filled the air.

Young American women dressed in beautiful Indian saris served the vegetarian fare. Giving thanks before consuming, the American worshippers of Lord Krishna stretched their bodies flat out on the floor in full prostration position, foreheads touching the ground, and with overflowing emotion they recited the ancient Sanskrit prayers.

I savored each bite, so exotic and new to my taste did I find the Indian cuisine.

A longhaired hippie guy with a heavy beard came into the temple and stretched his body flat out on the floor in front of the altar exactly as the others had done, forehead to the ground in full prostration position and recited the ancient Sanskrit prayers, displaying the same intensity of emotion I had witnessed pouring out of the saffron robed bald headed guys only moments earlier. A Hare Krishna in training, I correctly assumed. He too would soon make the temple his permanent home, shave his head, don the saffron robes and surrender his life to Krishna. As far as I could see, he was well on his way. He simply needed a little more time, I figured, before making the final move. After all, transforming oneself into a Hindu monk in America, one could only imagine, is no small modification to make in one's life. And yet, thousands of young people had already done it and many more would follow over the next several years until the movement reached its peak. I finished my delicious meal of Krishna prasadam, thanked my hosts, slipped back into my shoes and returned to the streets of Portland.

Wow! I marveled. I felt as if I had walked through a magic portal transporting me to ancient India and back again. My curiosity had been sparked. A childhood friend I had grown up with in Baltimore, he and his girlfriend had joined the Hare Krishna movement. Last I heard they had taken up residence in the temple in Laguna Beach, California. I planned to visit them. I suddenly wished to learn all I could about this mysterious religion of ancient India that had captured the minds of so many young people in the Western world.

## Chapter One

My concerns over finding a safe place to stay in a large metropolitan area such as Portland after the experience I had in Salt Lake City would soon fall completely off the radar. Several blocks after leaving the Hare Krishna temple a girl stopped me on the street and offered me a place to stay if I would hitchhike to the city of Eugene with her. She attended the University of Oregon in Eugene and shared an apartment with two other girls. She wanted to save bus fare, but didn't want to hitchhike alone.

In one instant, my plan of getting to know the city of my birth I had so looked forward to since the onset of the journey would be tossed to the wind. Instead, I would arrive in Portland, have lunch with a bunch of bald headed American Hindu monks dressed in what would appear at first glance to the uninformed as orange bed sheets, and leave without seeing anything.

Certain I had hit the jackpot, I gave up my long held plan and agreed to join her. Eugene is several hours south of Portland, a straight run down Interstate-5. Rides came quickly as they always do when accompanied by a young and pretty female. But the situation didn't unfold as I had hoped. Her boyfriend was waiting for her upon our arrival. A hitchhiking companion is all she wanted from me. She stuck to her word, though, and I had a comfortable place to stay for a few days, where I could rest my travel weary bones, and in excellent company, nonetheless.

Before I left Baltimore I met a girl who spoke to me about the alternative community of Takilma, Oregon.

I decided to make Takilma my next stop before returning to the Pacific Highway.

Traveling scenic back roads in the heart of Southern Oregon's magnificent forest landscapes, I reached the picturesque Takilma Valley, a paradise of nature with a river running through it, nestled against mountains filled with redwood trees.

"Welcome," the bearded guy with shoulder-length hair standing on the front porch of a dilapidated abandoned farmhouse from an era long gone hollered to me as I walked past. "You can stay here if you like. Everyone is welcome."

Two types of hippies lived in Takilma, I learned. Those who wanted nothing more than to get stoned and live in the woods, such as the half dozen or so hippies whose company I found myself in at present, and those with a strong belief in vegetarianism and the ideals of communal living, whom the stoners called the meadows people.

"Cross the river and see them," they said.

I had heard about the communal and back to the land movements out West, and the alternative communities. Now, I would witness them for myself.

I navigated the narrow river, hopping upon the many rocks jutting out above the shallow water line, and when I reached the other side I walked a stretch along a well worn path through the forest. Organic vegetable gardens grew in a beautiful meadow at the end of the trail. Like pioneers, idealistic young people from middle class America were scattered throughout the Takilma Valley, homesteading in log cabins, abandoned farmhouses, barns, teepees, and some had built tree houses. A new generation, unlike any other, questioning, searching, looking within, seeking a peaceful new way of life far removed from the trappings, turmoil, and conflicts of the modern world. Some would call it an impossible dream, but for a few fleeting moments in time, the dream seemed possible, nonetheless.

At night I slept in the house with the stoners. By day I wandered the forest, eager to soak up and take in the fascinating new ideas and creative new ways of thinking and living these most interesting of times had brought forth, seeking out and having conversation with the many adventurous young souls whose search had led them to this

*Chapter One*

beautiful place, hoping some bits of enlightenment might perhaps come my way. None did. But they were looking, at least, daring to be different, trying new and extraordinary ways to figure it all out. A week later I found myself back on the Pacific Coast. I arrived in the dimming light of dusk, leaving me no alternative but to sleep under the stars upon the Oregon Shore.

●

A rusty beat-up old rattletrap with the name of Jesus painted in bright multi-hued colors across the entire vehicle, front, back, sides, and top, pulled over and came to a stop. I didn't even have my thumb out. I was too busy munching endless handfuls of luscious, juicy blackberries growing wild and abundant along Oregon's scenic coastal highway. I couldn't get enough of them, so sweet, succulent, and delicious were they. I stood and stared at this strange old heap, giving my mind a moment to process what in the world had landed at my feet before I walked over and hopped in. A tall, lanky bearded fellow in his early twenties sat behind the wheel.

"I'm Pete," he said.

Pete had shoulder-length hair, a long and scraggly beard, and was clad in farmer's overalls, a white t-shirt, and construction boots.

"I'm going to wine country to make a little money picking grapes," Pete said, "and then I'm going to live on the desert and meet the Lord."

The ocean sparkled in the crisp autumn morning. Shiny agate stones lie like jewels upon the postcard perfect Oregon Shore. A storybook lighthouse sat upon a cliff jutting out to sea, veiled in a delicate morning mist. Magical rock formations and elegant boulders glimmered in the rising sun, carved and polished by eons of salt water splashes and foaming tides. I fixed my gaze upon the astonishing beauty of the Oregon Coast while at the same time trying my best to think of a response to Pete's plan of "meeting the Lord." Nothing came to mind, so I asked him about picking grapes instead, and if I could join him.

"I could use a few extra dollars," I said.

"Easily done," Pete replied.

We rolled on, the Oregon Coast becoming more magnificent with each passing mile.

"It's comin' up," Pete said.

And sure enough, there it was. I could hardly believe my eyes.

"Wow! I did it!" I blurted out as we sailed past the welcome sign and cruised across the border, into the great state of California.

"You sure did," Pete responded, his voice cheering me on, supportively letting me know that my achievement, although in reality carrying no significance, meaning, or point whatsoever, was still something remarkable and had not gone unnoticed.

"Never met anyone from Baltimore," Pete said.

"No one ever does," I replied.

My little road trip continued as we traveled down the Redwood Highway, where Northern California's breathtaking Pacific shoreline meets the tall redwood trees of the majestic Redwood forests. We veered inland about fifty miles south of the giant redwoods, arrived in the Napa Valley near day's end and slept under the stars in a large open field.

"We rise at the crack of dawn," Pete said. "We want to sign up early for the grape pickin'."

The rising sun climbed over the valley, unveiling a stunning landscape of lush rolling hills and gorgeous green meadows as we drove to the vineyards along a winding country road. We stood in line, received our baskets, and out to the fields we marched with scores of Mexican

## Chapter One

migrant workers to pick and fill our baskets with California grapes.

I had been picking no more than an hour when I decided to call it quits. I doubt a slower grape picker ever existed. Pete, on the other hand, was sure to make some money. He could almost keep up with the Mexicans and they picked lightning fast.

I wished Pete luck on his journey to the desert, thanked him for all he had done for me, collected the few dollars I managed to earn and returned to the road. A few hours later I found myself standing on a crowded street corner in the great city of San Francisco.

I had an address in my pocket. Images of stylishly uniformed doormen and brass buttoned elevator operators came to mind as I walked into the lobby of the grand old red brick building. But the once elegant lobby had become shabby and gray, the glamour of a bygone era had long since passed, and a run-down apartment building stood in its place.

I took the elevator to the fifth floor. I didn't know what to expect. Would she remember me? I met Jeanne, a friend of a friend, during a brief encounter in Baltimore. I told her of my plan to hitchhike to the West Coast and she in turn offered me a place to stay in the apartment she shared with her mother and younger brother in San Francisco, although I'm sure not for one moment did she believe I would actually show up. I hadn't spoken to her since, and now, here I stood, knocking on her door.

"Wow! You made it. Great! Come in," she said. But the look on her face gave her true thoughts away.

I don't believe it. You actually did what you said you were going to do. And now that you're here, what are we going to do with you? The look on her face in truth seemed to say.

I wouldn't have been in the least bit surprised had I been told I couldn't stay. After all, for all intents and

23

purposes, I was a stranger popping in on her family completely unannounced.

I had hitchhiked all the way from Baltimore, Jeanne explained to her mom, and I wished to spend a few days becoming acquainted with their legendary town.

Jeanne's initial uneasiness over my out of the blue appearance at her doorstep would find quick resolution when her mom, taking the situation in hand in a most comforting motherly manner, ushered me into the kitchen, sat me down and prepared for me a big fat ham and cheese sandwich with lettuce and tomatoes and a Coca-Cola with which to wash it down and told me in no uncertain terms that I was more than welcome to stay.

Had I not met Jeanne in Baltimore, I believe bypassing San Francisco would have been the wisest of choices to make, for one could imagine what bizarre situations and crazy characters I might have fallen in with in a city of San Francisco's size and colorful reputation had I decided to wing it on my own.

As it turned out, thanks to Jeanne's most generous mom, the time I spent in San Francisco would prove itself a tremendous success. And Calvin, Jeanne's brother. With nothing but time on his hands, no real friends, and no lack of pride in his famous hometown, Calvin latched onto me and took me around, making sure I saw all of the sights a tourist should see while visiting the celebrated city by the bay. I would have a one week stay in San Francisco costing me nothing and I would have my own personal tour guide to boot.

Santa Cruz, a small beach town about an hour away, would have the distinction of becoming my first stop out of San Francisco. Later in the day I found myself in the posh and beautiful village of Carmel, adjacent to Monterey, where the most dramatic stretch of coastline in America begins.

## Chapter One

Amidst an abundant backdrop of green forested hills, the famed white sands of Carmel sparkled in the midday sun. I roamed around the village with my backpack on my back, peering into the polished windows of the fashionable boutiques and art galleries, wishing I could afford to have lunch, a cappuccino, and dessert at one of Carmel's charming cafés. As evening drew near I set up camp upon the exquisite white sanded beach, watched the sun set over the Pacific Ocean and fell asleep to the sounds of the surf rolling in upon the shores of Southern California.

My eyes opened at dawn's first light. I lie still for a while, listening to the sounds of the morning tides rushing in. A cool salty mist covered the shoreline. Sea gulls flew in, looking for an early meal as dawn gave way to another bright and beautiful day in sunny Southern California. I climbed out of my sleeping bag, ate a peanut butter sandwich, packed up and strolled back to the coastal highway.

A pickup truck with a German shepherd riding in the back pulled over. "Throw your pack in the back," I heard a voice say. "There's no room for it in the front."

I threw my pack in with the dog and climbed aboard, introducing myself and thanking the driver and his girlfriend for picking me up.

"My name's Adam and this is Penelope," he said. "How far are you going?"

I told them about my journey.

"You're welcome to ride with us to Santa Barbara," Adam offered in reply.

Not long into the ride Adam suggested I sit in the back of the pickup truck for an optimal view as we travel through Big Sur, the legendary stretch of California Coast.

He pulled over to the side of the road and I climbed in the back with the German shepherd.

"And don't worry about a place to sleep tonight," Adam said, "you can stay with us in Santa Barbara."

Overlooking the Pacific Ocean, the winding road climbed to an altitude of five thousand feet, offering breathtaking views of lush forests, untouched beaches, and spectacular cliffs towering over the sea. Big Sur, a ninety mile stretch of California Coast, deemed by many as the most picturesque coastal drive on the planet. I sat in the back of the pickup truck, wind in my hair, held in a trance by the supreme splendor rolling past my eyes.

Santa Barbara sits between the Pacific Ocean and a four thousand foot high mountain range, creating a magnificent scenic backdrop to the beautiful Santa Barbara beaches. I was still sitting in the back of the pickup truck with the German shepherd when we cruised into town and pulled into the driveway of a two-story house.

I hopped down from the truck, grabbed my pack and walked inside, followed by the dog, his tail wagging as Adam called his name. A group of young people inhabited the property. A communal atmosphere pervaded, and all of the girls walked around topless all of the time, while within the confines of the house, of course, and each one was beautiful. It was the 1970s, California style.

I struck up a conversation with a guy who lived in a commune called the Brotherhood of the Sun, located in the mountains surrounding Santa Barbara.

"You're welcome to visit if you're interested," Richard said. "Visitors can stay for up to a week. If you want to stay longer, leadership will ask you to make a commitment."

I took Richard up on his offer.

"You can stay in my cabin. Floor space only though," Richard said.

"That's where I mostly sleep these days anyway," I replied.

On another beautiful day in sunny Southern California I hopped into Richard's car and up the winding mountain road we traveled. We reached the entrance to the commune, situated high above the town of Santa Barbara, and drove along a dirt road through the forest until we arrived at an area of small wooden cabins.

Richard shared a tiny one-room cabin with three other guys. The communal dining hall and the community bathrooms and showers were located within a short distance of the living quarters.

The founder of the Brotherhood of the Sun, Norman Paulsen, had been a student of Paramahansa Yogananda, a much revered holy man and teacher from India whose life is documented in the book, *Autobiography of a Yogi*.

In the late 1960s Norman Paulsen acquired property on top of a mountain in Santa Barbara and his vision of founding a spiritual community became reality.

I stood outside of Richard's cabin and filled my lungs with fresh mountain air. Drugs, tobacco, and alcohol, as well as newspapers, magazines, television, and radio were not allowed. Filling one's mind with news of the outside world was considered a hindrance to spiritual growth. The commune numbered around seventy-five at the time but would grow into the hundreds at its peak.

As a source of collective income, the commune members developed a vast acreage of land upon which to grow a wide range of organic vegetables. They also established a health food store and bakery operation in Santa Barbara. Both their organic produce and their baked goods, under the brand name Sunburst Farms, would achieve widespread distribution throughout the nation.

As evening approached I headed over to the communal kitchen and dining hall, a rustic, rambling, roughly built one-story wooden structure. Along the way I stopped to chat with a young couple busy building a small house in the woods.

"We've finally found what we've been looking for, a true spiritual community!" They said in voices bursting with idealism, convinced they were changing the world, certain of its lasting forever.

Nothing could have prepared me for the fabulous vegetarian dinner served buffet style in the communal dining hall. Organic grains, beans, legumes, nuts and seeds; Organic brown rice; farm fresh home grown organic vegetables and spices, and more, transformed into creative, healthy, hearty, wonderful vegetarian meals. Nowhere in my memory could I recall seeing anything like this. It certainly wasn't our mother's kitchen, that's for sure! But how had they figured it all out? Every morsel on the menu I found unfamiliar, and yet, my instincts recognized the superior health benefits inherent in such a diet, not only as a means of nourishing the body, but also the mind and the soul.

After dinner a group meditation took place. Taking my lead from the others, I sat in silence, cross-legged, eyes shut, and I wondered: How do these hippies living on top of a mountain in Santa Barbara, California know how to meditate? And I wondered how I too could learn.

The meditation session concluded with several long, sustained incantations of the sacred sound, OM, also written as AUM, rising from the silence, chanted in unison by every member of the group, sending mystical sound vibrations reverberating throughout the room.

The communal movement of the 1960s was in its heyday and still on the upswing in 1972. With unbounded enthusiasm, young seekers were rolling in and signing up every day. Witnessing large numbers of people the same age as myself making such a strong commitment, and one so far removed from our middle class upbringing astonished me, and it also left me feeling a bit envious, in a way, of the peace of mind I could only imagine comes to those who believe they have reached the end of their search and have found what they had been looking for.

## Chapter One

For a guy newly arrived from the East Coast without a clue, the flood of spiritual seekers whose presence I now found myself submerged in, the unfamiliar ways of thinking, and the unforeseen exposure to a spirituality far removed from traditional Western culture became overwhelming. Unusual thoughts began inserting themselves into my head, placing themselves at the forefront of my thinking, without warning, flooding my consciousness from a place unknown with burning philosophical issues begging answers. Who am I? What am I looking for? A startling new voice in my head began asking, shaking up my foundation and leaving me unsettled. Some would call it a spiritual awakening. To me it felt as if I had been hit in the head with a ton of bricks.

I had been in the commune for six days, participating in what I had begun to believe were the only God given abilities assigned to me at birth. These included: hanging around; walking around; looking at things; having random conversation, and eating delicious food for free. Now, the founder and spiritual leader of the commune requested to meet with me.

Norman Paulsen was a heftily built man with a heavy black beard and long black hair. An imposing, charismatic figure, Norman Paulsen was twenty years older, on average, than just about everyone else in the commune, the majority of whom were in their early to mid-twenties. Nothing happened in the Brotherhood of the Sun spiritual community without the approval of Norman Paulsen. The commune centered around Norman Paulsen's esoteric teachings, built and based upon a blending of Paramahansa Yogananda's Kriya Yoga, his own extensive philosophies, visions, and theories regarding God, creation, and the nature of the universe, and a determined belief that people should live peacefully together in collective colonies. He was, so to speak, the commune's guru.

"What are your plans?" he asked.

"I don't have any," I replied. "I'm just hitchhiking around."

"What are you looking for?" he furthered inquired of me.

"I'm not looking for anything in particular," I said; "I'm just looking."

And I was damn glad and damn lucky my brain came up with an answer instead of looking stupid by saying I don't know, thus allowing me to give at least a half-way reasonable response to this intimidating guy who had founded a commune, written books, and was well known and respected as a spiritual leader and driving force in the communal movement. He said I could begin the process of becoming a member of the commune; otherwise, I would have to leave, but I would always be welcomed back if I changed my mind. I thanked him and we shook hands.

The cautious footsteps of people stepping around me as I slept on the cabin floor in the narrow space between the two sets of bunk beds woke me up, as it did every day at dawn during my stay in the Brotherhood of the Sun. Shivering in the crisp mountain morning, I climbed out of my sleeping bag and followed the trail to the communal bathroom. I then returned to the cabin, packed up my belongings and headed over to the dining hall for my final breakfast in the commune. I made sure to stuff myself real good. I would soon be back to eating nothing but peanut butter sandwiches until someone or something else comes along to feed me something different.

With my backpack on my back I stood on the narrow mountain road leading out of the commune, waiting for a ride into town.

"Where are you going?" the red headed girl behind the wheel of a Volkswagen Beetle asked.

I told her about the house where I had stayed before coming to the commune.

## Chapter One

"I know where it is," she said. "Hop in, I'll take you there."

The Brotherhood of the Sun spiritual community would develop into one of the more successful and famous communes of the era. In studies, articles, and books written on the communal movement of the 1960s, the Brotherhood of the Sun almost always finds itself included. But impermanence, known to be inescapable, although never foreseen by the young, would sneak in and the change, unknown and unrecognized at first, would begin, ultimately taking the unprecedented idealism of a generation that came of age in the raging inferno between the civil rights movement and the Vietnam War fading down the corridors of time, along with the era to which it once belonged.

"Why are you leaving the commune? You're making a mistake. There's nothing out there. You should stay," the red headed girl said, her voice expressing genuine concern for my spiritual well being.

I answered her in the only way I knew how: "I can't stay in one place. I have to keep moving. I don't know why."

The spiritual seekers in the commune believed they had found themselves, and perhaps in some strange way, I had found myself too, although I'm sure it would appear the exact opposite to anyone paying attention to my baffling existence, but never in my life had I felt so at one with myself as I had since I hit the road.

The tiny vehicle with the engine in the back and the trunk in the front carried me down the mountain side, back to beautiful Santa Barbara by the sea.

From Santa Barbara I headed for Laguna Beach to visit my boyhood friend Marty, whom I had known since the second grade. Marty and his girlfriend traveled from Baltimore to California a year earlier and never looked back. They joined the Hare Krishna movement and moved into the temple, having made the decision to surrender their lives to Lord Krishna, the blue skinned God of ancient India.

I had traveled seventy miles from Santa Barbara, halfway to Laguna Beach, when an excessively talkative fellow named Ron stopped to give me a lift. I filled Ron in on the details of my journey and he in turn invited me over to his place.

"My girlfriend will fix you something to eat and you can spend the night," he said.

His on the spot invitation and manic manner made me think he might be crazy, but I went ahead and took him up on his offer anyway.

Ron and his girlfriend Jenny resided in a third floor apartment in a garden apartment complex.

"Want a beer?" Ron asked as soon as we stepped inside.

"No thanks," I said.

He showed signs of surprise, as most people do, when I told him I don't drink.

A friend of Jenny's had stopped by. Marie was a small girl in her mid-twenties. She wore her long black hair in one long braid reaching to the middle of her back. Marie was open and forthcoming and spoke to me of her troubled life. Marie had left her three-year-old daughter in the custody of her ex-husband when she moved from the state of Pennsylvania back to her home state of California a year earlier. She missed her daughter terribly, she said, but couldn't go back. I wondered why, but I didn't ask.

Marie and I soon found ourselves embroiled in the heat of passion on Ron and Jenny's sofa, while in the background, Ron and Jenny had begun to argue. Ron was already on his third beer, a point of contention between them.

"We should go to my place," Marie said, an offer I straight away accepted. Jenny then served me a delicious tuna salad sandwich. Lunch, as Ron had promised.

*Chapter One*

Marie had a tiny apartment with one room serving as both a bedroom and a living room. Marie didn't work. She lived on government assistance with additional help from her parents. She claimed to have emotional problems. I saw nothing wrong with her. She was a nice girl, and cute. We had a great time together. In the two weeks we spent together, her culinary abilities were the only fault I found, the full extent of which were limited to the following: frozen dinners, scrambled eggs, hot dogs, and lunchmeat sandwiches on white bread with slices of American cheese.

The road provided many opportunities for me to make new discoveries about myself. For example, from the commune to Marie, how easily and seamlessly I found myself capable of navigating from one extreme set of circumstances to another. Although I couldn't help but wonder if possessing such a curious talent didn't put my own mental state in question.

Marie drove me back to the highway on the morning of my departure. She wanted me to stay longer, but once again, the time had come for me to move on. I stuck out my thumb and by noon I found myself in Southern California's picturesque coastal town of Laguna Beach, looking for the Hare Krishna temple.

I walked along the beautiful Laguna Beach ocean front boulevard, following the directions I had been given by the clerk behind the drugstore counter until I came upon a small one-story house sitting on a hill. The lovely bungalow had been converted into a Hindu temple. I climbed a flight of steps, strolled past a well-tended flower garden and stuck my head in the door.

"Hare Krishna, come in," a saffron robed bald headed guy said.

❦

Greeted by the pleasing aroma of incense, I placed my shoes at the door and entered the tiny temple. An altar containing doll-like figures of the Hindu deities adorned with colorful costumes, flowers, and jewels formed the centerpiece of the room, same as I had seen in the temple in Portland. Several devotees, as the worshippers of Krishna are known, stood in front of the altar chanting the Hare Krishna mantra, with razor sharp intensity, ultra deep focus, and unending repetition. I addressed the small number of devotees in the room.

"I'm looking for a friend of mine. His name is Marty. He's from Baltimore," I said.

"He's living in the Los Angeles temple now," a female devotee responded. "We're driving up there in a couple of hours. You can ride with us if you like."

The Los Angeles temple, at the time one of the largest Hare Krishna temples in the country, served as the West Coast headquarters of the Hare Krishna Movement.

I rode the short distance from Laguna Beach to Los Angeles with three sari clad American girls looking as if they were straight out of India. All three sat in the front in the days when automobiles sat six. I sat in the back by myself.

"You should surrender unto the lotus feet of Krishna and live in the nectar of his mercy," the girl sitting in the middle said.

The content of her speech left me baffled.

"Krishna is the supreme personality of godhead," she continued, confounding me even more.

All three then began chanting, and they chanted the Hare Krishna mantra non-stop all the way to Los Angeles, approximately an hour's drive north of Laguna Beach. Their minds were consumed with nothing but Krishna and as I sat taking it all in, I began to understand why they called it Krishna Consciousness.

In 1965, at the age of 69, A.C. Bhaktivedanta Swami Prabhupada booked passage on a freighter from India to

## Chapter One

America. His sole purpose in making the journey was to introduce Krishna to the Western world. The mysterious Indian holy man, clad in the exotic garb of a sadhu, drew the interest of a handful of hippies in Greenwich Village and from there, in the most humble of beginnings, the Hare Krishna Movement came into existence.

The Hare Krishna people became a familiar part of the counterculture's colorful landscape as spiritual seekers across America joined the modern day religious movement and moved into the scores of temples springing up across the nation. The American worshippers of the blue skinned God of ancient India, the young men, clad in monks robes with small pony tails dangling from the backs of their clean shaven heads and the young women, clad in beautiful Indian saris, began showing up on the streets of America's cities in the latter part of the 1960s, singing ancient Hindu melodies, chanting, and dancing in euphoric excitement, accompanied by the exotic rhythms of their unusual musical instruments.

Welcome to the International Society for Krishna Consciousness, read the sign sitting in front of the Los Angeles temple. A large portrait of Lord Krishna in the company of a stunning Hindu Goddess whose name I would soon know as well sat adjacent to the welcome sign.

I stepped out of the car and approached the temple entrance. A devotee came near.

"Hari Bol," he said, his saffron robes flowing in the soft breeze. "Do you know what Hari Bol means?"

"No, I don't," I replied.

"It means chant Hare Krishna! It's a greeting in the energy of the Lord. Are you coming to the kirtan?"

"Sure," I said, even though I hadn't a clue what he meant by kirtan.

"It's nectar! Krishna's mercy is so great!" he said in a voice quivering with emotion.

Countless devotees lived in the Los Angeles temple on Watseka Avenue in Venice Beach, California and in apartments throughout the surrounding neighborhood, and nowhere could the energy and excitement have been more apparent and at a higher level.

The worship of Lord Krishna has been a well established tradition in India for thousands of years. In the Western world; however, the ancient religion of India would become a new religious movement, a rare event in history, and in 1972 the Hare Krishna movement was in its heyday and still at the height of its charismatic phase.

In a religious movement's charismatic phase, new converts are willing to surrender all worldly possessions and relationships, including family if need be, to follow their newfound beliefs, such is the level of exhilaration, zealousness, and euphoria.

I heard someone call my name. I turned around and in front of me stood Arlene, my childhood friend Marty's girlfriend. The last time I saw Arlene, about a year and a half earlier in Baltimore, she was an ordinary American girl in her final semester of college. Now she was wrapped in an Indian sari from head to foot, devoting her life to worshipping Krishna.

"Hari Bol," she said, astonished to see me standing on the steps of the Los Angeles Hare Krishna temple with my backpack on my back.

I told her about my journey and I told her I had come to the temple to see Marty and to learn about Krishna consciousness.

"Marty's not here right now," she said. "He's traveling around with other devotees. They're chanting on the streets of different cities and towns, talking to people about Krishna and selling books to raise money for the temple. He should be back in about two weeks, but it could be longer. You should see him, he's never been happier! You

*Chapter One*

should stay here and wait for him. I'll ask if you can stay in the temple until he returns."

"I'd like that," I said.

The size of the Los Angeles Hare Krishna temple stood in stark contrast to the tiny temples I had visited in Laguna Beach and Portland. The building appeared to have been either a church or a school transformed into a Hindu temple. I slipped off my shoes in the foyer and stepped inside. The blissful aromas of jasmine, sandalwood, and musk filled the air. Ancient Hindu paintings hung on the walls, portraying, in stunning intricacy of detail and brilliance of hues, a radiant, beautiful, magical, transcendental realm where Krishna and the entire mind-boggling mythological myriad of Hindu Gods and Goddesses reside, and where, according to the devotees, those who chant the holy mantra and devote their lives to serving Krishna will go after death, never to take birth again in the material world. In these exotic, mystical paintings, unlike any art work I had ever seen, Krishna is strikingly attractive, with androgynous features, eyes filled with love and compassion, skin the color of a perfect sky.

"You're looking at Krishna and Radha enjoying one of Lord Krishna's many transcendental pastimes," a devotee offered, giving me a brief explanation upon noticing my fascination with one painting in particular.

Never had I been exposed to such an extraordinary amount of puzzling lingo and mystifying information as I had in the few short hours since falling into the company of the Hare Krishnas.

The enthralling picture portrayed a radiant Lord Krishna playing a small wooden flute, with velvety skin tinted a most divine color of blue, and Radha, his dazzling eternal consort, representing the female energy of God. Both were clad in delicate flowing fabric of heavenly hue, floating on pink lotus petals in a celestial sea of lavender-green.

Each male devotee had a clean shaven head except for a small pony tail known as a shikha. Devotees believe this tuft of hair protects the topmost chakra out of which a devotee's soul leaves the body at time of death. Devotees also wore tilak, white lines made of clay from the banks of sacred rivers in India, running from the forehead down the front of the nose, symbolizing the devotee's surrender to Lord Krishna, in whose humble service the devotee has dedicated his life. All were clad in monk's robes. Unmarried men wore saffron. Married men wore white. All of the female devotees were clad in beautiful Indian saris.

"Prasadam," a voice called out.

I filled my plate with the wonderful vegetarian cuisine and sat crossed legged on the floor. A devotee sat beside me and proceeded to perform the devotional ritual required of devotees before partaking of Krishna Prasadam. He didn't do a full body prostration as I had seen displayed in the temple in Portland. He did a kneel-over instead, placing his forehead to the floor as he recited the ancient Sanskrit prayers.

"Hare Krishna, my name's Vijaya Dasa," he said upon completion of his prayers.

"Hare Krishna, I'm Steve," I replied.

"The prasadam's good, isn't it?" Vijaya Dasa asked.

"Delicious," I responded.

"Do you know what prasadam means?"

"Not exactly," I said.

"It means Krishna's mercy. And do you know why it is so delicious?"

Again, I told him I wasn't sure.

"Everything we eat is offered to Krishna first," Vijaya Dasa explained. "Krishna tastes the food, and from the nectar of Krishna's lips it acquires a transcendental flavor, thus turning it into prasadam, spiritual food."

"By living in the material world we continue creating karma, causing us to suffer through countless

## Chapter One

reincarnations. We must get out of the material world and end the cycle of birth and death so we can enjoy Krishna's eternal transcendental mercy. Surrendering our lives to Krishna and chanting the holy mantra is the only way back to godhead," Vijaya Dasa further explained.

I cleared my plate, scarfing down every delicious bite of Krishna prasadam. I thought about the curious term godhead. I had heard godhead and another curious term, nectar, used repeatedly since arriving in the temple.

"Let's go," Vijaya Dasa said, "The kirtan's about to begin."

I followed Vijaya Dasa into the ceremonial chamber. The temple's sacred room contained an altar far greater in size and lavishness than the other two temples I had been in. Sitting upon the altar were the customary doll-like representations of the Hindu Gods, known as the deities, ornamented in colorful costumes and jewels, adorned with an abundance of fresh flowers and peacock feathers. Several devotees stood by the deities waving sticks of incense in the air.

A group of devotees with unusual musical instruments had assembled for the kirtan. One played a harmonium, a small keyboard instrument about eighteen inches in length, similar to a reed organ. European in origin, the harmonium found its way to the sub-continent in the 1800s and became a part of Hindu religious ceremonies. Others played small finger symbols, producing pleasing, ear catching, high pitched rhythmic jingling sounds, and one devotee played the mrdanga drum, a two sided Indian hand drum. The harmonium player and the mrdanga drummer sat cross-legged on the floor. And those with finger symbols, some stood, ready to mix and move among the crowd and some would remain stationary, also sitting crossed legged on the floor beside the harmonium player and the mrdanga drummer. The devotional service commenced with a conch shell sounding three times.

The men and women of the Los Angeles Hare Krishna Temple came pouring in. Men stood on one side and women on the other. The room filled up, the mystical melodies of the East began to play, and I fell in love with the music of an ancient and foreign culture unknown to my ears until this moment. I stood, watching, taking it all in, captivated by a magical new world of sound and blown away by the emotional scene in front of my eyes. In joyous, uplifting harmony, the devotional songs of India were sung by scores of devotees as they swayed back and forth, waved their arms in the air, and, in divine ecstasy, began dancing around the room. And as the harmonium, the finger symbols, and the spiritual beat of the two-sided hand drum picked up the tempo, abandoning all inhibition, I joined in, swayed back and forth, waved my arms in the air, and, losing myself in a sea of monk's robes, bald heads, and colorful Indian saris, I began dancing around the room with them.

The musical portion of the ceremony came to an end and all present seated themselves cross-legged on the floor. The drummer and leader of the kirtan began to speak.

"Krishna is the supreme personality of godhead and he makes himself present in the form of the deity so the devotee can worship and serve him personally. A pure devotee surrenders all worldly attachment and keeps nothing but Krishna on his mind. Not only is Krishna's transcendental energy present in the mantra, but he is on our lips when we repeat his names." These were a few of the key points the kirtan leader expounded upon in his sermon.

He also told tales of Krishna's incarnation on Earth in India five thousand years ago and he recited verses in Sanskrit and in English from ancient Vedic scripture.

The vast majority of devotees were in their early twenties. They were intelligent, educated, middle class young people who had of their own choosing adopted a religion and lifestyle entirely foreign to our culture, demanding of them, without

## Chapter One

exception, unconditional surrender and absolute detachment from their past. They dressed in the exotic attire of the East and even changed their names, taking new names from the ancient Sanskrit language. The intensity of the moment defied description. Never had I seen anyone do anything so extreme with their lives. I felt as if my head would explode, so astounded was I by the changes these young men and women of my generation had put themselves through.

The deities were showered with colorful aromatic flower petals and put to sleep for the night, bringing an end to the evening devotions. Everyone then filed out of the sacred chamber and into another room where a night cap of delicious yogurt drinks awaited us.

I sat savoring my wonderful refreshment, known to Indian cuisine as a lassi, its flavor exotic and superb.

A devotee sat beside me and introduced himself. "I'm Srivas Das. I sure did get high on that kirtan. How about you?"

"I'm pretty spaced out myself right now," I said.

I told him about my devotee friends from Baltimore. And I told him I hadn't received an answer yet about the possibility of sleeping in the temple.

"No problem," Srivas Das said. "Krishna will take care of you."

I followed Srivas Das up a flight of steps to the male dormitory. Not one mattress did I see. The devotees slept on top of straw mats on the floor.

"Devotees live austere lives," Srivas Das said. "We renounce the material world and live only to serve Krishna."

The devotees never stopped thinking or talking about Krishna. When a devotee swept the floor, he would say I'm doing it for Krishna. When a devotee changed a light bulb, he did it for Krishna. Every action, every interaction, every movement, every breath taken was done for Krishna. Every conversation, every thought, every activity should focus solely on Krishna. Nothing else should enter the mind of a devotee.

Since arriving in the temple my brain had become inundated with an immense amount of unfamiliar stimulation and never before heard information and I had reached overload.

"Kirtan begins at four o'clock in the morning," Srivas Das said.

"I'm not getting eight hours tonight, am I?" I asked.

"A devotee never does," Srivas Das replied.

I awoke in the wee hours of the morning to the sounds of the Hare Krishna mantra: "Hare Krishna, Hare Krishna, Krishna Krishna, Hare Hare, Hare Rama, Hare Rama, Rama Rama, Hare Hare," chanted non-stop at record speed by a roomful of bald headed celibate Hindu monks as they buzzed about, taking cold showers and donning their monk's robes. Without exception, every one of them had been regular American guys only a short time ago.

The purpose of the cold shower is to cool down the temptation of sense desire, I learned. Everyone chanted the mantra with total abandon while the freezing water poured down upon them. Several devotees were off to the side taking turns shaving each other's heads. I took a deep breath and jumped in.

Srivas Das handed me a set of wooden Japa beads and a prayer bag as we headed down the steps for the morning devotional service.

"Japa is individual chanting. Kirtan is when we chant as a group to the accompaniment of music," Srivas Das explained.

The harmonium played an entrancing Eastern melody, the two-sided Indian hand drum tapped a spiritual beat, and the finger symbols sounded delightful sparkling jingling rhythms appearing in my mind as bright floating colors of yellow and orange. And as the intoxicating fragrance of incense and rosewater permeated the sacred chamber, scores of devotees singing in heavenly harmony

*Chapter One*

filled the room with the mystical songs of ancient India. The morning kirtan, an otherworldly experience in the delicate pre-dawn hour, had begun.

I floated out of the chamber at ceremony's end, the mystical melodies still playing in my head. What a way to start the day, and to think they do this every morning. I remembered what Srivas Das had said to me while we were sipping on our delicious yogurt drinks. He said he had gotten high on the kirtan. Now I understood.

A soft humming sound began vibrating throughout the temple. Japa, otherwise known as individual chanting, had begun. Each devotee is required to chant the Hare Krishna mantra 1,728 times every morning. In order to keep count, a string of 108 wooden beads known as Japa beads are kept in a small prayer bag worn over the shoulder. One hand is kept inside of the prayer bag while chanting and for each chant one rolls the thumb and index finger over one bead, moving on to the next bead with the next repetitive chant. Make a complete circle around the string of beads sixteen times and you've chanted the mantra 1,728 times.

I stood on the temple steps in the cool morning air. The sun was rising over the city of Los Angeles. Devotees filled every space, in the temple, on the porch, on the steps, in the courtyard, walking up and down the sidewalk in front of the temple, and all chanted the mantra non-stop for two solid hours, the allotted amount of time given each morning for completing the required 1,728 chants. With one hand inside of my prayer bag draped over my shoulder, counting every chant on my beads, I joined the morning ritual. In the event one is unable to complete the required sixteen rounds within the allotted two hours, the devotee must still complete them by the end of the day. And chanting more than what is required is always good. It gives one extra credit with Krishna.

With the morning rituals completed and morning prasadam served and consumed the devotees hustled off to their daily activities. Some worked in the vast book publishing operation, headquartered in Los Angeles, producing the many books written by the founder of the movement, Srila Prabhupada. And some worked in the incense factory, producing the Hare Krishna incense under the brand name Spiritual Sky. Others went into the community selling books and soliciting donations. And a smaller number stayed back, tending to the temple's needs. No one had outside jobs and no one associated with anyone outside of the temple. A pure devotee associates only with other devotees.

I had been given a few tidying up chores to complete around the temple, which took no time at all. I volunteered to work in the kitchen, but no one other than an initiated devotee is allowed to set foot in the kitchen, much less participate in the sacred duty of preparing prasadam.

With hours of free time on my hands I delved into the temple library, offering volumes of books to help further my understanding of this unusual religion. I found myself receiving an intensive crash course in Eastern religion, philosophy, and thought and I soaked it up like a sponge. My questions regarding birth, death, creation, and the existence of God, with all due respect, remained unanswered by the traditional religious teachings of my upbringing. But now, from a mysterious faraway land, I found fascinating new explanations for my mind to ponder and explore. The Eastern concepts of karma and reincarnation I found most attention grabbing, concepts new to our culture, and to which I had given no prior thought, but now found fascinating and deserving of serious consideration.

I had been in the temple for several days when a group of devotees invited me to join them as they prepared to take Krishna out of the temple and onto the streets of Hollywood's legendary Sunset Strip.

## Chapter One

The non-stop sound vibrations of the Hare Krishna mantra reverberated throughout the vehicle as we pulled out of Watseka Avenue and headed for Sunset Boulevard, where, according to the devotees, sense desire is worshipped and Maya, the goddess of illusion, reigns supreme. A second van followed, carrying another half dozen devotees.

"What we're doing now is called Sankirtan," a devotee explained. "We'll be chanting Krishna's names on the streets for all to hear, and everyone will benefit, whether they know it or not."

We reached our destination, piled out of the vans and with drums a pounding and finger cymbals jingling the American followers of the Hindu God Krishna skipped, danced, jumped, twirled, and sang the Hare Krishna mantra up and down the sidewalks of Hollywood's Sunset Strip.

I first saw the Hare Krishna people on the streets of Baltimore circa 1968. Who are these people? In sheer bewilderment I wondered. Never had I seen anything of this nature. Not many in the Western world had. The guys clad in monk's robes with shaven heads and little pony tails, and the girls clad in beautiful Indian saris, dancing and singing curiously ear catching melodies in an unrecognizable language accompanied by their unusual musical instruments. They were young, they were American, and they spoke English, and yet they were not of the world in which we lived. Everything about them was alien. How does one come to make such a radical change? In incredulity I marveled. And now, I find myself dancing and singing the praises of Lord Krishna on the streets of Los Angeles with them. It couldn't have been more surreal.

Several devotees engaged the curious crowd of bystanders, explaining Krishna consciousness to them, while the remainder of the group played their instruments, danced, and in rapturous joy sang the holy mantra. The devotees would stay in one place for about twenty minutes before skipping, dancing, jumping, twirling, and singing their way to another spot, the rhythmic jingling of the finger cymbals and the pulsing beat of the two-sided Indian hand drum making it known to everyone in their path that Krishna's pure devotees were coming through. After about two hours we piled back into the vans. The devotees were ecstatic. Sankirtan is the highest form of devotion to Krishna, I would learn.

The devotees continued chanting the mantra all the way back to the temple without pause. Their devotion to Krishna was inexhaustible.

Not for one moment did these people live in modern day America, an aspect of their lives I found most astonishing above all else. They lived in ancient India, one hundred percent, in their minds and in the physical environment they had created and within which they had encapsulated themselves, from top to bottom.

I had always found accepting one belief system as the absolute truth an impossible choice to make. But now I found myself thinking perhaps I truly had stumbled upon the absolute truth, so intense had this experience become. Every fiber of my being became filled with fright the moment this thought entered my mind, because the last thing I wanted was to become a Hare Krishna. But if what the devotees say is true, and Krishna in fact is God, what other choice would I have but to join them? These thoughts proved overwhelming, but they too would pass. Even the supreme personality of godhead couldn't compete with my itchy feet.

"It's difficult at first because we are all so attached to the material world. But no earthly pleasure can compete with serving Krishna and sitting at his lotus feet," the devotees would say. "Stay in the temple for six months and you'll never leave." I was beginning to believe them. The food alone had been the deciding factor for some, I had heard.

*Chapter One*

Does the nectar from Krishna's lips truly give the prasadam its transcendental taste? Or had the American worshippers of the blue skinned God of ancient India simply become master chefs in its exotic preparation? My inner skeptic had kicked in on several aspects of the experience, but the Eastern concepts of karma and reincarnation had taken root and a new spiritual foundation would establish itself in my mind, opening up a previously unknown world of mystical possibilities.

I had been in the temple for two weeks and Marty still hadn't returned. I prepared to move on, disappointed to leave without seeing my boyhood friend.

I said goodbye to Arlene. I tried to explain to her why I had to go.

"I can't commit to anything. I can't stay in one place. I need to keep moving," I said.

She was not sympathetic.

"You can't serve Krishna if you're living in the material world. You need to stay in the temple! Krishna is here!" she responded, her voice filled with urgency and concern for my spiritual well being.

"I promise I'll think about it. I need some time. I can't make a decision right now," I said in an attempt to soften my exit against her firm stance.

Arlene and Marty were always trying to convince their old friends from Baltimore to join the International Society for Krishna Consciousness. One already had and two more would soon follow, in time bringing the number to five.

I threw my backpack on my back and stepped out of the temple. As the devotees would say, I had stepped back into the arms of Maya, Goddess of the material world, also known as the great illusion.

I would not leave unchanged. I had opened myself up to a powerful spiritual experience and an incomparable learning experience as well. In a short couple of weeks, an in-depth education in Eastern religion, philosophy, thought, and culture had been planted in my brain. My introduction to vegetarianism, which began in the commune, had seen significant expansion, and the seeds of what would become my lifelong love for the music of India had been sown.

●

I carried five dollars into the Hare Krishna temple and I still had the same five dollars in my pocket when I left. With four thousand miles to go back to Baltimore, five dollars simply wasn't going to cut it, no matter how skillful I had become at making my money stretch. I needed to pick up a bit of temporary employment and Palm Springs seemed the perfect place. Interstate-10, the highway that would take me back to the East Coast runs straight through the famous desert resort town, about one hundred miles east of Los Angeles. At the most, I figured, I shouldn't need more than a couple of weeks, considering how much mileage I had gotten out of the small amount of money I had when the journey began.

One of those pint-sized Italian sports cars I never felt safe in pulled over to the side of the road. I squeezed in and the tiny two-seater took off, zipping across the desert, top down, wind in my hair, the magnificent San Bernardino Mountains in full view.

A fellow in his early thirties named Carl sat behind the wheel. I told him about my journey and of my hopeful plan to remedy my dire financial situation.

"I'm broke and I've still got a long ways to go."

"I live in Palm Springs," Carl said. "You're welcome to stay until my wife and kids return. We've been separated. She's coming back in two weeks."

We cruised into the elite desert resort and pulled into the driveway of a luxurious sprawling one-story home with

*Chapter One*

lemon trees in the front yard. A lucrative real estate deal had made Carl a wealthy man at a young age.

"There's food in the fridge, help yourself," Carl said as we stepped inside.

I had started out early from Los Angeles and my luck couldn't have been better. And now, with a full belly, a terrific place to stay, and the day still young, I set out to explore Palm Springs and look for a job. I walked past the lemon trees and headed into town. Sitting at an elevation of eleven thousand feet, the snow-capped peaks of the San Jacinto mountain range created a remarkable contrast to the palm trees and bright sunshine as I strolled along the exclusive desert resort's main boulevard in the afternoon heat.

I walked into a fashionable restaurant, asked about a job and began scrubbing pots and pans the following day, from eight in the morning until half past four in the afternoon with a half hour break for lunch. I wasn't paying rent and I was eating for free, both at Carl's house and at the restaurant, so I could save almost all of the money I earned.

Two weeks passed and Carl's wife returned with their two pre-school children. Payday at the restaurant was still a few days off. I could have stayed, but I knew Carl needed the time alone with his family. He had done enough for me already. And as it had been from the onset of the journey, I found myself humbled once again by the overwhelming generosity of a perfect stranger.

An isolated area of desert land hidden from view by a rugged tract of desert rocks on the edge of town became my home for the next three days after leaving Carl's house.

Three thousand miles of Interstate-10 lie ahead, through the Southwestern states of Arizona, New Mexico, and Texas, then along the Gulf Coast through the deep Southern states of Louisiana, Mississippi, and Alabama, delivering me to the state of Florida, from where I would begin the final leg of the journey, another eleven hundred miles north up the East Coast back to Baltimore.

The morning of my departure arrived. I crawled out of my sleeping bag at first light. I won't be shivering much longer, I reassured myself. And as the freezing desert night met the warming rays of the early morning sun, I threw my pack on my back, walked out to the highway and stuck out my thumb.

A fellow hitchhiker with whom I shared a ride offered me a place to sleep in his parents' home in Phoenix, Arizona on my first day back on the road.

El Paso, Texas at sunset is where I found myself at the end of the following day. I stood on the highway with my thumb out, hoping one lucky long distance ride would come along and carry me all the way through the night to San Antonio and I could sleep along the way, but the odds of that happening between the hours of darkness and morning's first light were not good. A long and dismal night awaited me.

One luckless hour passed. I abandoned my hitching spot and walked across the highway to a truck stop with an all night diner. Palm Springs had been good to me. I could afford to indulge. Putting my vegetarian conversion on hold, I chowed down on a good-n-greasy double cheeseburger and a double order of French fries, and after washing my meal down with a large Coca-Cola I tried my luck again on the highway. Another hour passed. I walked back to the diner, drank a cup of coffee and returned to the road, only to return to the diner after one more luckless hour.

I was stranded in El Paso, Texas and I could do nothing about it till sunrise, when, lo and behold, feeling sick in my stomach from too many cups of coffee and zero sleep, a car pulled over and came to a stop.

*Chapter One*

"Throw your gear in the back and hop in," the big bellied Texas good ole boy sitting behind the wheel hollered out the window as I approached the vehicle.

I placed my backpack on the backseat beside a couple of hunting rifles and climbed aboard.

"Henry's the name," he said.

Henry was clad in farmer's overalls with a green and yellow striped flannel work shirt. He wore a well worn cap bearing the name of a tractor company on his head, spoke in a Texas drawl so thick I could barely understand him, and looked as if he had just crawled out from under a bale of hay.

Nothing less than a precious gem at any antique car show in today's world, Henry's eight cylinder 1960 Chevy Impala two door sedan pulled back out to the highway and through the vast wide-open plains and prairies of the great Southwest we rolled, beneath the eternal skies of the lone star state, and I was carried straight through to San Antonio. And I was damn lucky to get one ride all the way, because endless empty hours of nothing but wild and boundless Texas ranch and cattle country is just about all that exists along this five hundred and fifty mile stretch of Interstate-10 running between El Paso and San Antonio.

Henry's conversation consisted of the following three subjects: farming, construction work, and heavy machinery, nothing more and nothing less. He could talk about each one without end, and he did, and not for one moment did he notice the difficulty I had understanding him, nor the trouble I had keeping my eyes open. He kept right on talking. I didn't have to say a word. All I had to do was grunt now and then so he'd think I was listening.

We arrived in San Antonio. A bit of sporadic dozing in Henry's car was all the sleep I had managed to get in over thirty hours. I thought about sleeping in the train station or the bus terminal and getting a fresh start in the morning, but with a few hours of daylight remaining I decided to take my chances and continue on to Houston instead, two hundred miles from San Antonio.

"Name's George. I'm just goin' a short ways up the road," the next driver to stop for me said.

"Every little bit helps," I replied.

George was a man of few words and I welcomed his quiet nature, because on this day of full-blown sleep deprivation I had scarcely a brain left with which to formulate a sentence. We cruised down the highway, silent, peaceful, and steady, when out of the blue all hell broke loose. Interstate-10 exploded into a flaming sea of sirens and flashing lights. George reached under his seat and pulled out a pistol as a convoy of Texas State Troopers sprang up all around us. My heart began pounding. I was terrified. Had he committed a robbery? Is he an escaped convict? Perhaps he's a serial killer. I'm either going to become a hostage or I'm about to be shot in the head. These were but a few of the panicked thoughts running through my mind in less than ten seconds. With gun in hand, George leaned over in my direction. I thought my heart would jump out of my chest. It was pounding so hard it hurt.

In his deep voice and slow Texas twang, George asked if I wouldn't mind putting the gun in the glove compartment for him. Frozen in a cold sweat, I took the weapon with a hand still shaking and followed through with his request.

I never did find out why George wanted the gun to go into the glove compartment as soon as he saw the fiery lights of the Texas State Troopers come blazing by. And he, in turn, remained completely oblivious to the emotional wreck I had become. George reached his exit and dropped me off. I stood on the highway, my head still in a daze, my heart still pounding. I wanted to get the hell out of Texas.

After a series of short rides with moderate spaces of time in between, the lucky long one carrying me all the way to Houston arrived.

## Chapter One

"I'm Roger and this here's Ralph. I picked Ralph up on the highway a little ways before I picked you up," the driver said.

Ralph, the other hitchhiker, with his brewery breath, tattoo covered arms, and missing front teeth had already begun making me nervous when he asked: "What are you doing in Houston?"

"Just passing through on my way to Florida," I replied.

"Got a place to stay in Houston?" he further inquired.

I told him I didn't.

"Stick with me," he said, "and you'll have a place to sleep tonight."

"Where do we go from here?" I asked as we stepped out to the sidewalk upon arriving in Houston. Darkness had fallen.

"We'll have to walk a couple of miles," Ralph replied.

At this point I could do nothing else but wonder what in the hell was I doing walking the streets of Houston in the pitch black night with a tattoo covered homeless wino whom I had just met and knew nothing about leading the way.

Questioning my own judgment, which certainly wasn't the first time, nor would it be the last, I followed Ralph into an abandoned apartment on the second floor of a rundown row house in a Houston slum. I wondered if we were trespassing. I knew the risk, but my desperate need for slumber superseded all logic at this point. I showered in a roach infested bathroom before drifting off to sleep on the floor in my sleeping bag with paranoid thoughts of my backpack disappearing in the night. But I had no need to worry. My backpack was still there when I awoke in the morning. Good fortune had found me once again, showing up this time in the form of a kind-hearted homeless drifter whose own luck seemed to have run out.

Bourbon Street was three hundred and fifty miles from Houston.

I stood on the side of the highway outside of Baton Rouge, Louisiana. Eighty miles remained before reaching

New Orleans. I began looking for a safe place to sleep, knowing how poor my chances were of getting a ride at night when the last thing I expected suddenly occurred. A young couple with a baby stopped to pick me up. And not only did they carry me the final distance into New Orleans, but they took me home with them as well.

"You'll have to cross the Mississippi River to visit the French Quarter," I was told. "We live on the other side."

I rode the ferry across the Mississippi River the following day and my tour of the famous French Quarter began. Showing admirable skills in the art of tap dancing, an aging street dancer grabbed my attention, his fast moving steel heeled feet tapping out rhythmic beats on the sidewalk. A crowd had gathered round. I stood and watched for a while and I dropped a few coins in his basket before moving on. The ear-catching sounds of Dixieland, Blues, and jazzy quartets echoed out from the spirited watering holes on Bourbon Street. There were plenty of girls around too. But did I believe those unavoidable, uncontrollable fantasies of an intimate encounter with a beautiful stranger of the opposite sex in the intriguing city of New Orleans I found flooding my mind had any chance of becoming reality? One can hope. But as I would discover, on this day, Lady Luck had no such plans for me.

I gave you the gift of a safe place to stay so you could have the golden opportunity of spending a backpack free day exploring the legendary city of New Orleans. And now you want more? I could hear Lady Luck saying.

"Actually, I do," I told her. I waited for a response, but none came.

I rode the ferry back across the mighty Mississippi before darkness fell and spent a second night with the generous couple and their baby. Unfulfilled fantasies notwithstanding, my visit to the Big Easy had still been a tremendous success, and my only expense had been two

## Chapter One

ferry boat rides and giving Mr. Bojangles the loose change in my pocket.

Continuing to travel along the Gulf Coast, I moved quickly through Louisiana and Mississippi, ending up outside of Mobile, Alabama at day's end. And as the remaining glimmer of daylight took its final bow and I prepared to roll out my sleeping bag in a patch of woods on the side of the road for the night, a Winnebago camper pulled over and came to a stop.

I hustled over to the colossal vehicle and opened the door. A man in his golden years named Jake sat behind the wheel.

"Climb on in," he said in a booming voice. I put my foot up on the running board and hoisted myself aboard. Three young guys sat at a table in the back of the rolling fortress drinking bottles of beer.

A native of Oklahoma, Jake spent his winters enjoying retired life living out of his Winnebago in Florida. He brought the three young guys along as drivers.

"They're useless!" he said. "They haven't been sober since we left."

I told Jake I too was on my way to Florida. He asked if I could drive. I told him I could.

"Great! Now here's the plan," Jake said. "We'll find a truck stop, or a parking lot, someplace where we can put down for the night and in the morning you, my friend, are driving us to Tallahassee. And from Tallahassee you're driving us to Tampa. Can you handle it?"

"Sure," I said.

The following morning I drove the humongous motor home from Mobile, Alabama to Tallahassee, Florida while Jake and the boys spent the day drinking beer, smoking cigarettes, and playing cards. We made regular stops at hamburger joints along the way. Jake picked up the tab at every meal. In Tallahassee we slept on the parking lot of a roadside restaurant. At daybreak, in the driver's seat again, I drove the remaining distance to Tampa, on the Gulf of Mexico.

"End of the line boys," Jake said, ready to retreat into his retirement paradise. I don't know what plans the other three guys had, but I continued traveling south until I reached the town of Naples. From there I resumed traveling east, through Alligator Alley, an eighty mile stretch through the Florida everglades, delivering me to the coastal town of Fort Lauderdale.

Upon the shores of the Atlantic Ocean I now stood, lost in a deeply pensive state of mind. My little road trip was coming to an end.

---

I walked around Fort Lauderdale hoping to find a floor to crash on. I figured sleeping on the beach in this town could easily land me in jail for vagrancy. I wasn't in California anymore. A man in his forties, slight of build and balding, stood in front of a small motel.

"You interested in working for a free place to stay?" he inquired of me as I strolled past with my backpack on my back.

"What would it involve?" I asked.

"Not much," he said. "Sweep the grounds, run a few errands, take out the trash. About two hours in the morning. The rest of the day is yours."

The guy looks awful peculiar, my instincts told me. But how choosy can one be when depending upon the charity of others to come popping out of nowhere? And so, I decided to go for it, despite my soon to be proven all too real misgivings.

I followed Walter into a small apartment attached to the motel's rental office.

"I'll have dinner ready shortly," Walter said, handing me a tall glass of ice tea. "How do you like your steak?"

"Well done," I responded, putting my vegetarian conversion on hold once again and putting the obvious question

## Chapter One

of what kind of a weirdo have I gotten myself mixed up with now in the back of my mind as well.

After dinner and upon Walter's request, I took a seat on the sofa in the living room. Walter set up a home movie screen and projector, as was the technology of the day, and I soon found myself watching a hardcore pornographic movie leaving nothing to the imagination. Walter sat beside me. That's when things really went to hell. Walter put his hand on my thigh. Like a bullet I shot to my feet.

Walter showed annoyance. His debauched plans had been ruined and in his twisted mind, I was at fault, I was the culprit, because I had rejected his perverted intentions.

"I'm taking a walk," I said. I had to get out of there. I had to think.

How disturbing was that? I can't believe it even happened. I knew something was wrong with that guy the moment I laid eyes on him. Why do I never listen to my own better judgment? These were but a few of the distressing thoughts flooding my mind as I walked along the ocean front boulevard on a balmy night in South Florida.

I continued wandering about Fort Lauderdale, the ever pleasing ambience of twilight at the shore easing my mind. At this point I saw no alternative to spending the night at Walter's place. I can handle the pervert for one night, I assured myself.

"Enjoy your walk?" Walter snidely asked upon my return, his nerd face wrapped in a maddening smirk.

I thought again about splitting. But I was dead tired; it had been a long day since leaving Jake's Winnebago outside of Tampa in the morning. And so, in spite of it all, I went ahead and crashed on Walter's sofa anyway.

"Leaving?" Walter asked as I headed for the door first thing in the morning, all packed up and ready to get the hell out of there. He looked me up and down. He had the creepiest expression on his face. It made my skin crawl. I couldn't believe I slept under the same roof with this guy.

I marched out the door, made my way to the highway and hitchhiked to Key West, a magnificent two hundred mile journey over a series of bridges connecting the tiny islands of the Florida Keys, including a spectacular ride over the famous seven mile bridge, one of the longest bridges in the world.

In Key West, a festive sunset celebration takes place every evening on the waterfront at Mallory Square. I heard about it along the traveler's grapevine. Although I believe hitchhiking four hundred miles out of my way for the sole purpose of watching the sun set at one particular earthly location simply because of the event's high degree of pop culture popularity would be considered downright questionable thinking by more than a few.

I arrived in Key West and spent the remaining hours of daylight exploring America's southernmost point.

A joyous, raucous, high spirited crowd clapped and cheered in celebration, bidding goodnight to the setting sun as it made its slow descent over the Gulf of Mexico, sending a dazzling display of captivating color dancing across the celestial sphere. The daily ritual came to an end, the crowd slowly dispersed and I still hadn't found a place to sleep. I had been certain I would, with the large gathering of people there, having a good time, passing bottles of wine around, but it didn't happen, to my utmost surprise, and I was at a loss.

Should I spend some of the money I made in Palm Springs and rent a room? I pondered the question, for with it came a life altering implication; namely, the undoing, downfall, and ruination of my perfect score of not having spent one cent on accommodations throughout the entire journey. Weighing my options carefully, I walked into the lobby of a cheap motel and inquired into the cost of a room for the night. Scrutinizing all outcomes, consequences, and

## Chapter One

ramifications, I made my decision. In approximately seven thousand miles of hitchhiking so far, and over a thousand yet to go, it would be the only time I would pay for a place to sleep.

I checked in, showered, turned on the television and climbed into bed. What a treat. My enjoyment; however, was short lived. I was exhausted and sleep came all too quickly. In the morning, surrounded by water and sunshine, I hit the highway and headed north. I was going home.

Interstate-95 runs the entire length of the East Coast, from Florida to Maine. I had no doubt a long distance ride would come along at some point in the journey, although I didn't expect it to happen as fast as it did, nor could I have imagined how perfect it would be. As I once again passed through Fort Lauderdale, a van with Vermont tags carrying five young people, two girls and three guys, pulled over and came to a stop. The door on the side of the van opened up and in I climbed. Two passengers sat in the front. The other three sat on the floor in the back where the seats had been removed.

"How far are you going?" a voice in the crowd inquired.

"Baltimore," I replied.

"We're driving non-stop to Vermont," another voice in the crowd said as they shuffled about, making room for me among themselves and the luggage.

All five were followers of Sri Chinmoy, a holy man from India and a popular guru of the day. They were returning to Vermont after attending a gathering held in Miami for Sri Chinmoy and his flock of American disciples.

When speaking about Sri Chinmoy the disciples referred to him as "our guru." Otherwise, they appeared as regular everyday folks. They wore no special garb, nor did they limit their conversation to their spiritual path alone, and they didn't try to talk me into becoming one of them.

I told them about my journey. I spoke of all the beautiful places I had seen and how humbled I had been by the overwhelming generosity extended to me by my fellow Americans. And I spoke of my own introduction to Eastern spirituality in the Krishna temple in Los Angeles, and of my experience in the commune in Santa Barbara.

My goal when I set out from Baltimore had been to see the Rocky Mountains, the Grand Canyon, and the coasts of Oregon and California, and I would have been more than satisfied accomplishing these objectives alone. But the journey evolved far beyond anything I could have ever imagined.

Cruising north on Interstate 95, we rolled through Florida and Georgia, stretching out in the night side by side in our sleeping bags, packed in like sardines, everyone except the designated driver, of course. South Carolina, North Carolina, and Virginia came next.

"Where in Baltimore do you want us to drop you off?" the driver inquired as we closed in on the Maryland line.

"I don't want to inconvenience you guys," I responded.

"No problem," the disciples replied.

What I really wanted was to stay on the road, where everything was unfamiliar and new. Didn't matter where I was going, or in what direction I was heading. The road itself had become the journey. No past, no future, only the present. Every moment a fresh start, a blank slate. Now, I was back in familiar territory, returning to my former self, and I wasn't sure I even knew who that person was anymore.

*Chapter Two*

## A BRIEF DESCRIPTION OF MY CIRCUMSTANCES AND WHEREABOUTS IMMEDIATELY PRECEDING THE JOURNEY

Lenny Jackson was a likable but somewhat shady character with an appearance reflective of Mediterranean descent and a facial resemblance to the actor Harvey Keitel who played the pimp in "Taxi Driver" with Robert De Niro.

I first met Lenny while strolling about the historic Baltimore City neighborhood of Charles Village near Johns Hopkins University on a pleasant evening in the spring of 1972. We stopped to chat and developed an immediate rapport.

At the time, my mind had fallen into a state of uncertainty. A long term relationship had abruptly ended. Within days I would have nowhere to live. Upon hearing of my predicament and often finding himself in similar situations, Lenny gave me his address, without hesitation, and offered me a place to stay in the apartment he shared with two other guys a few blocks from where our first meeting took place.

I popped over the following day. Lenny introduced me to his roommates, Barry and Morris, two Jewish guys Lenny knew from City College, a high school for academic achievers, and by all appearances it most certainly seemed as if the achieving had stopped there.

A boisterous loudmouth, Morris wore a huge white man's afro on his head and bore a resemblance to the guitarist Frank Zappa.

Barry was an exceptionally good-natured fellow. His short height and prematurely receding hairline caused him to suffer from bouts of insecurity. He needn't have, but no one could convince him otherwise. Barry's part time job as a telephone counselor on a suicide hotline made him the only one of the three with any visible source of income.

Getting stoned and listening to music occupied much of the day for these guys. And Lenny would smoke a joint anywhere. He would light up sitting on the stoop. He would smoke walking down the street. He never worried about getting busted. Lenny had served in a combat unit in Vietnam that suffered heavy casualties. He was lucky to be alive. In his mind he had earned the right to smoke a joint anywhere and anytime he pleased.

Charles Village is an area comprised of early 1900s three story row homes converted into multiple apartment units. No one presently living in the small two bedroom apartment could make an exclusive claim on the place because the original inhabitants were no longer there. The place had been passed down from one misfit to another. For this reason, no one could object when Lenny invited me to move in.

Meeting Lenny and moving into the apartment opened up an entirely new world for me. Not only were my new roommates a curious bunch of characters, but the apartment itself had become a magnet for people living on the edge, people who didn't fit in. A steady stream of potheads

*Chapter Two*

and acidheads; travelers and transients; the gender confused; misfits and street freaks; hippie girls and crazy girls, and some normal girls too, would find their way into our living room throughout the summer. And I met Elaine, a student at Johns Hopkins University. Elaine lived in the apartment next door and became my girlfriend shortly after I moved in; hence, taking my crazy idea of hitchhiking across America off the back burner and putting it into action became an even more difficult decision to make.

Summer's end drew near. Autumn approached. If I was going to follow through with my plan, I needed to act. The weather would turn against me if I didn't leave soon.

Acquiring a backpack and a sleeping bag became my top priority, neither of which had I ever possessed. They were also the components with the biggest price tags, leaving me to begin the journey with barely one hundred dollars in my pocket. Of course, I didn't have to buy a goose down, the most expensive sleeping bag, but I knew I would regret my decision if I didn't.

I would travel only with the simplest of necessities, keeping my backpack light. In addition to my sleeping bag, these bare essentials would include: one extra pair of jeans and several days' worth of tee-shirts, socks, and underwear; one light jacket; a plastic poncho; a towel and a bar of soap; a fork and spoon; a camping knife; a flashlight; a canteen filled with water; a jar of peanut butter; a loaf of bread; a bag of nut and dried fruit mix, and a map of the United States.

Elaine drove me to the highway on the morning of my departure. We said our goodbyes and I stepped out to the road. Am I crazy? I asked myself. I sure am! I answered, and then I took a deep breath and stuck out my thumb.

## Chapter Three
# HOME

I stood on a street in downtown Baltimore where the five disciples of Sri Chinmoy had dropped me off. My final ride of the journey had been with the followers of an Indian holy man, a fact I contemplated as I picked up my feet, on a freezing December day, and trudged back to the last place I had called home. My little road trip had come to an end.

"Fritz!" Lenny said, standing in the doorway, shocked by my unexpected arrival. My middle name, Fred, is the English translation of Fritz, my German Grandfather's name. Lenny began calling me Fritz after I made the mistake of giving him this information. Thank goodness he was the only one of my friends to do so.

I walked into the apartment. I didn't have to say a word. I simply moved right back in and it wasn't long, to my utmost dismay, before I felt as if I had never left.

A bewildering question overwhelmed my mind: What am I doing back in Baltimore? At a loss for an answer, I sank into depression. I also began working on a solution.

Feeling lost and hopeless was not a state of mind I wished to linger in too long. As soon as spring arrived, I thus decided, I would relocate to Ocean City, a bustling beach resort on the Maryland Coast, find gainful employment, save my money and travel to Europe in the fall.

Getting back on the road was the only justification for my continued existence in this world that made any sense to me at all.

At the age of eighteen, I spent my first summer on the Maryland Shore working as a dishwasher at Phillips Crab House. I shared a tiny cottage with two co-workers located in the back of a large apartment house one block from the boardwalk, between Fifth and Sixth Streets. My rent totaled ten dollars a week. The cottage had a toilet and a sink inside, but no shower. The only shower available to us was a cold outdoor shower attached to the back of the apartment house originally put in place so guests could rinse their feet off when they came in from the beach to avoid tracking sand into their rooms. A ramshackle wooden enclosure had been added for privacy.

Four years later I spent the summer in Ocean City again, working as a busboy at the Embers, a sprawling restaurant with six large dining rooms and a nightclub with live entertainment. I hoped to return to the Embers, but as a waiter this time, the only way to make real money at the beach.

I wished to set myself up with a seasonal summer job where I could work four or five months, live at the beach while doing so, and have the remainder of the year free for travel. I knew I could achieve this goal at the Embers because I knew how the management operated. Employees in good standing, if they wished to return, were invited back year after year. I was desperate to make my plan work.

I headed for the beach in early spring. I thought I might still have a chance to get hired at the Embers, but to

## Chapter Three

my disappointment, they had completed their staffing for the season. Openings wouldn't come up again until people began leaving for college toward the end of the summer. I landed a job at Phillips by the Sea in the meantime, working in the kitchen preparing appetizers.

When I first arrived in Ocean City, I lived in a large three-story boarding house. The landlady, who also owned an Italian-ice shop on the boardwalk, had a crazy system of renting to more people than she had room for. I gave up trying to get a bed at night and slept on the floor instead. In the month of June I moved into a beach house with five surfing fanatics who went surfing every morning after staying up half the night drinking beer.

The summer season moved along, Labor Day approached, and I still hadn't saved a dime for my trip to Europe. Sure, I had hitchhiked throughout the United States on next to nothing, but one can't hitchhike across the ocean, and running out of money in a foreign country is a situation I would never want to find myself in.

Through my unwavering persistence, Alessandro, the suave Italian headwaiter, finally agreed to hire me, but as a busboy. He said he would promote me to waiter next year.

This I couldn't let happen. I'd be going nowhere at season's end if I did. Left with no alternative but to tell an untruth, I told Alessandro I had gained significant waiter experience in other restaurants since working as a busboy at the Embers several years earlier, a story, I'm sure, he had heard many times before.

I began on a weekend at the peak of the season, the worst possible time for someone with no waiter experience to find themselves on the floor for the first time. The doors opened, the hungry beachgoers came pouring in, and I knew in a flash the deep trouble I was in. The hostesses seated my tables, bang, bang, one after the other, barely able to stagger them because so many people came in at the same time. The experienced servers could weather the storm, but I became stuck, as they say in restaurant jargon. I was stuck big time!

I had been assigned four tables. One table grew more impatient by the minute waiting for their entrees to arrive while another wondered where in the world could their desserts possibly be hiding and a third table wondered if their appetizers were in the house at all. And to make matters even more demanding, all three had requested drinks and table number four had requested their check. The pressure became unbearable. My anxiety reached new peaks. Serious thoughts of dropping everything, calling it quits and walking out crossed my mind, so stressful had the situation become. And to top it off, as if the situation hadn't deteriorated to an absurd enough point already, the family waiting for their check couldn't wait any longer and walked out without paying, setting the stage for even further ludicrousness as the most bizarre restaurant transaction in restaurant history unfolded.

My customers left me a note with their hotel and room number, instructing me to stop by later and collect the money. Facing them embarrassed me, but I felt enormous gratitude also, since the restaurant made its servers pay out of their own pockets when customers walked out on their checks.

One year ago pretty much to the day I began my journey across America, a journey of spiritual awakening, and now I find myself running around like a madman inside of an exclusive restaurant dressed in full black tuxedo with a white shirt, frills, and a black bow tie, serving gourmet dinners, pouring fine wine into polished glasses, and serving mixed drinks garnished with olives, maraschino cherries, and slices of orange. Could anyone's life be any more absurdly incongruous? I don't think so, my perplexed inner voice replied.

My anxiety shot through the sky when I saw Alessandro approach at the end of my nerve-racking first night.

## Chapter Three

I'm done for. I've been exposed. I'm an imposter and Alessandro knows it. Alessandro was the quintessential waiter. Medium in height, he was muscular, handsome, debonair, and carried with him an abundance of self-confidence. Alessandro had more natural suave than anyone I had ever seen. I, on the other hand, had none.

I didn't want to get fired. This job was my ticket to travel. I knew I could become a successful waiter, given the right amount of time and practice, although getting fired may have been easier to emotionally endure than hearing Alessandro speak to me about my disastrous performance. To my enormous relief, he neither fired nor reprimanded me.

Instead, he put his arm around my shoulder and in his heavy Italian accent he spoke the following reassuring words: "Don't worry, tomorrow will be better."

There are those rare times in one's life when one is given exactly what one needs in a moment of despair. I believe I can say with unwavering certainty this was one of those times.

A cool and gentle breeze blew in from the sea as I strolled along the boardwalk. The perfect amount of pristine puffy white clouds delicately laced an immaculate blue sky. Labor Day had passed and the boardwalk stood practically empty. The once hustling, bustling, crowded summer resort felt like a quaint New England village in the autumn scented September morning.

The disaster of my first day on the job would soon pass into memory. A few more shifts and I felt as if I had been waiting tables forever. The genetics of suave and polish may have passed me by, but I would learn the job well and become a reasonably good waiter, nonetheless.

Mid-October rolled around and the restaurant closed its doors until next year. In the final two months of the season, in the true spirit of frugality, I managed to bank one thousand dollars. I returned to Baltimore for a brief visit with family and friends, booked a flight to Europe and soon departed for New York City to catch my plane.

## Chapter Four
# CROSSING THE ATLANTIC

Bordering on France, Germany, and Belgium, the Grand Duchy of Luxembourg is one of the tiniest countries in the world, with an area slightly smaller than the state of Rhode Island.

At the budget cost of a mere one hundred dollars, one could fly aboard an Icelandic Airways Boeing 727 from New York City to Luxembourg. The airline of the small North Atlantic island nation of Iceland offered the cheapest fares to Europe at the time.

How frugally can one human being live on the road on the other side of the Atlantic? I needed an answer and I needed it fast, because on this trip, food, lodging, and transportation would prove themselves an expense to be dealt with. Unlike my previous outing when I was taken in and fed throughout much of the journey. No doubt, generous people exist in all corners of the planet, and with all due respect and it is purely my humble opinion, but only in America I believe could the benevolence I experienced have taken place to such an extent.

71

I rode the bus from the airport to historic Luxembourg's youth hostel. Had I not found the youth hostels affordable, I would have indeed been screwed, because no viable alternative existed on my budget. To the question of diet, through my rare and peculiar ability to subsist on the same minimal variety of foods for long periods of time the answer would come.

Upon the soil of the old world my feet now tread, where the most supreme of cheeses are made and the finest of breads are baked. It was a no brainer. I would live on bread and cheese with a café au lait and a European pastry thrown in on occasion. One must treat oneself now and then, even on a budget such as mine. And last but not least, the question of transportation, to which I could think of only one solution. I would try my luck hitchhiking, as I had done on my journey across America. In addition, and to my good fortune, the exchange rate in Europe was excellent at the time.

Unable to sleep more than an intermittent couple of hours on the night flight to Luxembourg, I found myself deep in the throes of sleep deprivation. But rather than give in to slumber's nagging temptation, I chose to spend the entire day on my feet instead, wandering throughout tiny Luxembourg. Founded in the ninth century, Luxembourg's charming old world cobbled lanes and medieval architecture kept me energized, sparking my imagination with captivating tales of Europe during the middle-ages.

The following day I boarded a bus for the short ride to the German city of Frankfurt. From there my tour of the European continent would begin.

I spent one night in the Frankfurt youth hostel. The following day I headed for Paris. On an invigorating autumn morning under crisp October skies, I stood on the autobahn with my thumb out, watching the little European cars whiz by.

## Chapter Four

A vehicle driven by a young German in his early twenties named Helmut soon pulled over and came to a stop. I climbed aboard and in my best German I introduced myself and informed Helmut of my intended destination.

"How do you know German?" Helmut asked.

"My parents came from Germany," I informed him.

"Are you Jewish?" Helmut inquired, after a short pause.

"Yes," I replied.

Both the German and English languages found their way into my head during the formative language learning years, although I'm sure German was the language my baby brain heard first, a logical assumption, I would think, since my parents would have been the only people talking to me during this stage of my life. The German language established roots, but those roots were not allowed to grow, because once I began speaking, I only spoke English. I would continue hearing my parents speaking German to each other throughout my growing up years, and they would speak both languages to me, but even when they spoke to me in German, I would still only answer in English. As a result, I learned to understand the German language, but I struggle to speak. Passive knowledge versus active knowledge. The German language became stuck in an early developmental stage in my brain, the stage where a child has a fair level of understanding but is only beginning to speak.

Unlike a second language one learns through study but forgets when not used, my German abilities have remained the same since childhood, despite having few opportunities throughout my adult life to hear or speak the German language. There's a little German boy living in my head. But as he readied himself to fly, an English speaking child came along and pushed him aside. The English speaking child grew up learning his language well. The little German boy is still waiting for his turn to speak. I'd like to give him the opportunity. I'm looking forward to meeting him.

## An Extraordinary Tale of Travel

My difficulty in expressing myself in German beyond basic conversation made me hesitant to give Helmut the full details of my family's ordeal under the Nazi regime. And the sensitivity of the subject matter gave me another reason for pause. After all, only one generation had passed since the end of the Nazi era. I wasn't sure which way to go with it, until Helmut began speaking perfect English, as many Germans do. I then proceeded to tell him about my German family, almost all of whom perished in the Holocaust.

My father was born in 1910 in Gorlitz, a small German town on the Polish border. Gorlitz grew out of a medieval village established in the eleventh century. My Mother was born in 1911 in the great German city of Berlin. I grew up with one foot in the old world and one in the new. My ancestral history on both sides of the family lies firmly rooted in Germany. They were Jews, but they were also proud Germans. Several of my family members served in the German Army during the First World War, including my great uncle on my father's side who was killed in France in 1914 at the age of twenty-five. Through countless generations my family had been devoted, well established citizens of Germany, active in all areas of German life, and then came the horror of the holocaust.

Only a few members of my family fled their native Germany during the Nazi era. Among them were my newlywed parents, my father's younger brother, and several cousins. And as the window of time to escape narrowed to a sliver before the door was shut for good, both of my widowed grandmothers miraculously managed to flee. The remaining family members were rounded up, crammed into freight and cattle cars and transported by rail to the death camps. An extended family of over forty people. Children among them. None survived. All lost their lives in Hitler's gas chambers.

*Chapter Four*

    Forced to stand, packed in so tight were they, pressed against each other with scarcely room to breathe, and without food or water throughout the entire nightmarish journey. For the old and infirm, the journey itself was their death sentence. Such was the fate of my great grandmother, a small and frail woman in her eighties. Unable to tolerate the train ride from hell, she died in route. By way of the phenomenal work of the international Red Cross, my parents would in time receive a full accounting of our family members' fates.

    Eighty percent of our family had been murdered by the Nazis and my parents, having grown up in the comfort and security of affluent households with loving parents and loving extended families, committing no crime, were forced to become refugees, to lose their country, and to struggle for years. They would ultimately live good lives in America, but the loss of home and loved ones was much too traumatic for the emotional scars to ever fully go away.

    The Holocaust was a consistent theme in my life growing up. My parents would talk about their families and their towns in Germany. They could never completely come to terms with what had happened and all they had lost. I could only imagine how devastating it must have been when at war's end they first heard the news. Six million, the final count, and the majority of their friends and family were among the annihilated. All of the aforementioned and the pain that never left could do nothing less than have a profound effect upon the offspring of people who have had history's most horrifying and insane misfortune fall upon them. One can't avoid being wounded oneself by events so deeply wounding one's parents.

    I began to wonder if I had made the right decision in telling a native German the horrific tale of my family's plight under the Nazi regime and I hoped I hadn't made Helmut uncomfortable. Then again, why should making a native German uncomfortable on the subject of the Holocaust cause me unease? Perhaps because I understood who bears the guilt. Helmut's parents' generation bear the guilt. Not Helmut's generation, nor any subsequent generation, born after the war into a new and changed Germany. I could have used some advice. But few understood what it meant to grow up in the shadow of the Holocaust.

I needn't have worried. Having made my acquaintance pleased Helmut. He considered our conversation a rare opportunity. After all, it's not every day a native German meets someone like me. Our conversation then turned to less serious subjects for the remainder of the ride, which, by the way, was a terrific ride, carrying me a good distance across Germany, ever closer to France.

My final ride into Paris came as a young Frenchman driving a Citroen stopped to pick me up. Unlike Helmut, the Frenchman spoke not one word of English.

"*Paris*," I said as I climbed into the tiny French car.

"*Oui*," he answered.

"*Merci*," I replied.

"*No parle Anglais*," he said.

"*No parle Francais*," I responded.

Our feeble attempt at communication made us both laugh as the Frenchman steered his little car back out to the highway. In silence we rolled through the beautiful French countryside, making no more impossible attempts at conversation.

"*Au revoir, merci*," I said as I stepped out of the tiny vehicle upon arriving in Paris.

"*Au revoir*," the Frenchman, amused at my efforts, responded with a smile.

I walked a bit along a classic wide Parisian boulevard before taking a seat at a sidewalk café. Refreshing myself with a cold bottle of sparkling water, I sat, in quiet fascination, observing life on the streets of the world's most charming

## Chapter Four

city. Spellbound, I listened to the French language spoken all around me, wondering if it sounds as beautiful to its native speakers as it does to those of us who don't understand it.

By and large, accommodations in European youth hostels in the 1970s consisted of co-ed dormitories filled with narrow beds, bunk beds more often than not. And as an added bonus to the affordable lodging, guests could enjoy toast with delicious European marmalade, a small glass of juice, and a cup of tea every morning. The light fare, known as a continental breakfast, was complimentary and standard at all European youth hostels.

Finding my way to the youth hostel in the great city of Paris was the immediate challenge at hand. I would have success, but locating the metro, finding the right platform and boarding the right train, and figuring out where to get off proved no easy task, with no directions and so few English speakers among the French to help guide my way.

A diverse variety of physical locations housed the European youth hostels. So far I had found no consistency in structure or design. All were unique. A sprawling one-story state of the art modern red brick building with a beautiful indoor fountain sitting in the center of a fashionable lobby housed the Paris youth hostel. A stone built structure sitting on a cobbled lane served as Luxembourg's youth hostel. The interior had been modernized, but the original medieval exterior had been left untouched. And a three-story mansion, rustic and old, its character intact, but its former grandeur now left only to the imagination, served as the site of the youth hostel in the German city of Frankfurt.

Her eyes stared straight into mine from every angle, no matter where I stood. Such was the magic of the Mona Lisa. My tour of Paris began in the morning with a trip to the legendary Louvre. I had one painting in mind to see, and had I seen nothing more than Leonardo Di Vinci's timeless masterpiece, I would have been satisfied, but I ended up getting lost, both literally and figuratively, lost in the Louvre's endless haunting hallways, deep majestic rooms, and vast elegant chambers, abundant with artistic expression of every shape, style, and form from every recorded century and civilization of man's existence on the planet Earth. The Louvre is much more than a museum. The Louvre is a city, a fabulous city of art.

I walked the historic lanes of Montmartre, the world's most famous artist's colony, rising in splendor at one hundred and thirty meters above the metropolis, overlooking Paris at its highest point and thought of by many, both past and present, as the most charming district in Paris. I let my imagination run wild, envisioning what colorful camaraderie and captivating conversation there must have been in Montmartre's sidewalk cafés when Montmartre was the Bohemian capital of Europe and the likes of Vincent Van Gogh, Henri Matisse, Renoir, Picasso, Edgar Degas, Toulouse-Lautrec, and Salvador Dali, to name a few, called Montmartre home, and what wild nights there must have been in pursuit of wine and woman and all matters of merry making in the bistros, brothels, cabarets, and dance halls of nineteenth century France.

Ever since I crossed the great saltwater sea, images of long-ago times, eras, ages, and epochs began rolling past my eyes and an exhilarating new reality had taken shape in my mind. I had made an incredible discovery. With a little imagination and a love of history, one in fact can travel through time, to whatever century or civilization one wishes to explore.

I toured the twelfth century Cathedral of Notre Dame. Taking over one hundred years to complete, the Cathedral of Notre Dame is the largest cathedral in Europe and an unparalleled example of Gothic era architectural design. Even those not familiar with the cathedrals of Europe

*Chapter Four*

have heard of the Cathedral of Notre Dame, brought to even greater fame by French author Victor Hugo in his landmark novel, the Hunchback of Notre Dame, a stirring statement of class, attitudes, and injustice in fifteenth century France.

I wandered the world's most elegant boulevard, the Champs-Elysees, and I strolled along the River Seine. I paid a visit to the Arc De Tromphe, and I took a trip to the top of the Eiffel Tower. I fell in love with sidewalk cafés and I drank too many cups of café au lait accompanied by a few too many French pastries. The original plan of a treat now and then seemed to have flown right out the window in Paris.

You'll have to cut your ration of bread and cheese in half for a week to make up for the money you spent indulging yourself in Paris, my inner voice, coming this time from the financial wizard part of my brain, declared. And I knew full well these were orders I had no choice but to follow.

Temperatures took a drop, forcing me to bundle up as I journeyed north into the Netherlands. At one point in the journey I found myself trekking through a small Dutch village from one end to the other in order to get back to the highway from where I had been dropped off. Cheerful crowds of Netherlanders were out and about. Children played on the sidewalks. Bicycles, a vital mode of transportation in Europe to this day, hurried along on busy bicycle only paths running parallel to and in between the sidewalks and the streets, carrying people of all ages, sizes, shapes, genders, and stations in life. And the language had changed. Dutch was now the people's spoken word.

Wrapped snug and tight in a winter coat with a wool hat slipped over his head and a backpack on his back, exhaling visible vapor into the nippy northern air, a stranger from another land marched through a tiny town in the land of windmills. The friendliest smiles and the heartiest hellos greeted him every step of the way.

I arrived in Amsterdam in the early evening after a long day of hitchhiking through France, Belgium, and Holland. The official youth hostel had no vacancy, but the famous Dutch city provided plenty of other spots where a budget traveler could rest his weary head. One such place was a huge old factory building, a gray and cheerless three-story brick structure, circa the early 1900s. I tried to imagine what kind of factory it could have been. A depressing one, no doubt about it. The vibes never left the building. And with those thoughts, images came into my mind. One enormous room covered each of the structure's three floors. I envisioned each room filled with sewing machines, all going at once, and at each sewing machine sat one lonely seamstress, working for pennies from morning till night. A sweatshop in the days of the industrial revolution. Now, narrow bunk beds packed each of these three rooms. And the vacancies were few. Seemed everyone had Amsterdam on their list.

I soon hit the streets of the historic city. Amsterdam's bustling night life was in full swing. I strolled into one of Amsterdam's legendary cafés and stood among the crowd. A chalk board listing cost and origin of hashish available for sale hung on the wall. Two guys in their mid to late twenties approached and struck up a conversation with me in English. One was an Israeli and the other was a Jew from Morocco who had lived in Israel but said he didn't like it there. At the time, I had no knowledge of Amsterdam's reputation as a haven for unsavory characters and small time criminals, many of whom were on the run, as I would later have good reason to believe these two were.

The Israeli was a prematurely balding short guy and his personality seemed to have gone missing. His friend, the

## Chapter Four

Moroccan, had an engaging personality and did most of the talking.

They invited me to accompany them to a gathering at a friend's house. My instincts told me accepting their offer might not be such a good idea, but I went ahead, fell right back into my inexplicable pattern of ignoring my own better judgment and joined them anyway.

We left the café, walked a couple of quick city miles along the celebrated streets of Amsterdam and entered a house where a small group of people had gathered inside. And of those assembled within, not one was anything less than shady, suspect, and of questionable character. Dutch is the official language of Holland, but everyone in this house spoke French. The Israeli and I were unable to communicate, but the Moroccan spoke perfect French, having grown up in a country that for many years had been under French colonial rule.

A huge joint made its way around the room. The Europeans, I discovered, liked to make joints the size of cigars, mixing the intoxicating ingredient with tobacco. In this case the intoxicating ingredient consisted of extremely potent hashish. The joint came my way and I took a puff. A guy using hand motions because he spoke no English communicated to me to hold on to the joint for a while, so I took a few more puffs before passing it on. The Moroccan and another seedy looking character were engaged in conversation in French. They stopped for a moment, and with strange smiles upon their faces they both looked over at me at the same time, laughed, looked back at each other, spoke a few more words in French, turned back toward me again and laughed some more.

This hashish was some pretty wicked stuff, and I'm prone to paranoia anyway when I get stoned, but this disturbing interaction pushed me straight over the edge, planting in my mind the belief that people were talking about me and conspiring against me. The joint came my way again. I took several more puffs. I knew doing so would only serve to increase my paranoia, but I also knew what a big deal they would make out of it if I took a pass.

An annoying loud-mouthed guy turned in my direction and began shouting at me in French. The room burst into hysterics as I stood, frozen, staring at him, mute and unable to respond while he carried on. I wanted to get out of there, but I was dependent upon the Israeli and the Moroccan to lead the way back and I had no idea how long they planned to hang around.

I was lost somewhere in Amsterdam in a strange room filled with international outcasts. I couldn't understand one word of anything coming out of anyone's mouth, and a powerful paranoia held me in its grip.

A complicated matter can paranoia be. How much of my paranoia was in truth reality and how much of it could I attribute to the hashish?

"I have a gun and I'm going to kill you if you don't give me your money," the Moroccan said as he and his weasel buddy stopped in front of an abandoned house on our way back.

A dreadful fright swept over me. My suspicions had proven themselves correct.

Horror-struck, I could do nothing more than stand in place and stare at them. My heart began pounding. They could kill me right here, hide my body in this abandoned house and in all probability get away with it. One transient murdering another transient in a city filled with transients. Who would know or even care?

I didn't see a gun, and I thought the odds of a bluff were good, but I was taking no chances. I offered them the small amount of Dutch guilders I had in my wallet, which amounted to about twenty U.S. dollars.

"Here, take it!" I said, breaking into a cold sweat.

"That's all the money you have on you?" the Moroccan asked.

*Chapter Four*

"Yes," I said.

They looked at each other with blank stares on their faces.

"We're not going to kill you," the Israeli said.

The Moroccan confirmed his statement and we continued our trek back to town.

"We're sorry," they repeated several times, patting me on the back, trying to calm me down and console me.

I couldn't speak. My heart hadn't stopped pounding. What kind of idiots are these guys? First, they try to rob me and threaten me with death, and now they're apologizing. Do they have any idea of the emotional trauma they have caused me?

I got away from the crazy bastards as fast as I could the minute I recognized our location and hurried back to my hotel, only to find the doors locked and not scheduled to reopen until six o'clock in the morning. My grip on reality, tenuous under normal conditions, had now been pushed straight over the edge.

The bunk bed warehouse finally opened its doors. I couldn't get into my sleeping bag fast enough. I couldn't recall ever having had as bizarre a day as the one I just had. In one twenty-four hour period, I hitchhiked from Paris to Amsterdam, met up with the Israeli and the Moroccan, thought I was going to be murdered, and spent the damp wee hours of a chilly October night loitering on a dark deserted street somewhere in the Netherlands waiting for dawn to arrive.

I awoke at noon, showered, and headed back out to the streets of Amsterdam. I had learned a valuable lesson, one I wouldn't soon forget. I needed to take note. Everything had changed. I had veered off the recognizable highway. I had of my own choosing taken an unfamiliar exit, landing me square out in a world I could no longer call mine.

I passed through the red light district, where a fascinating assortment of women put themselves on view, like a shop display, in the stylish sitting rooms of narrow eighteenth century attached dwellings running along Amsterdam's famed canals and cobblestone streets. The legal prostitutes came in a variety of race, ethnicity, and nationalities.

I motioned to one through her lacy curtained picture window. She opened the door and let me in.

She was a petite woman of Caucasian descent with long straight jet black hair. She wasn't half bad looking, even with a face reflecting a hard road traveled, which made guessing her age difficult. Her small size, which gave her a certain cuteness, also factored into the difficulty. I also couldn't figure out her nationality. She spoke broken English with an accent I didn't recognize, leading me to believe she came from one of those mysterious regions in Eastern Europe, deep in territory controlled by the Russian Communists, locked behind the Iron Curtain, where everyone is watched, travel not allowed, every movement controlled, and only those willing to risk prison or even death sometimes manage to escape. Where families would huddle round their radios waiting to hear news from the West, beamed to them by radio free Europe, giving them hope they too would one day be free. As a kid I would see re-enactments of these despairing scenes on television in commercials asking for donations to keep radio free Europe running during the height of the cold war.

I inquired about the sexual acts she offered and what the cost of these pleasurable activities might be. She was eager, friendly, and forthcoming at first, thinking she had a customer. Her mood changed fast, though, giving way to an unsmiling, no nonsense all business disposition and I was quickly shown the door when she realized I was only fooling around, wasting her time, having fun with my curiosity.

I stepped out of the one woman brothel and continued my walking tour of historic Amsterdam. I toured the Rembrandt and Vincent Van Gogh museums, the latter

## Chapter Four

having the world's largest collection of the brilliant but tormented Dutch artist's paintings on display. And I toured the Anne Frank house, where the fourteen-year-old Jewish girl, her parents, older sister, another couple, their teenage son, and a single man had been hidden away in an attic by courageous Dutch citizens risking their own lives to save Jews during the Second World War. The house has been preserved as a monument and museum by the government of Holland.

On a fateful day in August, 1944, after two years in hiding, their luck ran out. The Nazis had found them. They were arrested and shipped to a death camp. Out of the eight people who had been in hiding, only Anne Frank's father, Otto Frank, survived. He returned to the house after the war and found his daughter's diary. The teenager's writings would become the famous Diary of Anne Frank, published in multiple languages, made into a Hollywood movie, and adapted to theatre, having a run of over seven hundred performances on Broadway in the 1950s.

I would run into the Israeli and the Moroccan on several more occasions as I wandered in and out of the cafés during my stay in Amsterdam. At first, I found myself having homicidal thoughts toward them, which I believed were more than justified, but as they were by far the sorriest bunch of losers I had ever met, I soon found myself taking pity on them instead.

From Amsterdam I hitchhiked back through Germany, first to historic Nuremberg, and from Nuremberg I hitchhiked to Munich, Germany's third largest city and capital of the German state of Bavaria.

I spent the night in the Munich youth hostel and traveled by bus in the morning to the town of Dachau, about ten miles outside of Munich, where the Dachau concentration camp remains untouched, exactly as it had been found by the American soldiers who liberated the death camp at the end of the Second World War.

Dachau stands among the smaller concentration camps, its initial purpose the imprisonment and disposal of Hitler's political opponents in the early days of the Nazi regime. In time, the Nazis would send Jews to Dachau as well, but the majority of my family murdered in the Holocaust lost their lives in the Nazi death camp known as Auschwitz, the most hellish place to have ever existed upon the face of the Earth.

A shipment is arriving was the term the Nazis used to describe a train load of Jews arriving in the concentration camp, headed for the gas chambers. One shipment would have been more than enough to take care of my father's small town, whose population of eight hundred Jews was reduced to zero. My Berlin relatives in all likelihood would have been shipped from Berlin's notorious Grunewald station, where trains packed with Jews bound for the killing camps in the East departed on a regular basis during the height of the genocidal years, each trainload on average carrying between fifteen hundred and two thousand doomed souls at a time.

The Dachau concentration camp still stands, as many of the former death camps do throughout Germany and Poland, as a testament for the world to see, and as a memorial, lest we forget the ultimate horror ethnic and racial hatred can bring upon innocent human beings.

I entered Dachau, walked into a gas chamber and stood, somber and silent, within its four deadly walls. Nearby were the horrific conditions under which tens of thousands of innocent prisoners had been forced to live, where they had been beaten, tortured, and starved to death, crammed by the thousands into barracks made to hold only a few, and close at hand were the cremation ovens the Nazis used to reduce millions of innocent people to ashes throughout the terrifying reign of Adolf Hitler's Third Reich.

Bringing my visit to the Dachau concentration camp to its conclusion, I passed rows of flower bouquets lined up

*Chapter Four*

against a wall on my way out. A memorial for the French victims of Dachau was in progress.

A dreary sky hung overhead on a damp and cool November day. I arrived back at the hostel in the nick of time as a driving rain began to fall, slapped sideways by a cold hard wind. Winter drew near, and I planned to stay one step ahead of the approaching change of season by heading south, to Italy, but first I would take a trip into the Alps, the spectacular European mountain range reaching altitudes as high as 15,000 feet.

The storm passed in the night. Blue skies greeted me in the morning. Energized by a crisp autumn chill, I began my journey into the mountains, to the Bavarian village of Oberammergau.

Deemed by a respectable global consensus as the most magnificent castle the world has ever seen, King Ludwig's castle, sitting on a hill surrounded by the beauty of the German Alps, came into clear and perfect view as I traveled the winding mountain road.

Oberammergau, the quintessential Bavarian village, is one of the most enchanting places I have ever seen. It is a magical place where German woodcarvers make small wooden toys in old fashioned wood carving shops and delightful hand painted murals depicting traditional Bavarian themes, bible stories, and colorful scenes from children's fairy tales such as Hansel and Gretel and Little Red Riding Hood decorate the exterior of small houses and mountain chalets.

Red cheeked Bavarian milk maids in dirndl dresses and the wonderful cheeses and butters made from their delicate hands danced in my imagination as I hiked the scenic mountain roads surrounding Oberammergau, enjoying postcard perfect scenes of exquisite alpine meadows and splendid rolling pastures where the Bavarian bovine grazed.

## An Extraordinary Tale of Travel

On a brisk early mountain morning, wrapped snug and tight in my winter coat with my wool hat slipped over my head and my backpack on my back, I began the downhill trek out of Oberammergau after spending several days in the fairytale Bavarian village. I decided to walk a few winding mountain miles before sticking out my thumb. I could have walked forever. So picturesque, so enchanting, so timeless was it there. I almost expected Heidi, the fabled children's storybook character, to come running out from the hills at any moment during my stay in Oberammergau.

I would fall in love with Germany, it simply couldn't be avoided, despite what had happened in this land and the effect it would always have upon me.

Once again I spent the night in the Munich youth hostel. The following morning I boarded a train heading for the Austrian Alps. I decided to take a break from hitchhiking until I reached Italy.

A miserable combination of rain, cold, and wind had the beautiful Austrian mountain town of Salzburg in its nasty grips and a blanket of dark clouds kept the snow capped peaks of the Austrian Alps hidden from view. I wished for one decent day, I would have settled for a fraction thereof, upon which to enjoy Austria's majestic alpine beauty and to explore the historic Austrian town of Salzburg under favorable conditions. But Mother Nature would not cooperate.

I remained stuck inside of the Salzburg youth hostel for three days, waiting and hoping for the wicked storm to lift. On the fourth morning I gave up and headed for the train station.

I met Pam on the train to Venice. An American girl from Boston, Pam and I were traveling in the same direction. We were both heading for the Italian port city of Brindisi on the Adriatic Sea. From Brindisi, Pam would travel by boat to the Greek island of Crete. I planned to visit the Turkish city of Istanbul before catching a flight to Israel,

## Chapter Four

via Athens, where I hoped to live and work on a communal farming settlement known as a kibbutz until springtime.

Chugging and whistling through the Austrian Alps over winding alpine passes we rode the mountain rails, rolling toward the Italian border. I asked Pam if she would like to hitchhike from Venice to Brindisi with me. I figured a female companion would significantly increase my chances of successfully hitchhiking through Italy. She agreed without hesitation.

We arrived in Venice in the afternoon. From the train station we rode a water taxi to the youth hostel. The city of Venice is built upon a group of tiny islands in the Adriatic Sea linked by a network of canals. All transportation is done in small boats, water taxis, waterbuses, gondolas, or on foot.

We checked into the youth hostel and soon set about exploring Venice on foot. We navigated small bridges, walked along ancient cobbled corridors, and strolled medieval lanes. We sat on a bench in pigeon filled St. Marks Square admiring the magnificent twelfth century Basilica di San Marco, known in the English speaking world as the Cathedral of St. Marks, among the most beautiful cathedrals in Europe and one of Europe's finest examples of Byzantine era architecture. Dusk approached. We didn't think it possible one could be more enchanted, until, in twilight's shimmering afterglow, our eyes fell upon gondolas dreamily drifting down the Grand Canal.

We dined on a superb gourmet dinner, authentic Italian, of course, at a white table cloth covered table for two in a small Venetian café, charming and cozy, adorned with sparkling wine glasses and polished silverware. I told Pam my budget would not allow me to repeat our fine dining experience and Pam agreed it had been too much for her budget as well. Her response surprised me because indulging had been her suggestion and I went along because I didn't want to say no.

Pizza, we thus decided, cheap, tasty, and nourishing, and in plentiful supply in pasta land, would serve as our staple for the remainder of our journey through Italy.

Three days in Venice and we were back on the road, heading for the Italian city of Florence, birthplace of the renaissance. The time had come to get back to the basics. Two train rides and one gourmet dinner totaled more than enough money spent. We hit the highway and Pam stuck out her thumb.

A trucker soon pulled over and came to a stop. Pam climbed in first. I thought it best she sit next to the driver. After all, who could doubt the reason he picked us up in the first place. The driver talked to us non-stop in Italian even though we couldn't understand one word, and excitedly grabbed Pam's thigh a few times, to which she maintained a commendable attitude.

Pam was a good looking brunette, twenty-three years of age, standing above average in height for a girl and solidly built. An air of New England sophistication I found both charming and inadvertently comical surrounded her.

Our first ride dropped us off halfway to Florence and before we knew it another large tractor-trailer stopped to pick us up. I wondered how much luck I would have had hitchhiking through Italy by myself. I doubt rides would have come this fast, or anywhere near.

We arrived in Florence and walked the legendary streets. The same historic passageways the great artists of the renaissance once tread, in carriage and on foot. We were looking for the youth hostel when we came upon a guesthouse known as a pensione. More often than not a pensione is the proprietor's own residence, offering private rooms at a cost even a budget traveler can oftentimes afford. I told Pam I had heard excellent stories about this type of lodging, hoping she might be willing to give it a try.

*Chapter Four*

    We approached the entrance to the narrow centuries-old house, situated within rows of similar centuries-old attached dwellings lining cobbled lanes. An elderly woman opened the door. She spoke not one word of English, but we still managed to figure out that we could afford the room with the two of us sharing the expense. The plan met Pam's approval and up a creaky flight of steps we climbed following our aged host. One small wooden table with two wooden chairs and a double size bed with clean linens and soft pillows filled the small but tidy space. A pair of tall and narrow windows framed with the lost art of intricate hand carved wooden trim, no doubt a unique style within the framework of a long ago architectural era, offered a view of the old world below.

    It had been a long day since leaving Venice. Our tour of historic Florence and its abundance of medieval churches, cathedrals, and great works of renaissance art would begin in the morning.

    The bathroom had no shower. Instead, a skinny hose had been attached to the slow running faucet of a deep bathtub standing on tarnished brass legs about six inches off the floor. I climbed in first. Pam had to wait for the hot water to heat up again before she could take her bath after I froze halfway through mine. Had I known, I would have used the wet yourself, turn the water off, soap up, turn the water on again and rinse off method. But how was I to know the hot water would run out so fast. Western Europe slipped away and hot water, as I so rudely discovered, could no longer be taken for granted, at least not by those who travel on a budget such as mine.

    We settled in and a done deal couldn't have seemed more certain, when, to my disbelief, Pam exclaimed: "We have to stop! I can't do it!"

    I hadn't heard those words uttered since my teenage years. We're adults, this isn't supposed to happen.

    Stunned, I asked: "How come?"

"Because I'm a Christian Scientist and I need to remain a virgin until I get married and I can only marry a Christian Scientist," she said.

As expected, I would continue giving it the good ole college try anyway, on all of the nights we spent together, as any red blooded American boy would, and on every one of those nights the identical scenario would unfold. She would appear in every way as if she wanted to go through with it, and in the very last second she would ask me to stop, and I, the reluctant gentleman, respected her wishes. I also wanted neither the guilt nor the responsibility for causing her to break her religious vows.

"What are the odds of you finding a Christian Scientist guy you would actually want to marry? How many Christian Scientists can there be out there? You're the first one I've ever met."

"I'll find one," she said.

For the rest of my life, I would wonder if she ever did.

Several days later we were back on the road, heading for Rome. Pam was enjoying her unexpected adventure of hitchhiking through Italy, despite the horny Italian truck drivers who couldn't keep their hands to themselves.

The immeasurable wealth and depth of European history, art, and architecture found in this land will leave all whose eyes fall upon even the slightest amount enthralled and with their educations significantly advanced. But spending my time wandering the enchanting avenues and boulevards, soaking up Italy's one of a kind culture and charm is what I loved most of all.

Several days in Rome and we were off to Brindisi, expecting once more to get a ride with a trucker, but the opposite happened instead when an Italian sports car with its top down pulled over and came to a stop.

We approached the tiny two-seater. A young Italian guy who spoke fluent English sat behind the wheel. He

*Chapter Four*

said he could take us all the way to the coastal town of Bari, about fifty miles north of Brindisi. Pam climbed in the front, next to the driver. I squeezed into the tiny crawl space behind the two tiny front seats, barely able to move as we embarked upon a breathtaking journey across Southern Italy. Scenes as on an artist's canvas came alive as we traveled, with the wind in our hair, through miles of gorgeous Mediterranean landscapes dotted with timeless Italian villages, rich with vineyards and olive groves. We reached the town of Bari on the scenic coast of the Adriatic Sea by day's end. The Italian port of Brindisi, from where Pam would set sail to the Greek islands, was now only a short train ride away.

Our ship set sail at midnight. Upon the calm waters of the Adriatic Sea we slept on a canopied double size bed with fresh linens and puffy pillows in a first class cabin with a sparkling clean bathroom and plenty of hot water, the latter a luxury I would learn to do without as eastward I did roam.

At day break, upon arriving at our first docking point, I packed up, said goodbye to Pam and put my feet on Greek soil. Pam continued on to the island of Crete. Before I stepped off the boat, I told her, with the utmost of sincerity, that I truly hope she finds her man in the not so distant future.

A ramshackle shack housed the border checkpoint. Nothing more existed in this place of pure desolation I had blindly chosen as my entry point to the Greek mainland. I handed my passport over to the border guard. My backpack and side bag were searched, my passport stamped and returned to me, and I was free to go.

Close to five hours would pass before a comfortable and surprisingly inexpensive coach finally showed up. The crowd of Greeks waiting for the bus didn't seem bothered one bit. As for me, the only foreigner among them, the infinite wait nearly drove me to the brink of madness.

Gorgeous vistas of lush rolling hills rich in olive groves and captivating scenes of Greek peasants laboring the Earth with horse drawn plows rolled past my window as I journeyed through the timeless Greek countryside, heading toward the city of Thessaloniki.

Public transportation had taken a drastic drop in price, beginning with the beautiful first class cabin Pam and I had been able to afford on the boat crossing the Adriatic Sea, much to our pleasant surprise. This welcome change couldn't have come at a better time, for surely hitchhiking the roads of this sparse region I now found myself passing through would have meant standing stranded with my thumb out for painfully protracted periods of time.

Gathering information at this point in the journey had taken on a critical importance, but not one seat on a filled to capacity bus held one soul who spoke English, including the driver, so my questions went unanswered. This convoluted set of circumstances had me in a predicament because I hadn't a clue what time I would arrive in the city of Thessaloniki and I didn't want to arrive in the middle of the night.

I've got to have myself safely tucked away before dark, with a worrisome urgency I decided. I figured any village or town would do, since I had no idea where I was anyway.

In addition to the sudden affordability of transportation, I could now also afford to stay in real hotels, such a significant drop had costs taken overall since crossing into Greece. A lovely family run guesthouse in a picturesque small Greek town with an enchanting Mediterranean ambiance and an alluring Latin courtyard is where I would find myself spending the night, having made a random choice of location by simply telling myself: You're getting

## Chapter Four

off at the next town while it's still light out, with no inkling whatsoever of what I might find there.

I completed the journey to the Greek metropolis of Thessaloniki the following day. I stepped off the bus, put my backpack on my back and proceeded to hunt, as always, for the cheapest accommodations I could find. I hadn't walked but a few blocks along a bustling Grecian boulevard when my eyes caught sight of a neon sign precariously dangling over a dilapidated recessed doorway hidden between rows of smoky shish kebob restaurants. And as the word hotel spelled out in glowing neon colors came into view, I knew I had found what I was looking for.

I walked through the entranceway and continued along a skinny corridor leading to a dimly lit lobby where time looked as if it had stopped circa 1920. I booked a room for the night and with a few hours of daylight remaining I set about exploring the city of Thessaloniki.

Among the oldest cities in Europe, Thessaloniki is the second largest city in Greece, next to Athens, and its importance during the days of the Byzantine Empire is surpassed only by Constantinople.

In the morning I headed for the train station. An English couple joined me as I walked out of the hotel. They too were catching the train to Istanbul.

"We're traveling overland to India," the Englishman said.

The ancient silk road to the Orient had become the hippie trail to India. A budget backpacker could travel through Turkey, Iran, Afghanistan, and Pakistan, all the way to the sub-continent, spending as little as one hundred dollars.

The British couple and I walked to the train station together. Four others, a Canadian guy, another Englishman, a Frenchman, and an American girl from California joined us upon our arrival. All were boarding the early morning train to Istanbul and all except me were on their way to India.

Wow! I marveled. These people are traveling from Europe to India by land. They're taking busses and trains all the way to India. I so wished to join them, but I didn't think it a good idea to go so far away with the amount of money I had left. I put the overland journey to India on my list and it would eventually take place, but not for another four years. My journey east, for the time being, would have to end in Istanbul.

The train was old and dirty, unlike the ultra clean and modern trains in the prosperous nations of Northern Europe. All of us Western travelers were ushered into one train car together, containing multiple compartments with two benches in each compartment. We spread out and made ourselves comfortable.

We traveled all day through the Greek countryside, pulling up to the Turkish border past nightfall. The train came to a halt, our train car was separated from the rest of the train and we were left sitting motionless on the tracks without a clue. Uniformed Turkish officials soon came aboard, took our passports and herded all seven of us into one compartment together.

I was marooned in a no-man's land on the border between Greece and Turkey. Stranded in a lone train car in the middle of nowhere in the middle of the night somewhere between where Europe ends and Asia begins.

Hours passed. Our train car hadn't budged, our passports hadn't returned, and we still hadn't a clue, when a jolting and a bumping and a thumping and a loud clanking and a banging rocked our train car. The mother ship had arrived. They hooked us up, the whistles sounded, our passports came back to us and we were on our way to Istanbul at last.

Twisting and contorting, we settled in, seven people with seven backpacks trying to get comfortable and get some sleep in a compartment designed for two people to sleep in.

## Chapter Four

We arrived the following afternoon. From the train station we walked to Istanbul's ancient Sultanahmet district.

Seven weary Western travelers with backpacks on their backs trudged past the famed Pudding Shop. The ancient Sultanahmet district, old Istanbul, the heart and soul of the Ottoman Empire, is where the overland journey to India officially began.

The smells, the sounds, the muezzin's haunting, mystical melody echoing across an exotic skyline of domes and minarets, calling the faithful to prayer, told me in no uncertain terms that I had truly entered another world.

My first introduction to the Eastern world's unique universe of cheap hotels came as we walked into a dilapidated building, marched down a shadowy hallway, and entered a smoke filled room at the top of a dusty flight of steps. Two young Turkish guys sat at a shabby table, smoking cigarettes, drinking tea, and playing a game of backgammon. They jumped to their feet as soon as we appeared and ushered us into the available rooms.

A bare, stained, junk pile mattress rested upon a beat up makeshift wooden frame. I covered it with my plastic poncho and threw my sleeping bag on top. A small tattered table covered with a solid coating of dust sat beside it. Not much else could fit in the tiny room. When the final Sultan of Constantinople was run out of town, housekeepers and maintenance men, it most certainly seemed, had all taken a hike with him. The walls were filthy. Paint was peeling. Dirt caked the window sills. The bathrooms were dank and smelly, and the shower would freeze you to the bone. But at sixty cents a night, who's complaining?

A knock came to my door. "Let's go to the Pudding Shop," Cindy, the American girl, said.

A petite hippie girl in her early twenties, Cindy had embarked upon a journey to India by herself.

## An Extraordinary Tale of Travel

Known for its rice pudding and a host of other delicious Turkish desserts, and also serving full course meals, the Pudding Shop, situated in the center of the Sultanahmet district, had become a legendary gathering place for India bound Western travelers. The owners of the Pudding shop, two Turkish brothers, had even created a special space in their restaurant for a bulletin board where travelers could receive and post messages. The famed magic buses that ran from Amsterdam to Katmandu were often seen parked on the street outside of the Pudding shop.

Young Western budget travelers packed the Pudding shop. Most were heading overland to India. Some were coming back. A number of them were enjoying sweet Turkish treats, while others dined on their evening meal. And in every major Western European language spoken, they were gathering information and sharing stories of the road.

For a brief moment in time, in a world that no longer exists, a traveling sub-culture of young international wanderers traveled freely, safely, and without worry throughout the Islamic world. The ancient silk road to the Orient had opened up to adventurous independent Western travelers in the 1960s, only to have world events shut it down by the end of the following decade.

The road is a world entirely unto itself, known only to those who have genuinely tread the path, and in all humility, I believed I had reached a point in my wandering life where I had earned the right to claim myself a member of the club, so to speak, until I arrived in Istanbul in early December, 1973 and found myself witnessing the road taken to a level far exceeding anything I could have ever imagined. Every day new backpackers arrived in Istanbul, while others boarded busses heading deep into the Eastern world.

With worry-free abandon, I could now partake of everything the local culture had to offer, so cheap had the world become since I arrived in Istanbul. What a liberating

## Chapter Four

feeling after the frugality I had been forced to impose upon myself throughout most of the journey so far. For even less money than I would spend in Europe sleeping in youth hostels and living on cheese and bread, I could now eat three full course meals a day, including dessert, and I could afford unlimited nights in a hotel, albeit filthy and dilapidated, but a real hotel, nonetheless. On my first night in Istanbul; however, although I could have afforded a full dinner menu, I choose baklava and rice pudding as my evening meal instead.

An abundance of sights, sounds, and smells unknown to our Western minds burst at us from all directions as Cindy and I slowly navigated the weaving, winding, seemingly never ending psychedelic pathways of Istanbul's Grand Bazaar. A myriad of exotic shops lined the hypnotic corridors of an ancient Eastern marketplace enclosed within a magical covered labyrinth. Cafés, kiosks, shouting push cart-vendors, and mysterious dark-eyed Turkish men smoking tobacco out of beautiful big bowled Turkish water pipes filled the spaces in between.

An ever-increasing chill descended upon the city as Cindy and I walked back to the hotel after our mind blowing journey through Istanbul's Grand Bazaar. I took a freezing shower on a freezing night in Istanbul and I learned another valuable lesson in the process: Never enter a bathroom bare foot in the Eastern world. I would never again travel without a pair of rubber flip-flops.

We spent the remainder of the evening in the hotel's dingy sitting room, huddled round an old rusty wood stove, drinking hot cups of tea, trying to stay warm as mice skirted past.

A dilapidated hotel in a poor Eastern country on a winter's night without heat and a mouse darting about the room is not the best place for an intimate encounter, but we had no other place so we didn't let it stop us.

In the morning we ate breakfast at the Pudding Shop. After breakfast we parted ways. Cindy had business to take care of; namely, obtaining an Iranian visa and booking her bus ticket to Iran. I headed over to explore the four hundred-year-old Topkapi Palace, the world's largest and oldest surviving palace, from where the great sultans of Constantinople, with harems of five hundred concubines, ruled over the Ottoman Empire.

The December mornings and nights in Istanbul were wintry cold, but the hours in between required nothing more than my well worn flannel shirt to keep me comfortable.

From the sultan's palace I walked to Istanbul's fabulous harbor on the Bosporus Strait. Istanbul, known as the gateway to the East, is the only city in the world spanning two continents, one side in Asia and the other side in Europe, separated by the Bosporus strait, the world's narrowest strait and the sole connection between the Mediterranean and the Black Sea, making Istanbul a vital international port through which hundreds of ships pass through daily.

Packed with upscale international shops, fashionable restaurants, and colorful cafés, Istanbul's world renowned harbor teems with tourists, merchants, and seafaring men of many nations, their ships taking respite in the port of Istanbul for a stretch before sailing on into the Mediterranean or heading toward the Black Sea. I traversed the bridge across the Bosporus on foot, wandered about on the Asian side for a while, and after having had breakfast on one continent and lunch on another, I changed continents again and returned to Sultanahmet.

Cindy's day of departure arrived. On a chilly December morning I accompanied her to the bus depot where she would board the bus for the three day journey to Tehran. In envy and admiration I watched as Cindy's bus disappeared from view, becoming even more determined to board the same bus myself one day.

## Chapter Four

Attended to like a king, I was scrubbed, rinsed, and massaged upon a steamy raised marble platform. After seeing Cindy off, I decided to treat myself to an authentic, too wonderful for words ancient Turkish bath. In pure hedonistic pleasure, I remained stretched out in the exquisitely tiled palatial chamber upon the luxurious marble platform in the splendid steamy watery warmth long after the royal treatment had ended. When I returned to my private cubicle, a delicious pot of hot tea sitting upon a silver tray awaited me. I dried off, dressed myself, and sat in pleasing solitude, drinking hot tea from a sparkling tulip shaped glass, sweetened with little sugar cubes.

The Turkish bath left me with one humongous appetite. I strolled down to the harbor, and from a street vendor's push cart I ate a fried fish sandwich as I stood on the water's edge, watching merchant ships, ferry boats, and ocean cruises move between two continents.

What kind of fish? I hadn't a clue other than to say, a helluva good sized one, and delicious, freshly caught and deep fried in its entirety in a pan of sizzling, bubbling, albeit questionable oil. And the whole crispy delicacy was served between two hearty slices of bread, freshly baked, as it has been for centuries, in the brick and stone earthen ovens of the old world.

As it does five times a day throughout the Islamic world, the Muezzin's call to prayer echoed across the city once more. A crowd of men moved past and into a mosque to pray, when a man grabbed me by the arm and pulled me into the mosque with him as I walked back from the harbor to Sultanahmet. We knelt down upon beautiful Turkish carpets, faced Mecca and prayed and when prayers ended we slipped back into our shoes and walked back out to the street. In his excitement my friend began speaking to me in Turkish. I couldn't understand one word, but the joy he felt in having me go into the mosque with him, kneel before

Allah and pray could not be mistaken. We shook hands and smiled at each other. "*Tesekkür ederim,*" I said. Thank you in Turkish, the only Turkish I had learned.

Authentic international student identification cards made here, the sign said, directing those interested to the second floor of yet another rundown building in Sultanahmet. In my mind, the structural disrepair found in the ancient Sultanahmet district only served to give the historic section of Istanbul even more character. I climbed up a flight of creaky dusty steps to find a heavily mustached Turk who looked as if he belonged in a 1940s spy movie sitting in a tiny cluttered room behind an old tattered desk.

"You want student identification card?" he asked.

"Yes," I replied.

"I will need passport, passport picture, and name of school," he said.

I handed him my passport and one of my extra passport pictures and I told him to use the University of Maryland as the name of the school. He said come back in one hour.

I just gave my passport to a complete stranger in Istanbul, Turkey. Have I lost my mind? Once again I questioned my own judgment and with more severity than ever this time, I might add, as I walked back down the steps, out to the street and into a smoky café filled with tough looking Turkish men sporting enormous black mustaches making their already dark and secretive eyes appear even more mysterious.

They were drinking strong Turkish coffee, playing backgammon, and puffing tobacco out of fabulous pure works of art Turkish water pipes that multiple men could and were smoking out of at the same time. Without a doubt a breed of humans I had never made contact with before. And the uncanny velocity with which their backgammon moves were made drove this point home even further. In sheer wonder, I watched. Yes, it is true, they've been

## Chapter Four

playing backgammon in this part of the world long before Jesus walked the Earth. Still, no mortal should have the capability of playing backgammon this fast. It boggled the mind. Their moves were made at lightning speed without a millisecond of a thought.

I passed the time drinking cups of hot tea. I couldn't handle Turkish coffee. It gave me the jitters that lasted all day. Fascinated, my eyes remained fixed upon those beautiful water pipes and the unknowable men who puffed upon them three and four at a time while playing backgammon at the speed of light.

An angst-ridden hour worrying about my passport finally passed. Eager to lift the burden of anxiety I had so ridiculously inflicted upon myself, I raced back, breathing deep sighs of relief to find the mustached Turk sitting in his tiny space, behind his cluttered desk, same as I had left him, doing the work of a master forger. I retrieved my passport and picked up my international student Identification card, a perfect replica of the international student identification cards legally issued from actual universities. And it only cost me fifty cents.

The document's objective is to provide student travelers with discounts on their transportation needs. I tucked my new student identification card away in my passport bag which I wore around my neck underneath my shirt, hoping the forged certificate would meet its intended purpose.

I returned to the Sultanahmet district, strolled into the Pudding Shop and looked at the dozens of messages pinned to the crowded bulletin board. People were looking for rides, some were looking for riders, and others were telling their friends when and where to meet them in places like Kabul, Delhi, Katmandu, and Goa.

Volkswagen van going to Thessaloniki and Northern Europe, leaving from the Pudding Shop Friday morning at nine o'clock, one message read. Perfect! I could hang out in Istanbul another two days and spare myself the difficult train ride back to Thessaloniki.

●

Two British guys, and the drivers, a young couple from Holland, stood waiting in front of the Pudding Shop by the red and white Volkswagen van when I arrived on the morning of my departure.

We boarded the vehicle and rolled out of the city that sits between two continents, leaving the magical domed landscape of ancient churches, medieval mosques, and mystical minarets behind.

We traveled all day, through rural Turkish villages and small Turkish towns, crossed the Greek border, entered the city of Thessaloniki and came to a stop on an empty boulevard where all that remained to brighten up the darkness of a cold and lonely winter's night in Northern Greece were the glowing colors of a neon sign, precariously dangling over a dilapidated recessed doorway hidden between rows of smoky shish kebob restaurants, spelling out the word, hotel. The Dutchman knew the trail well, and now, I did too.

I awoke in the morning to the sounds of an icy wind howling outside my window. I washed up, packed up, bundled up and stepped out to a big surprise. Two inches of snow covered the ground. I made my way to the highway and stuck out my thumb, the winter wind biting and the arctic air chilling me to the bone. I figured I shouldn't have any trouble hitchhiking between the two largest cities in Greece, Thessaloniki and Athens, a distance in the neighborhood of five hundred kilometers.

Three workers from a construction site across the street from where I stood began walking toward me. As they neared, I noticed one guy had a knife in his hand.

## Chapter Four

The guy with the knife came close, began yelling at me in Greek and wildly waved his knife around like a crazed animal while his two companions stood by and laughed. Frozen by both the cold and by fear, I could do nothing more than stand motionless and watch. He carried on with his maniac behavior for what seemed like an eternity. Time stands still when you think you're about to die. One of his companions finally stepped in, spoke a few words and to my enormous relief, the madness came to a halt and the three lunatics walked away, laughing hysterically.

I began walking as fast as I could, stopping only to stick out my thumb whenever a car approached. I was bundled up solid, still freezing though, and by the time a car pulled over my face had become numb.

I hustled over to the waiting vehicle. A Greek man, his wife, and two young daughters had stopped to pick me up. He and his family were returning to Athens after living in Germany for several years where he had been employed as a guest worker. I climbed into the back seat next to the two young girls, ages seven and ten.

A rather unusual conversational experience began to unfold as we both did our best to communicate in German. I believe he initially thought he had picked up a native German and I hoped he wasn't too disappointed. I certainly wasn't. I had a ride all the way to Athens, I was thawing out, and I didn't have to worry about those idiot construction workers anymore.

Much of my time in Greece had been spent in transit and a majority of the traveling occurred during the daylight hours. A staggering amount of the beautiful Greek landscape would pass before my eyes, from the Adriatic Sea to the Turkish border and from Thessaloniki in Northern Greece all the way to Athens in the South. And what a difference a day makes. In Northern Greece I nearly froze to death. In Athens I didn't even need a jacket.

The section of Athens where my Greek friend dropped me off couldn't have been better suited to meet my needs, with inexpensive lodging, cafés filled with fellow travelers, and airline offices. I'm certain he had gone out of his way to do so, an extraordinary act of kindness, considering how much driving he had done in one day and how restless his children had become.

The following day I booked a flight to Israel on the Israeli National Airline. I presented my international student identification card and received a discount. I would never use the document again. No one else would honor it. Perhaps it wasn't as perfect a forgery as I had thought. I believe the Israeli Airline agent knew but let me get away with it. I did save twenty dollars. Not a bad return on an investment of fifty cents. Two days later I boarded a flight to Tel Aviv, a short hop across the Mediterranean Sea.

*Chapter Five*

# THE HOLY LAND

Israeli soldiers guarded the airport as we taxied down the runway. Only six weeks had passed since the end of the Yom Kipper War.

From the airport I rode a bus to the Tel Aviv youth hostel, accompanied by an American girl named Ellen. A college reunion taking place in West Jerusalem had summoned Ellen to the Holy Land.

I checked into the youth hostel, placed my backpack in a locker and hit the streets on a beautiful, sunny, spring-like Mediterranean afternoon, exploring Israel's largest city and strolling upon the shores of the Mediterranean Sea.

The following day Ellen and I made the short trip from Tel Aviv to Jerusalem. Jerusalem is divided into two sections. East Jerusalem is the legendary city of the ancient world, also known as the old city. West Jerusalem is the modern section, much of its development taking place after the establishment of the present-day State of Israel.

Ellen's friend Susan, one of the college reunion's five attendees, had undertaken rabbinical studies in West Jerusalem. From the bustling bus depot we walked to Susan's apartment, the reunion's planned location. Ellen had invited me to join her for a place to stay in the holy city.

James and Kathy, a married couple, and Tom, Susan's former college boyfriend, had arrived the day before. All had flown in from the states. The five friends had formed a close bond while attending university together in the late 1960s.

Ellen introduced me to her friends, but I didn't stay long. My restlessness to explore the ancient city of the Bible could no longer be contained.

I passed through the stone gates of the ancient walled city, leading me to the temple mount, where King Solomon's temple once stood, and from where the great kings of the Old Testament ruled over the ancient Kingdom of Israel.

King Solomon's temple, the first temple, built in the tenth century BC, stood an estimated four hundred and fifty years, until it's destruction at the hands of Nebuchadnezzar, the Babylonian king. The second temple met its destruction at the hands of the Roman Empire in the year 70 AD. One massive wall of the second temple still stands. A hallowed destination of religious pilgrimage, this mighty remnant of the second temple is the holiest place on Earth for the Jewish people.

Crowds of devout Jews stood at the sacred temple wall, lost in prayer, rocking back and forth as they read aloud from Hebrew prayer books held in their hands.

The magnificent Mosque of Omar, also known as the Dome of the Rock, stands adjacent to the ruins of the second temple. Jerusalem is the third holiest place in Islam. Mecca is first and Medina second. According to Islamic belief, Mohammad ascended to heaven from a rock resting beneath the Mosque's golden dome.

## Chapter Five

Neighboring the Dome of the Rock one finds the Al-Aqsa Mosque, the largest mosque in Jerusalem. In the Old Testament, Abraham prepares to sacrifice his son, but changes his mind. Islamic teaching believes this event took place on the spot where the Al-Aqsa Mosque now stands. Both the Mosque of Omar and the Al-Aqsa Mosque are built on the temple mount, where the great temples of the ancient Kingdom of Israel once stood.

Navigating the ancient corridors and winding passageways of a crowded and colorful Arab bazaar, I soon found myself setting foot upon yet another location of untold historical measure: The Via Dolorosa, also known as the Stations of the Cross.

I tread the revered path, following the footsteps of Jesus as he carried the cross to his crucifixion. Hallowed ground for three of the world's five great religions, jewel of empires rising and vanishing through the ages, no other place on Earth holds as much significance to so many people as the sacred city of Jerusalem.

Shadows fell upon the hills of the holy city. As if traveling through time, I returned to the modern world. In the evening I joined Ellen and her friends for dinner. Authentic Middle Eastern, of course, and my love of falafels would find its beginning.

The reunion had set the stage for the playing out of a personal drama; namely, the unfinished business between Tom and Susan, to be played out before the eyes of everyone. For Susan; however, the business was already finished. But Tom refused to see the obvious. A hopeless case of denial held him in its grips.

Tom believed he and Susan would stay together after college, but Susan chose a different path. To everyone's surprise, Susan decided to become a rabbi. And to everyone's further surprise, she enrolled in rabbinical college in Israel and relocated to West Jerusalem. Tom hoped the reunion would rekindle her feelings for him, but Susan had moved on to a new life, a life Tom would have found impossible to take part in. The differences in their cultural backgrounds presented obstacles too great to overcome.

We had been invited to spend an evening with a group of Susan's fellow students from the rabbinical College. The six of us piled out to the street on a cool star filled December night in West Jerusalem and walked to her friends' apartment, only a few blocks away. Susan knocked, a future rabbi opened the door and in we strolled, greeted by more future American rabbis and a pipe full of Lebanese hashish making its way around the room.

One of the guys in the group, not a rabbinical student, became annoyed with me because I thought he had said Russian jewelry, when in fact he had said Russian Jewry. He spoke about his trip to Communist Russia where he had engaged in the perilous act of distributing religious books to Russian Jews, taking a huge risk of landing in a Russian prison. He also said he planned to go back and do it again. In my view, taking such a risk amounted to nothing short of an absolute act of lunacy, but I kept my opinion to myself.

The evening passed, the hour became late. We bid Susan's friends farewell and walked back to Susan's apartment. Ellen didn't come with us. Engaged in the process of seducing one of the rabbinical students, she stayed back.

All of us slept in the living room, which doubled as Susan's bedroom. A curtain covered the entrance for privacy. Her roommate, also a rabbinical student, occupied the small one bedroom, one bathroom apartment's only actual bedroom. I rolled my sleeping bag out on the floor in Susan's room and crawled inside.

The shining rays of the morning sun bursting through Susan's window facing east, rising over the holy city, woke me up early, or perhaps the noises emanating from Susan's

## Chapter Five

bed startled me out of my sleep instead. The future female rabbi was having an orgasm. I guess she figured as long as Tom was there she might as well get laid. I pretended to still be asleep until the action ended. I assumed James and Kathy, the married couple sleeping on the floor beside me, did the same.

A week passed. The reunion came to an end. And for Tom, reality could no longer be denied. He knew he would never see Susan again, even though she slept with him during his visit. Steadfast in her plans for her new life, Susan couldn't have been happier. Tom's misery didn't bother her one bit. The last image I have of the soon to be permanently dumped fellow is of him sitting on the edge of the bed with his hands between his knees and his head hung low.

Once again the time had come for me to move on. I thanked Ellen for offering me a place to stay in someone else's apartment, and I thanked Susan for her generosity in allowing it to happen. The golden opportunity of spending a rent free week in Jerusalem had been mine, including side trips to several more ancient biblical locations nearby, among them the Mount of Olives, Bethlehem, and King David's tomb.

I could have felt uncomfortable among such a tight knit group of old friends, but this would not be the case. To the contrary, not once did I feel unwelcome. I believe the generous reception I received was in no small measure related to a skill I developed on my journey across America. The art of not wearing out one's welcome is an ultra important survival skill for those who travel in a manner such as mine. It is a two-fold talent, requiring one to maintain a pleasant, unassuming, humble presence in combination with knowing when and for how long to disappear during the daylight hours.

## An Extraordinary Tale of Travel

The tale of Masada begins in the year 73 AD, seventy-five years after the death of King Herod. As legend has it, an estimated one thousand Hebrew fighters occupied King Herod's abandoned desert palace, built upon an isolated fifteen hundred foot high rock cliff overlooking the Judean Desert and the Dead Sea. The rebels transformed the former royal hideaway into a fortress from where one final desperate stand would be made against the Roman Empire.

Armed with battering rams, the legions of Rome laid siege to Masada and broke through the fortress walls, bringing the final defense of the ancient Kingdom of Israel to an end. As defeat drew near, the rebels and their families committed suicide rather than face capture and slavery at the hands of Roman soldiers.

Buried by two millennium of shifting desert sands, a comprehensive excavation of Masada would finally come to pass in the 1960s, unveiling one of history's most significant archeological discoveries.

I boarded the bus out of Jerusalem and headed into the Judean Desert, to the ruins of Masada, a short distance southeast of the holy city.

Upon arrival I decided to spend the remainder of the day at the youth hostel. I would get a fresh start in the morning exploring the ruins. The hostel was filled with young European and American kibbutz volunteers, giving me plenty of people to hang out with. Their kibbutz had provided a sightseeing expedition for them as part of their volunteer program.

The Dead Sea is the saltiest body of water on the planet and the lowest point on Earth, situated nearly 1400 feet below sea level. The following morning I stood upon the banks of the biblical Dead Sea. The narrow blacktop desert highway that had carried me from Jerusalem to the ancient sands of Judea delivered me to the legendary shores. From the ancient salt lake I made my way over to the base of

## Chapter Five

Masada and my trek up the winding trail to the top of the plateau began. I was not alone. I was in the company of a bus load of tourists and the kibbutz volunteers I had already met at the hostel.

All those wishing to see the ancient ruins would need to come prepared for an invigorating fifteen hundred foot hike. The Masada cable car had not yet come into existence.

Masada would be the second historic path I would tread since arriving in Israel, the Via Dolorosa in Jerusalem, where Jesus carried the cross to his crucifixion, having been the first.

I stood on the summit of Masada. With a panoramic view of the Judean Desert and the Dead Sea at my fingertips, I strolled throughout the captivating world of ancient Roman art, artifacts, and architecture the miraculous unearthing had brought forth across the plateau.

Elegant palace pillars; the king's throne room; harem room; living quarters for the king's concubines; Roman style baths; servant's quarters, and the finest tiled chambers and floors. Every extravagant, luxurious amenity, comfort, and indulgence the powerful monarch of an ancient kingdom could wish for, and the innumerable relics telling the smaller tales of every day domestic life in biblical times, all revealed in the vast vestiges of Masada. The desert sun poured down upon me as I explored every inch of the ancient world the great king's opulent sanctuary once held.

The following day I hitched a ride to Tel Aviv with the kibbutz group's tour bus. Distances in Israel are short. The entire country is not much larger than the state of New Jersey.

In Masada, infinite miles of arid desert landscape surrounded me in every direction. A few hours later I stood enjoying cool ocean breezes upon the shores of the Mediterranean Sea. Nowhere in all of my travels would I experience so great a diversity of nature within such short distances of each other as I would in Israel.

The Israeli kibbutz, Hebrew for communal farming settlement, is a collective community, primarily agricultural, and is the world's most successful and lasting attempt at communal living.

The following day I walked into the kibbutz placement agency with the intention of becoming a volunteer on a kibbutz. As a volunteer I would receive room and board through the winter in exchange for my labor. Many young people came from Europe, Canada, and America, and some came from as far away as Australia and New Zealand to live and work on the communal farming settlements. Most placements are pre-planned, either on an individual basis or in organized groups. Only a small percentage of volunteers arrive on their own, as I had done. A woman approached and directed me into her office.

"What can I do for you?" she asked in heavily accented, yet otherwise flawless English.

I told her of my wish to work on a kibbutz in a part of the country where the weather stays warm year round.

"I can send you to a kibbutz in the Negev, near the town of Beersheba," she replied.

◉

I stood on a highway in the Holy Land with my backpack on my back and my thumb out, heading for the shores of the biblical Red Sea. A pleasing Mediterranean breeze blew in on a bright and beautiful Mediterranean morning. The journey south would take me through the Negev Desert, to Eilat, Israel's southernmost city. I had decided to do a little more sightseeing before reporting to the kibbutz.

Hitchhiking was a popular and acceptable means of transportation in Israel with rides coming quickly, and communication presented no problem at all. Nearly everyone spoke English. My first ride out of Tel Aviv took

## Chapter Five

me to the biblical city of Beersheba, known as the city of Abraham, on the northern edge of the Negev.

I made a quick stop in Beersheba, taking a short break from the road. I would have plenty of time to explore the town at a later date. The kibbutz to which I had been assigned was only a half hour away by local bus. I refreshed myself with a soda at a roadside restaurant before heading out to the desert highway.

Rough, rocky, bone-dry and baked, the rugged terrain of the Negev covers half of Israel. It is a vast and desolate region bordering on Egypt's Sinai Desert, home of Mt. Sinai, where Moses, it is said, received the Ten Commandments.

Two hundred and fifty kilometers of wild desert wasteland lie between the town of Beersheba, steeped in ancient biblical lore, and Eilat, one of the few places in the Holy Land with no history prior to the founding of modern day Israel.

Once nothing more than a distant military outpost on the Gulf of Aquba guarding Israel's access point to the Red Sea, Eilat had developed into a thriving vacation resort, with its year round sunshine, desert beaches, and beautiful coral reefs.

A car soon pulled over. An American couple, Sonia and Jeffrey, had stopped to pick me up. Young and adventurous, and idealistic, they had immigrated to Israel and had started new lives in the uncharted territory of Eilat.

We cruised across the unforgiving landscape on a smooth black top desert highway. The desert sun blazed in a brilliant blue sky. The world was empty, except for an endless horizon stretching out to the edge of infinity and the eternal ghost of Father Abraham tending to his flocks. A camel caravan came into view, slowly stepping across the barren desert wilderness. As if in a dream, a window of time had opened up and a surreal glimpse of the ancient world appeared before me.

I figured I would have no other choice but to spend the night sleeping on the desert beach, but Sonia and Jeffrey took me home with them instead, to their small apartment in Eilat. The hitchhiking Gods had not forgotten me. They had followed me across the Atlantic, and in their infinite compassion they chose to follow me across the Mediterranean as well.

I stood upon the banks of the Red Sea. Biblical waters welcomed the ancient sands beneath my feet. The desert kingdoms of Jordan and Saudi Arabia lie on the opposite shore and Egypt was only a few miles down the road. Somewhere along this legendary coast God parted the waters, as the age-old tale is told, allowing Moses to lead his people out of slavery in Egypt.

They got the hell out, finally and fast. And with the Pharaoh's army in hot pursuit, the people watched in awe as a path allowing their escape miraculously appeared, and when they reached the other side they watched in awe again as the waters came crashing back and drowned the Pharaoh's men. But their journey was far from over. They would spend many years wandering in the desert, following Moses. He said he could deliver them to the promised land and they trusted in his word. And who could fault their faith. No doubt they would have followed him to the moon after the mind blowing spectacle they had witnessed.

Quite a task I had assigned myself hitchhiking the Negev from Beersheba to Eilat and back again in such a short space of time. But how could I come all the way to the Holy Land and not see where the amazing Moses event so embedded in our childhood brains by our Sunday school teachers took place? And even if I had no way of knowing my proximity to the precise location of its miraculous happening, I believe I can still say with a fair degree of certainty that I was at least somewhere in the neighborhood.

*Chapter Five*

The Israeli kibbutz is a democratically governed self-contained independent community based on joint ownership of property.

The driving force of a cohesive solid center born of true adversity, coupled with an authentic ancient tribal connection, gave the European refugees the key ingredients by which to create, against all odds, a successful and lasting communal movement that would become the back bone of a new nation. Conversely, I believe the absence of the aforementioned elements is in large part the reason why the well intentioned American communal movement of the 1960s could not find success beyond one extraordinarily idealistic generation. And as the fascinated observer and amateur student of communal life and communal movements I had become, those are, for whatever their worth, my humble, semi-educated thoughts on the matter.

Local transportation carried me the short distance from Beersheba to Kibbutz Nir Yitzach. I stepped off the bus, threw my pack on my back and strolled into the communal farming settlement that would become my home for the next four months. A warm desert breeze whistled through the trees.

"Shalom," the Israeli woman in charge of the volunteer program said as I handed her my papers from the agency. "Come, I'll show you to your quarters."

We walked along a paved pathway passing scores of small houses spread out in countless neat rows upon lush and fertile acres of green and gardened landscapes. The same terrain had been arid, harsh, desolate land in the Negev only one generation earlier.

"This is where the kibbutz members live," she said.

All medical and dental care is provided free of charge throughout a member's life and the kibbutz even had its own dental clinic. Upon receiving this information a light bulb lit up in my brain and I wondered if I could have my teeth attended to for free during my stay in the kibbutz. I would have success. I simply needed to bug the right people.

The dentist didn't believe the kibbutz should bear the expense of a volunteer's dental care and he wasted no time voicing a strong opinion on the matter, but he did an excellent job despite his opposition. I had three cavities and I would have all three fixed at no cost to me.

A swimming pool, tennis courts, a community clubhouse, and playgrounds for the children were but a few of the many amenities enjoyed by the members of the kibbutz. And I learned an astonishing fact. The kibbutz water supply comes all the way from Lake Tiberius, an immense fresh water lake in Northern Israel, better known as the Sea of Galilee. Pipes are run a staggering two hundred miles, bringing water to the parched terrain of the Negev, making the barren land bloom with thousands of acres of vegetable fields, fruit orchards, and citrus groves.

We continued walking until we came upon a group of old wooden barracks with a military watchtower standing nearby.

"The founding members lived here in the early days," my host said. "We use the buildings now as living quarters for the volunteers."

At the time, the kibbutz had nine volunteers. A group from Holland, six girls and one guy, made up the majority. An American guy and a guy from Scotland who would become my roommate made up the rest. The volunteers ranged in age from late teens to mid-twenties. Lebanese hashish had also found its way to the volunteer quarters of Kibbutz Nir Yitzach. Jan, the teenage Dutchman, had a sizeable supply in his room and offered to share his stash with his fellow volunteers.

My quarters consisted of a bare bones room in one of the old wooden barracks containing nothing more than

## Chapter Five

two skinny cots on opposite sides of the room and a couple of wooden shelves hammered into the wall upon which to store one's belongings. The common showers and toilets were nearby.

The only other Jewish volunteer was an American guy named Alan. As a student radical in college during the 1960s, Alan traveled to Cuba in spite of warnings by the American government, an unusual pursuit a small number of radicals were taking part in at the time, the logic of which I have never understood, and I have since wondered if he ever regretted his youthful show of solidarity for the romanticism of a Latin American revolution whose leader, after winning the revolution, became a far worse tyrant than the fascist he overthrew.

Alan also spent a year in the state of Mississippi teaching underprivileged African American kids to read, a more reasonable endeavor and one which he spoke of with exceptional pride.

Alan had undertaken the study of the Hebrew language. Classes were offered to volunteers and new immigrants. With single minded determination he worked at achieving his goal. Alan had no plans to use the language for religious purposes, nor did he plan to stay in the country when his time in the kibbutz ended. In light of both the former and the latter, I couldn't help but wonder why would a person put forth the tremendous amount of effort, energy, discipline, and concentration required to learn a foreign language from scratch when no conversational use for said language exists anywhere else in the world outside of the one tiny country of its origin? I would in time receive an answer to my question, in a most unusual way and at the most unexpected moment.

In the kibbutz, everyone awoke at dawn. The kibbutz members numbered in the hundreds and all ate breakfast, lunch, and dinner in the sprawling communal dining hall together. Every meal was a social event.

After breakfast a wagon pulled by a tractor transported the volunteers to the orchards. Our jobs were to pick fruit and prune trees. Alan didn't work in the orchards like the rest of us. He worked with the kibbutz men on the heavy machines, plowing, planting, and harvesting. Climate conditions were perfect. Everything I had wished for in a place to plant myself through the winter. Flawless deep blue skies, hot days, cool and refreshing mornings and nights. We worked every day except Saturday, the Sabbath in Israel.

Popular among the volunteers was adoption by an Israeli family. The Dutch girls all had one such family and so did Alan.

"It's a great way to get to know the kibbutzniks," they said.

They enjoyed and looked forward to socializing, drinking tea, eating cookies and cake in their adopted kibbutznik's homes one or two evenings a week. I took a pass, certain I would feel uncomfortable, worried I would run out of things to say, and I believed after a few visits I would lose interest and I wouldn't want to go anymore. And then I worried I would hurt my adopted family's feelings because it would appear as if I had rejected them.

Looking back, I can only ask myself one perplexing question: Why would the prospect of sitting on a sofa in a welcoming family's living room give me such a boatload of insecure thoughts?

Conversations of short duration in a host of random circumstances, situations, and locales as opposed to a planned and structured social call worked best for me. In the dining hall; for example, I made the acquaintance of countless kibbutzniks by simply having conversation with the person sitting next to me or across from me and different people sat in those spots at every meal. And by wandering about the kibbutz in my free time, of which I

*Chapter Five*

had plenty, stopping to have snippets of conversation with those whose paths crossed mine.

Jan the Dutchman and William, my Scottish roommate, also took passes. William took a pass because drinking ale in the pubs of Scotland, the bloody blokes he drinks with, and the game of soccer comprised the full extent of his conversational skills. And Jan the Dutchman was always stoned on the Lebanese hashish he had purchased in the holy city before arriving in the kibbutz. Thankfully, there were two other misfits among the group of volunteers.

I had been working in the orchards for two months when the volunteer coordinator asked if I wouldn't mind working in the chicken house, which should have been named the mad house. The chickens were given growth hormone shots. We had to chase the baby chicks around, hundreds of them, and give them their injections. The growth hormones gave the chickens humongous appetites. They ate voraciously and grew at an unbelievable speed.

A Polish survivor of Auschwitz concentration camp ran the chicken house. He had the numbers tattooed on his forearm. I was in awe of the guy. I couldn't even begin to imagine what he had been through in his life. What he had seen. What he had been forced to endure. Barely out of his teens, he watched his entire family perish. In the selection process which took place immediately upon completion of the torturous train ride to hell, his parents and younger siblings were sent straight to the gas chambers. The Nazis selected him for slave labor, which is how he managed to survive.

He spoke Polish, Hebrew, and Yiddish, but no English. Yiddish is a language spoken by Eastern European Jews. The origin of Yiddish is an ongoing subject of debate and research among linguistic scholars. With early roots in German, stretching back over a millennium, incorporating words from the languages of the many regions where Jews had dwelled through time, Yiddish grew into a unique and rich language of its own, producing an extensive wealth of literature, poetry, and music, until the Nazis obliterated the irreplaceable centuries old world of Eastern European Yiddish culture.

He also had a fair knowledge of German, as many Yiddish speakers of his time did; hence, between the German words I could comprehend and the Yiddish words that were close enough to German that I could figure out, I could understand roughly half of what he said and somehow I could get the gist of at least half of everything else. Our convoluted method of communication would tie my head up in knots, but it got the job done and he was able to successfully direct me in my tasks.

On one of my excursions into the nearby town of Beersheba I saw our chickens hanging in an outdoor market. The sight disturbed me and after only two weeks of working in the chicken house I requested another assignment. I felt bad to tell him, he had grown fond of me and we worked well together. Of course, I knew from the start raising chickens for slaughter wasn't for me, but I couldn't say no when they asked if I would please work in the chicken house.

My next job involved collecting all of the dumpsters in the kibbutz and dumping the garbage in a land fill about a mile out into the desert. Needless to say, neither working in the chicken house nor driving the garbage tractor were jobs with a waiting list of people knocking down the door. In light of this fact it became clear to me what the kibbutzniks had in mind. They were trying to stick the most undesirable jobs on the volunteers so they could get out of doing those jobs themselves. And another realization struck: Out of the four guys in our group why was I the only one they approached about working in the chicken house or driving the garbage tractor? Was I wearing a

*Chapter Five*

go ahead, take advantage of me sign? Did I look like that much of a sucker?

On the other hand, I had been given the rare and special opportunity to spend time with and get to know a survivor of Auschwitz Concentration Camp. Perhaps I had been the fortunate one after all.

I drove the garbage tractor for several weeks before requesting to go back to work in the orchards. I missed the camaraderie of my fellow volunteers.

By now one must be thinking: What about the Dutch girls? Well, it wasn't happening with the Dutch girls. They were inseparable. They only wished to have a great time with each other during their big adventure living in the kibbutz. Any attempt to isolate any one particular girl's attention away from the group was doomed to fail, except for one, whom I discovered was messing around with an Israeli guy. I picked up on it one day while standing next to them in the food line. They were speaking to each other in a whisper. I nosily glanced at them out of the side of my face, trying to be as discreet as I could, straining to hear their conversation. I could tell they were making plans. They must have done it at his place, because I don't recall seeing him in the volunteer's living area.

She behaved toward me in a flirtatious manner. The opportunity presented itself, but I choose not to respond. The Dutch girls had become like sisters to me. I didn't want to run the risk of altering the group dynamic. It didn't seem worth it for what I considered somewhere in the vicinity of a three on a scale of one to ten. But down the road, in the rear view mirror of my mind's eye, she would begin looking better to me and I would promote her several notches up the scale. And I would replay the situation over and over in my head, wondering what the hell was I thinking and why did I care about the silly group dynamic, and finally I would kick myself as I added one more to my list of missed opportunities.

Bedouins are a borderless, desert dwelling nomadic people who journey by camel caravan throughout the deserts of the Middle East. A Bedouin family appeared one day, camped on the edge of our kibbutz. Alan, Jan the teenage Dutchman, and I decided to pay them a visit. We walked out to the desert where the Bedouins had set up camp, a short distance from the volunteers' living quarters. Five Bedouin children tended to the camels and goats. We peeked inside of the tent and saw an Arab man clad in a long white robe with full Arab head-dress sitting cross-legged on the ground. He motioned for us to come inside and sit with him, and as we entered he yelled out in Arabic to his wife, a small woman with a dark, sun beaten tattooed face who soon came into the tent and served us each a delicious cup of tea.

"Tea good?" the Bedouin asked.

"Yes," we responded.

Our host's English didn't go much further. Alan and the Bedouin began having a conversation in Hebrew while Jan and I sat watching and sipping our drinks. Bedouins are an Arabic speaking people. Out of necessity many have developed a working knowledge of Hebrew. He and his family were on their way to sell a couple of goats in the Bedouin market in Beersheba, we learned.

Watching Alan and the Bedouin engaged in conversation forced me to take a fresh look at the way in which I had viewed his dedicated effort to learn a language he would in all likelihood rarely if ever use again.

Alan's opportunities to put his hard work to use once he leaves the Holy Land will become near non-existent. But it won't matter, because successfully communicating with this dude from the ancient world in a tent on the desert in the Middle East with three camels parked out front will become one of the most precious memories he will ever have and he will cherish it forever. In one brief conversation

## Chapter Five

his admirable, inexhaustible efforts to learn the Hebrew language will have been rewarded a thousand-fold. And I too received the gift of a treasured memory, in the witnessing and sharing of a priceless moment.

We finished our second cup of tea, thanked our host and exited the tent, passing his wife's timeless tattooed face as we walked back to our compound.

Although not initially by intention, but delving into my heritage had become inescapable, considering my family history in relation to the earthly locations I had been led to on this journey. But a different cultural direction; namely, my attraction to the East, would also demand its due attention. It began with my introduction to Eastern religion and culture in the Hare Krishna temple in Los Angeles. It resurfaced in Istanbul. But my experience sitting in the tent on the desert in the Middle East drinking tea with the desert sheik bearing a resemblance to the king of Saudi Arabia would fire up my desire to travel deep into the Eastern world more than ever.

The tour the kibbutz had promised the volunteers had been scheduled to take place several weeks prior to my departure, which I had planned for early May.

We boarded the bus and headed deep into the Sinai Desert, to Saint Catherine's monastery, the oldest working Christian monastery in the world and the location of two sacred Old Testament sites. First and foremost, the fourteen hundred-year-old monastery sits at the base of Mt. Sinai, the desert mountain where Moses is said to have received the Ten Commandments. And the second is the site of the burning bush. As the biblical tale is told, through the burning bush God spoke to Moses.

Israel's capture of the Sinai Peninsula in 1967 during the Six Day War made visiting Mt. Sinai and Saint Catherine's monastery possible. The journey into the Sinai also allowed me to add one more country to my list.

Technically speaking, I was in Israeli occupied territory, but in actual fact, I had entered Egypt. In a few years time the two nations would sign a peace treaty and the Sinai Peninsula would be returned to Egypt.

From Saint Catherine's Monastery we traveled to the tip of the Sinai Peninsula and camped out on the Red Sea's Egyptian desert shores. From there we traveled to Masada. And although I had already been to Masada, I didn't mind going back. In fact, we could have gone anywhere; of no consequence would it have been to me, such a good time was I having traveling with my friends from the kibbutz. And with the newly arrived German group, our numbers nearly doubled.

In Masada, rather than stay in the youth hostel, we camped out among the ancient ruins and watched the sun rise over the Judean Desert from a height of fifteen hundred feet.

Swimming in the Red Sea gave us our only opportunity to have at least a semblance of a bath during the entire excursion. It remains a mystery to me, but lodging had been left out of the itinerary. The young Israeli guys from the kibbutz who drove the bus and acted as our guides were getting big kicks out of putting us to the test. No doubt if a planning committee existed at all, they were the sole members.

Before heading back to the kibbutz we made one last stop at an Israeli Army desert outpost and rode camels in the desert under the supervision of the Israeli Army's camel patrol. I believe the generous hospitality extended to us by the Israeli soldiers was in large part motivated by the opportunity to spend time with the Dutch and German girls.

## Chapter Five

My backpack sat on the ground beside me under a hot desert sun as I stood waiting for the bus to Beersheba.

Alan, my Scottish roommate, and the Dutch group were also heading home, leaving the German group to take our place. Ten young Germans, evenly mixed, comprised the group of German volunteers and I had sparked the interest of one cute female in the bunch. And I wouldn't have cared in the least bit about the group dynamic with her. But I hardly got the chance. As my luck would have it, my stay in the kibbutz came to an end a few weeks after her arrival.

In the kibbutz, all of my needs had been taken care of. I was provided with three square meals a day, a roof over my head, a bed to sleep in, and a job. I didn't need money, I never carried keys, and I had no decisions to make. I had finally found the perfect communal life.

From Beersheba I caught the bus to Tel Aviv. I would travel by bus for the remainder of my stay in Israel. I would soon be home and back to work, so I didn't mind spending what little money I had left on the convenience of public transportation.

The time had come for me to fulfill my family obligation. I couldn't put it off any longer. My parents expected it of me. I would have some serious explaining to do if I didn't visit the relatives during my five month long stay in Israel. First on the list was a cousin on my father's side and his wife, living in an apartment in Tel Aviv. They, like my parents, had also fled from Nazi Germany.

I arrived at their door, took a deep breath and knocked, my insecurity rearing its head once again. I'm twenty-six years old, why does this type of situation still make me feel so anxious? The same reason I declined having an Israeli family adopt me in the kibbutz, I reminded myself. My discomfort in the presence of the older generation would not fully go away until, by some weird freak of nature and the unavoidable passage of time, I would wake up one day to the frightful realization that I had become one of them.

The door opened. I entered and took a seat in a chair in their living room. Over hot tea and cookies we talked. Surprising myself, I became relaxed and at ease.

They spoke about their children and grandchildren. They asked about my parents and about my experience in the kibbutz, and they asked about my plans for the future.

"I'm going to continue traveling," I said.

I appreciated not having too many questions thrown at me on the subject of my life, which I'm sure appeared to them as quite puzzling. For someone who lives in their own head to the extent to which I did, the curious quizzing always made me feel uncomfortable, because I found my existence nearly impossible to explain.

My German relatives had attained a remarkable command of the English language and never having lived in an English speaking country made their fluency all the more impressive. And I would hear of the sadness their family had been suffering through, of which I knew nothing about until this moment. Their son-in-law had lost both of his legs six months earlier in the bloody conflict with their Arab neighbors that came to be known as the Yom Kipper War.

From Tel Aviv I traveled north. I had a few more ancient biblical locations I wished to visit before my departure, and another set of relatives on my mother's side living in a kibbutz in Northern Israel.

Arab shepherds herded goats along the rocky hillsides as I passed through the biblical town of Nazareth, where Jesus spent his boyhood. I was on my way to another legendary location, the biblical town of Tiberias, on the shores of the Sea of Galilee. Jesus is said to have spent much of his three year ministry in Tiberias and many of his miracles are believed to have been performed there.

## Chapter Five

In Tiberias I slept in the youth hostel, but I still managed to take advantage of the lavish amenities offered in this major tourist town by spending a portion of each day loitering on the magnificent terraces of luxurious five-star water-front hotels enjoying splendid views of the Sea of Galilee, which isn't really a sea at all, but rather an enormous fresh water lake, thirteen miles long and eight miles wide, surrounded by the scenic green rolling hills of Northern Israel.

From Tiberias I continued traveling through the Galilee, to the ancient village of Safed, one of Judaism's four holy cities. Jerusalem, Hebron, and Tiberias comprise the other three. A center of Judaic studies and Jewish mysticism, Safed is known as the home of the Kabala. The village of Safed is also one of a handful of locations in the Holy Land that remained inhabited by Jews during the two thousand years of exile.

In the ancient Galilean village, colorful cobbled corridors wind and twist past delightful centuries-old attached stone houses sprinkled with intriguing medieval synagogues, quaint cafés, cozy restaurants, and a world renowned artist's colony whose creative inhabitants dwell along the timeless footpaths, their charming galleries and boutiques snugly situated within the confines of the enchanting tiny stone houses. Offering magical views of the Galilee from its highest point, the picturesque village of Safed will do nothing less than leave all who visit hopelessly entranced.

From Safed I traveled to Israel's third largest city, Haifa, on the Mediterranean Coast, completing my goal of traveling the length of the narrow country, from the southernmost tip of the Negev to Northern Israel near the Lebanese border. I spent one night in the Haifa youth hostel. In the morning I took the short trip from Haifa to the ancient town of Akko, a UNESCO world heritage site with a recorded history dating back four thousand years.

Akko, also known as Acre, is renowned for the excavated ruins of past civilizations, including the conquering Crusader's medieval city, unearthed near intact. In addition, large cannons and stonewalled fortresses decorate Akko's Mediterranean shores, having been throughout the ages a major gateway to the region where many battles over control of the Holy Land took place.

From Akko I traveled to kibbutz Gal'ed in Northern Israel's beautiful Megiddo region, home to the relatives on my mother's side of the family.

Elsa was one of my mother's many cousins in Germany. They had been best friends as girls growing up together in pre-war Berlin, a time my mother spoke of with what I could only now imagine to have been a heartbreaking nostalgia.

Elsa had joined a group of young Jews fleeing Nazi Germany on a boat bound for the Holy Land, under British control at the time. Their ship sailed into the Haifa harbor, but they were not allowed to disembark. Instead, the British forced them to remain on board the ship for several months under threat of deportation back to Germany, where they would have met certain death.

Allowed entry at last, Elsa and her future husband, whom she had met on the journey, would join other young Jewish refugees from Hitler's Germany and from scratch, under extreme adversity and with almost no resources they would go on to build a beautiful, thriving communal farming settlement, turning into green and fertile land the rocky earth that had for centuries sat unattended.

Elsa and her husband would raise three children and would spend the remainder of their lives living in kibbutz Gal'ed.

Once again I found my German relatives' command of the English language remarkable. Survival for the European refugees meant learning two new languages at the same time. In order to deal with the Brits, who showed little sympathy to their plight, they would need to learn English, and Hebrew, which the European refugees would bring back to life, turning the ancient tongue used for countless centuries as a language of prayer only into the spoken word of a new nation.

I was shown to my quarters, a small rustic guest cabin surrounded by thousands of acres of fertile fields, thriving fruit orchards, and the green rolling hills of Northern Israel.

My relatives did everything they could to make me feel welcome and at home. But in my mind I could hear them thinking: What exactly are you doing with your life? We'd like to know. Could you explain it to us?

Uh, well, no, actually, I can't, because I haven't a clue myself. I was thankful they didn't ask. It was a conversation I didn't want to have. I knew having the luxury of living as I did was incomprehensible to them. Their lives were way too serious and their responsibilities far too great. Still, through all of their trials and tribulations, my Israeli relatives remained the most kind and gracious people one could ever hope to meet.

They had been at the forefront of the twentieth century's most defining moments, an unprecedented chain of earth-shaking historical events that would change and reshape the world, with their lives on the line since their youth, and the lives of their children as well. How fortunate for me to have such people as members of my own family, allowing me the rare opportunity of staring history point blank right in the eye.

After spending three days with my relatives in beautiful Kibbutz Gal'ed, I returned to the planet's most celebrated city. I wanted to see Jerusalem one more time before going home.

Once again, I followed the footsteps of Jesus as he carried the cross to his crucifixion, and once again, I stood at the sacred temple wall, and one more time I heard the mystical melody of the Islamic call to prayer echo across the holy city.

## Chapter Six
# CULTURE SHOCK

The Air Belgium flight landed in Brussels several hours after taking off from Tel Aviv. Through Belgium and France I traveled by train, returning to tiny Luxembourg. A day later, aboard an Icelandic Airways Boeing 727, I journeyed across the Atlantic a second time, and from the Big Apple a greyhound bus carried me the final distance home.

I had been on the road for seven months. I traveled through nine European countries, ventured as far eastward as Istanbul, lived on a kibbutz, and traveled throughout the Holy Land. I did pretty darn good on the meager amount of money I saved in only two months waiting tables at the beach, giving myself a pat on the back as I stepped down from the bus, walked out of the station and found myself standing, once again, upon the ever uplifting streets of Baltimore.

I decided to head for my parents' house first before looking up my friends. Should I take a cab or should I take the bus? Twenty dollars remained of the one thousand dollars I began the journey with. Although I would have much preferred it, the taxi would have taken at least half. The bus only cost twenty-five cents.

Riding through Charm City's grim inner city neighborhoods in a Baltimore City public transit bus, watching the large lumbering vehicle stop at every dismal decaying corner as it wound and twisted through miles of city slums, threw me into a state of culture shock and I believe I experienced a momentary psychotic episode. Like a bolt of lightning, it hit, and suddenly, time stood still, nothing seemed real, the world began moving in slow motion, and waves of anxiety permeated my being. I can't say how long this unlike anything I had ever experienced hallucinatory state had my mind in its grips. Perhaps only seconds, although it seemed like an eternity. Distorted time, high anxiety, altered spatial orientation, reality gone missing, all classic symptoms of severe culture shock. I wanted to run back to where nothing was familiar. I was comfortable there. I didn't even know the meaning of culture shock until I returned to Baltimore.

Several days later, after spending time with family and old friends in the neighborhood, I returned to the Maryland Shore.

I stepped down from the bus, retrieved my belongings, placed my feet upon the boardwalk and gazed at the sea. Soon, I would once again find myself in full tuxedo, serving drinks, dinner, and dessert to the hungry masses spending Memorial Day weekend on Maryland's beautiful Eastern Shore.

I arrived at the beach with barely any money and no idea where I would sleep. But the kindness of co-workers would see me through until I found a permanent place to stay.

A busboy named Tony, also in need of permanent shelter, said he knew of a two bedroom house up for rent sitting

## Chapter Six

on the bay at Thirty-Seventh Street. We joined forces the following day and sought out the landlord.

A more ideal living situation I could not have imagined. The house overlooked the entire expanse of the bay. Miraculously, we managed to talk the landlord into letting us move in without the advance payment he initially demanded. He agreed to give us several weeks to get the money together.

Tony's Cousin Rosemarie came for a visit and decided to stay. She began working at English's Chicken and Steak House and became our next roommate. A few days later one of Rosemarie's co-workers, Michelle, became our fourth and final roommate. We were now set for the season.

In the middle of July Lenny Jackson came down from Baltimore and moved in with me. Two years earlier Lenny had given me a place to stay in my time of need, even though he had only met me the day before. I needed to return the favor. The girls didn't mind, and Tony seemed okay with it at first, so I figured I had some time before he began wearing out his welcome.

Lenny arrived at the beach with his new friend, Miguel, a student from Venezuela. He had talked Miguel into driving him from Baltimore to Ocean City. I told Miguel of my interest in visiting South America. In generous response, Miguel invited me to stay with his family in Caracas. He had finished school at the University of Baltimore and was heading home. He said I could come down anytime.

I had set my sights on the Eastern world, but I saw a journey to Latin America in my future as well. The order in which these journeys would take place had not yet been determined. Miguel's invitation, the golden opportunity of an invitation from a native, provided a prompt answer. I would take Miguel up on his offer and fly south to Venezuela after the season ended in October. I made my decision in one conversation with a guy I had just met and knew nothing about.

Lenny had been camped out in our living room for over a month, having a grand vacation at the beach, with no intention of looking for a job. What little patience Tony had to begin with had now flown right out the window. But Michelle had fallen for Lenny, saw to it that he didn't go hungry and insisted he stay. It became a complicated and polarizing situation, the kind my friend Lenny was good at creating, inadvertently, of course, and I was caught in the middle, wanting nothing more than to work, save my money and get back on the road.

Labor Day neared and I took a second job as a desk clerk at the Surf and Sands, a beautiful ninety-room ocean front motel complete with a swimming pool and a bustling coffee shop serving breakfast and lunch. I hadn't been able to save as much money working at the restaurant as I had hoped. Now, with a second job, I would be guaranteed to meet my goal.

Beginning at eight o'clock in the morning, I sat behind the motel's desk, six days a week, eight hours a day, checking guests in and out of their rooms and working the switchboard, as was the technology of the day.

Two brothers in their early forties owned and operated the motel. On occasion, the younger brother would send me out to run errands in his Corvette. And through this experience I would come to the undeniable conclusion that nothing cooler exists on the face of the Earth than sitting in the driver's seat of a white Corvette cruising down a coastal highway with its top down on a sunny day at the beach.

The brothers were strict. They ran a tight ship, making sure their motel maintained the highest of standards. But they also showed compassion.

I experienced their understanding when I presented them with my dilemma. I had a scheduling conflict. My schedules overlapped. My shift at the motel ended at four o'clock. My shift at the restaurant began at the same time. This predicament forced me to make an unusual request of the brothers. And they agreed to honor my request, allowing me to leave my post early so I could arrive at the restaurant on time.

The process would proceed as follows: I would change into my tuxedo in the motel's bathroom fifteen minutes prior to the end of my shift, leaving my desk clerk outfit, conservative slacks and button down dress shirt, hanging in a closet in the motel's office. Clad in a black tuxedo with a white shirt, frills, and a black bow tie, I would pedal my banana seat bike with the high handlebars the short three blocks over to the restaurant. When my evening of waiting tables came to an end, I would return to the motel, change out of my tuxedo and back into my desk clerk outfit, leaving my tuxedo hanging in the same closet where my desk clerk clothes had been. With the long day over at last, I would pedal home, get some much needed sleep and in the morning I would begin again. A grueling daily grind lasting seven weeks, but it would pay off in the end.

Mid-October arrived. The restaurant and the motel closed their doors until next year. With my mind firmly focused, steadfast in its singular purpose, my goal had been achieved. I was on my way to South America.

## Chapter Seven
# SOUTH OF THE BORDER

Miguel picked me up from the airport and drove me to his home in the neighborhood of California Del Sur, a fashionable suburb of Caracas. I had based my decision to come to Venezuela on this guy's word. Not once did I think to doubt him when he said I could stay with his family for an extended period of time. But as soon as I entered the house a disturbing reality became evident: I had made a terrible mistake.

"You can spend the night, but you'll have to leave in the morning," Miguel's father declared.

My plan had been to stay at Miguel's house in Caracas for a few months. From there I would fly to Panama and from the southernmost tip of Central America the journey north by land to the American border would begin. Living with Miguel's family would give me the opportunity to acquire the essential Spanish language skills I would need for the journey, the central, most critical component in making the plan work.

What a disaster! I couldn't recall ever having felt so stupid. Not for one moment did Miguel actually believe anyone would take him up on his offer. But he had never met anyone like me, and now here I am in Caracas, Venezuela looking like an idiot.

Morning came. Feeling quite the fool, I prepared to head back to the airport and board a flight to Panama.

"I have a friend," Miguel said. "His name is Paco. You might be able to stay with him. He lives in the neighborhood and he speaks pretty good English."

We drove through the Caracas suburb of California Del Sur. The lovely single homes with second floor terraces were modern, clean, open and airy. Lush rain forest landscapes bursting with the brilliant colors of tropical flower gardens adorned each house. Palm trees lined the streets.

Miguel stopped the car when he saw a gathering of guys he knew standing on a corner. He spoke a few words and the entire group began climbing all over each other, scrambling to get a better look at me. One would have thought my space ship had landed from Mars.

"They're asking if you want cocaine. They think you came here for drugs," Miguel said.

"Tell them I'm a traveler and I've come to see South America."

Miguel translated and the whole bunch burst into hysterical laughter, holding their bellies and slapping each other. They thought my response was the funniest thing they had ever heard. "Adios, Gringo," they shouted, still laughing uncontrollably as we drove away.

Miguel pulled over and parked the car in front of a house a few blocks from where I had been offered cocaine, laughed at, and called a gringo.

"Paco lives here," he said.

We stood on the front porch. Miguel rang the bell. A short middle-aged woman with curly black hair and a sweet slightly age lined dark complexioned face opened the door.

"Is Paco home?" Miguel asked.

"Si," Paco's mother responded. We followed her upstairs to Paco's room.

Paco was a tall fellow in his early twenties. He had a slim physique, a clean shaven face, and he kept his tight knit dark brown curly hair cut close. The sight of a gringo standing in his room put Paco's mind into a state of shock. Miguel explained the situation to him. Staring at me in disbelief, Paco sat on the edge of his bed and gave thought to this most unprecedented state of affairs.

"I'll let you stay in my room if you promise to write down the words to all of my favorite Rolling Stones' songs," Paco said upon ending his brief period of perplexed contemplation.

"No problem, I know most of their songs anyway," I replied.

Paco loved the Rolling Stones. The walls of his room were plastered with pictures and posters of the legendary rock band.

Paco excused himself. He returned several minutes later with the okay from his parents.

"You can sleep there," Paco said, directing my attention to an extra bed in his room once belonging to his younger brother who had moved into their sister's room after she had married and moved out.

My poorly thought out decision to take Miguel up on his offer could have easily landed me high on the list of biggest blunders ever made in the history of human travel. But thanks to Paco's family taking me in, my disastrous mistake would instead become nothing more than a mere footnote in the strange story of my life.

Relieved to have unloaded me, Miguel made his exit. Still in a state of bewilderment, Paco invited me out to the terrace, reached through an entrance attached to his room and from where a clear view of the mountains surrounding Caracas could be seen. It was a perfect day, eternal summer, as every day of my stay in Latin America would be. Paco studied me with insightful eyes.

"I don't understand how you could come to Venezuela as you have. You don't speak Spanish and you only knew one person in the entire country, and his family didn't even want you there. You must be crazy," he said. I couldn't have agreed more.

Paco had been hoping to become friends with a native English speaker, but had begun to give up on the idea, thinking it impossible, when, one day, out of nowhere, a Gringo appeared in his room, moved in, and stayed for three months.

I told Paco of my interest in learning Spanish.

"We can help each other. I've learned most of my English in school and from listening to the Rolling Stones," Paco said.

Under pressure from his father to choose a profession, Paco had undertaken studies in hotel management. His future career required fluency in English. He had reached a good level, but having regular conversation on a day to day basis with a native speaker is what he needed most of all to further his progress.

Paco loved the Rolling Stones and above all he loved Mick Jagger. He had an unplugged standup microphone in his room set up for the sole purpose of imagining himself as the famous rock star. We walked from the terrace back into Paco's room. Paco stood in front of the microphone, turned up the music and began singing along to the Rolling Stones, imitating, with uncanny accuracy, Mick Jagger's unique dance moves, gyrations, and facial expressions, lost in his own world, not giving a damn what others might think.

## Chapter Seven

An older brother, the aforementioned younger brother, and an aunt, known to everyone as Tia, also lived in the house with Paco and his parents. At first I thought Tia was her name, until I learned Tia is the Spanish word for aunt. By then I too had been calling her Tia and would continue to do so for the duration of my stay. Everyone in Paco's family had facial features and skin tone reflecting indigenous influences, and no one in the family, other than Paco, spoke one word of English.

Paco's family employed a live-in servant, an adorable eighteen-year-old Indian girl standing no taller than five feet, with beautiful long shiny black hair and silky smooth golden brown skin. Under the direction of Mama and Tia, she helped clean and cook and sent the money she earned home to her family in the village. I fell in love with her the minute I saw her. She was so damn cute. I kept it to myself, though. I would have been seen as a lunatic had I told the guys of my infatuation with a servant, a girl from the jungle, no less. No words were shared between us throughout the duration of my stay, but the sweetest ever present big bright shining smile and the innocence in her beautiful brown eyes spoke volumes.

Paco attended classes almost every day, although not once did I see him open a book at home. The remainder of his time he spent either with his girlfriend, or in his room listening to the Rolling Stones and imitating Mick Jagger. Elena was a pretty girl of medium height and slender build with soft black hair falling fashionably upon delicate shoulders. Unlike the historical mix found in Paco's family, Elena's pure Spanish descent could not be mistaken. A quiet girl, sweet and demure, Elena displayed a subtle Latin sexiness she wore naturally. She and Paco's older brother's girlfriend, a genuine, well-endowed Latin beauty, were exact opposites. Not a man on Earth could keep his head from turning when that buxom Latin bombshell walked by. She made sure of it. Nothing subtle about her!

Word of a Gringo living in Paco's house spread throughout the neighborhood. I became an object of great interest, a celebrity of sorts one might say. Neighborhood guys Paco had grown up with began stopping by, including some of the same guys I had seen on my first day in Miguel's car, the guys who had gotten such a kick out of the sight of me. Everyone wanted to know the reason I had come to Venezuela, a question to which I could give no clear response because the answer lie deep within the complicated confines of the curious life I lived in my head.

All of these guys, without exception, arrived at Paco's door carrying pre-rolled joints, eager to welcome the Gringo to their country by getting him stoned.

Paco had known these guys his entire life and a great deal of mutual respect existed between them, but he didn't hang out with them. He didn't hang out with anyone but his girlfriend. Paco was a loner, he too lived in his own head, and he recognized the same characteristics in my personality, which I believe not only influenced his decision to allow me to stay, but also became the reason we bonded so quickly. Destiny had brought me to Paco's door, of that I am certain.

Paco welcomed these guys into his room when they came to see me. He would act as translator and although he didn't partake, he would allow us to go out on the terrace and smoke joints. These visits occurred daily at first, gradually tapering off before coming to an end after several weeks. And I must say, I felt relief when the visits ended. They had begun tiring my mind and I also didn't want to smoke every day. But to refuse such well intended offerings of welcome and friendship would have been seen as disrespectful, and so I stayed stoned on top notch Columbian for most of my first month in Venezuela.

The visits would end, but I would still see these same guys hanging around the neighborhood. It couldn't have

## Chapter Seven

been more surreal. I found myself hanging out on street corners in South America, and little by little I began speaking Spanish, learning new words every day, trying them out, without inhibition, on anyone who would listen, engaging the amused ears of the kind and patient people of the neighborhood of California Del Sur with a Gringo's well intentioned efforts to learn and speak the Spanish Language.

I would be known only as the Gringo during my three month stay in Caracas. Only Paco's parents and Tia called me by my given name.

Time passed in the neighborhood of California Del Sur. Christmas arrived, and New Year's Eve came next, and the streets of California Del Sur on New Year's Eve were filled with people going in and out of each other's homes as the entire neighborhood celebrated together on a warm, star filled Venezuelan night. Nowhere in my memory had I seen hospitality taken to such heights. Every door in the neighborhood remained open into the wee hours, and inside every home a delightful flower decorated holiday table full of fruits, drinks, delicacies, and desserts welcomed all.

I woke up on New Year's Day thinking about my plans. My restlessness could no longer be contained. The road was calling. A friend of Paco's parents owned a home on the Caribbean island of Curacao, part of the Dutch Antilles, a chain of islands in the Caribbean formerly under Dutch control, a few hours by ferryboat off the coast of Venezuela. She, her two children, and Tia planned to go there on vacation and I had been invited to join them.

I worked hard learning Spanish during my stay in Caracas. In addition to my unending questions, which Paco would answer with heroic patience, I also spent time studying grammar and memorizing vocabulary, and I would spend hours walking around the neighborhood, engaging in conversation with everyone and their mother about everything and nothing, for the pure sake of practicing and learning. I didn't care what I sounded or looked like or how many mistakes I made. I kept plugging away. Continuous non-stop effort was the only way to make it happen and I was determined. I arrived in Caracas with no knowledge of the Spanish language. I would leave Caracas with a passable ability to engage in basic conversation and taking care of my food, lodging, and transportation needs as I traveled through Central America and Mexico on the journey back to the American border would present no problem at all.

Paco was a night owl. He liked to stay up after everyone else in the house had gone to sleep. He would go into the kitchen and prepare a midnight feast for both of us, delicious leftovers Mama and Tia had cooked for dinner, and we would talk until two.

The morning of my departure arrived. Per our usual routine, we had stayed up late talking. Paco wanted to leave it at that. He wouldn't get out of bed. He didn't want to say goodbye. Kindred spirits destined to meet for a brief moment in time. I had drifted into Paco's life, lived in his room for three months, and now, I was drifting out.

The family friend, Silvia, sat behind the wheel. Silvia had lived in America and spoke perfect English. Tia sat in the front beside her. I sat in the back seat with Silvia's two children, a boy and a girl, ages five and nine, respectively. Conversing with children, I discovered, is a great way to learn a foreign language. Children speak slowly and use basic vocabulary. I could understand almost all of their conversation. They were right on my level. Learning a new language made me feel as if I were a child learning to speak all over again.

We rolled through the Venezuelan countryside, through small Venezuelan towns, rural villages, and breathtaking tropical rain forest landscapes. I would finally get a good look at South American life outside of Paco's suburban

*Chapter Seven*

neighborhood, which I seldom left during my three month stay, other than one family outing to the beach, several trips with Paco when he picked up his girlfriend from the apartment she lived in with her parents in the city, and the solitary walks I would take in the wistful morning air of never ending summer.

On these excursions, I would hike several miles outside of the neighborhood to a bustling sidewalk café on a wide tree lined Spanish boulevard in the midst of a colorful commercial district. And there, indulging myself on delicious fresh tropical fruit drinks and luscious fresh tropical fruit filled pastries, I would sit, in welcome anonymity, lingering long at my table, observing life on the streets of a beautiful South American city.

We arrived upon the docks, boarded the ferryboat and set sail upon the Caribbean Sea at sunset, to the island of Curacao. Several hours later upon the moonlit horizon the surprising appearance of a small Dutch village came into view, lit up in the darkness of a Caribbean night.

Commonplace among the indigenous population of Curacao is the ability to converse in English, Spanish, and Dutch, the three major European languages brought to the Caribbean during the colonial era, while also speaking an island dialect known as Papiamentu, a fascinating fusion of the aforementioned European Languages.

As a world renowned duty free port, the island of Curacao sees a steady stream of ships of many nations sail into its harbor. As a popular Caribbean vacation spot; however, it takes a back seat to the booming business enjoyed by its sister island, Aruba, also part of the Dutch Antilles and a major tourist destination. A curious place, the island of Curacao, and well off the beaten path.

The only time Silvia and Tia left the house was to go food shopping and the house sat too far inland for me to walk to the beach. All of our time; therefore, to both my disappointment and puzzlement, we spent either in the house or outside in the yard.

On our third day on the island I came down with a whopper of a cold. I could do nothing more than spend my time flat on my back, sneezing, blowing my nose, and hacking away, and I could barely breathe. Silvia and Tia worried about the children and so did I. Their vacation would be ruined if the children became ill and I knew they would put the blame on me.

One expects women to instinctively demonstrate a nurturing nature, but not these two. The mere fact that I had taken ill, this alone irritated them to no end and overrode any sense of compassion they might have had.

Silvia wasted no time transporting me to the Dutch Royal Airline office to book my one-way flight to Panama City the minute I showed signs of recovery. She couldn't wait to unload me. I had been on a Caribbean island for over a week and not once did I see a beach. In the middle of this catastrophe; however, one consoling factor did emerge. It didn't cost me anything. Room and board had been provided.

The Dutch Royal Airline jet touched down on the runway and taxied to a stop. I had arrived in Panama, the southern-most country in Central America. I retrieved my backpack, breezed through security and stopped to cash a travelers check before boarding a bus waiting outside of the airport marked Panama City. It felt good to be in my own space and on the move again.

I took a hotel room on a bustling boulevard at the far reaches of the Pan American Highway and in the steamy tropical noonday heat I set about exploring Panama City. Street vendors stood on every corner selling delicious fruit flavored popsicles I quickly became addicted to. They only cost an American nickel.

Not since the ice cream man came rolling down my narrow one-way Baltimore City street with his truck full of frozen goodies on the lazy hot and humid summer days of my childhood had I bought a popsicle for a nickel. And when I say nickel, I mean an actual American nickel. Panama had no currency of its own. They used American money instead, and making the experience of using American money as currency in a foreign land even more surreal were the prices in Panama, not seen north of the border since before the Second World War.

I would keep my stay in Panama short, and I would move quickly through Costa Rica, Nicaragua, Honduras, and El Salvador as well, until I crossed into Guatemala. In Guatemala I would venture off the beaten path, into the interior and begin taking a good look around, and I would do the same in Mexico until I reached the American border. Every one of the countries along my route merited extended stays, but I needed to narrow my itinerary down, because, as conventional wisdom tells us, when one tries to see too much, one ends up not seeing much of anything at all.

From Panama City I headed for San Jose, capital of Costa Rica. Quiet, clean, and cared for with pride, San Jose is a perfect blend of modern Latin American culture and old world Spanish charm. Costa Rica has eluded the turmoil, war, and oppressive dictatorial regimes plaguing the region for decades and its citizens enjoy a standard of living far exceeding the majority of their Central American neighbors.

Comfortable coaches ran from Panama to Guatemala, departing every morning from the capital city of each Central American country along the route, arriving in the capital city of the next country by day's end.

From Costa Rica I headed for Managua, capital of Nicaragua, the next country on the journey through Central America and where the poverty of the region would finally be revealed. I found a cheap hotel not far from the bus depot accompanied by several other backpackers who had been on the bus with me.

In the morning I strolled the streets of Managua. I walked past the crumbling remains of fallen buildings and I stepped over cracked sidewalks, a stark reminder of the major earthquake the city experienced three years earlier, causing tremendous damage, much of which still hadn't been repaired. The government is believed to have stolen most of the international aid money.

At the time, Nicaragua was governed by the Somoza family, a corrupt totalitarian regime passing the power down through several generations. The fascist hereditary dictatorship held an iron grip on the nation and cared not an ounce for the people's needs. A dark cloud weighed heavily upon the land. A brutal civil war loomed. In a few years time the Somoza family's tyrannical rule would at long last come to an end, but not before rivers of blood flowed through the streets of Managua.

There wasn't much to do in the Managua of 1975, other than walk the grey streets of a forlorn and forgotten city, which I found intriguing nonetheless, despite its bleakness, or perhaps because of it.

Heading for the nation of Honduras next, the comfortable coach cruised up the Pan American highway. Ready for the junkyard, but ending up south of the border instead, old American cars and trucks rolled along beside us, sharing the road with beasts of burden hauling heavy loads in a range of dilapidated wagons and carts. We passed through impoverished villages where families lived in one-room shanties and young children in tattered clothing stood under the baking mid-day sun selling slices of watermelon from roadside stands. The third-world was at America's doorstep.

Remaining steadfast in my plan, I stayed one day in Tegucigalpa, the spirited capital of Honduras. From Tegucigalpa I boarded a bus for San Salvador, capital of El Salvador, the most populated country in Central America and the final stop before reaching Guatemala.

Because of the Miguel disaster, I came within one inch of leaving Venezuela the day after I arrived. Had I been forced to follow through, I would have found myself making the journey north with not one word of the Spanish language under my belt. How difficult taking care of my day to day needs would have been, not to mention how many priceless opportunities to communicate would have been lost had Paco's family not taken me in.

Thoughts of Paco and of the time I spent in Caracas would surface daily in my mind. I wrote several letters. Sadly, he didn't respond and as happens so often with friendships made on the road, we lost touch.

Scores of American, European, and Canadian budget backpackers filled the sprawling one-story hostel in Guatemala City, where a traveler could get a bed and three meals a day for a dollar. I gathered information fast. Guatemala is a great backpacker's country, I learned.

With my itinerary set, I ventured off into the land of the Maya. I would stop first in the colonial town of Antigua, a world heritage site founded in 1541, encircled by three spectacular volcanoes. A grand display of the historic architectural design of colonial Spain lines the cobblestone streets of Antigua, one of the original capitals of the Spanish colonial empire.

I hooked up with a fellow American backpacker on the bus from Guatemala City to Antigua. Larry carried a guitar and sang contemporary folk songs. He sang and played well, but when it came to speaking Spanish, Larry refused to learn even one syllable. "I just can't do it!" he would say in frustration.

We rolled into Antigua and found inexpensive lodging located in a spot where all points of interest could be reached on foot.

Clad in vibrant, eye-catching, multi-hued native garb, showcasing their phenomenal weaving skills, the Mayan Indians of Guatemala filled the streets of Antigua with a regal rainbow of woven magic, revealing a genius of design and a brilliance of tints, tones, and hues only the Mayan Indians of Guatemala hold the secret to and the likes of which are not to be duplicated anywhere else on the planet.

Direct descendents of the ancient Mayans, the indigenous people of Guatemala inhabit the towns and villages dotting the landscape of Guatemala's scenic Western Highlands, a picturesque mountainous region with over thirty volcanoes and a majestic mountain lake certain to take your breath away.

Earning their living through farming and by their unparalleled artistry, the Mayan Indians comprise half of the nation's population and without question rank among the most colorful and fascinating people in the world. It took no stretch of the imagination to understand why I would see countless more backpacking travelers in Guatemala than I had seen in all of the other Central American countries combined.

Two Spanish speaking girls sat unaccompanied at a table in the crowded tourist café Larry and I had randomly entered. In Spanish, I ask if we could please sit with them.

"Si," they responded in unison.

Ana and Isabella were two college girls from Mexico City. They were both twenty-one years old, had an adequate knowledge of English, and seemed open to our companionship. Ana and Isabella were doing a bit of traveling during their school break, against the wishes of their strict Catholic families. A few days later the four of us set off together for the journey into the Western Highlands, to the Mayan mountain village of Panajachel, sitting a mile above sea level on the banks of Lake Atitlan.

Our bus rolled out of the Antigua bus depot mid-morning, bumping and weaving along the hairpin curves and passes of the narrow, winding mountain roads, remaining packed throughout the journey with a steady flow of Guatemalan Indians, clad in traditional indigenous dress of brilliant tribal colors, speaking ancient Mayan languages, and carrying a myriad of goods to sell in various marketplaces throughout the mountain towns and villages, including chickens and roosters, which is how the busses in Guatemala, old American school busses with hard uncomfortable seats and shock absorbers that had long ago stopped working, came to be known as the chicken busses. The chicken busses were painted in bright colors with artistic design in an attempt to make them look beautiful, at least on the outside.

Of slender build, Ana stood a few inches above five feet, her long silken black hair accentuating a beautiful olive complexion.

My unending efforts to learn Spanish amused Ana. She had unlimited patience and didn't mind answering my many grammar and vocabulary questions. Ana and I sat next to each other on the bus, which put Isabella in a bad mood, because she would have preferred sitting next to her friend, and Larry's lack of interest in Isabella only made matters worse. Perhaps Isabella's acne bothered him. Although I must say, I still thought she was cute. Or maybe he would rather have been the one sitting next to Ana, who resembled a young Sofia Loren, the famous Italian actress and a stunning Latin beauty in her youth.

## An Extraordinary Tale of Travel

We pulled into the Mayan mountain village of Panajachel after traveling all day through rugged mountainous terrain over treacherous roads on a bus made for school children traveling short distances. We retrieved our backpacks, which had been tied to the roof of the bus, and set about finding the cheapest accommodations in town. Of the Mayan villages sitting upon the shores of Lake Atitlan, Panajachel, dating back to the ninth century, is the largest and most popular among travelers.

We located the budget backpacker's hostel, a one-story dilapidated wooden structure with one large room containing wooden benches without mattresses. The proprietors also offered floor space, and there seemed no limit to the number of people they were willing to squeeze in on the floor when all of the benches were occupied. The hostel's toilets were nothing but rough wooden platforms built over holes in the ground. I made sure to wear my rubber flip flops, a pair of which I have not traveled without since the first time I stepped barefoot onto the slimy floor of a cheap hotel's bathroom in a third world country, a mistake one does not make twice.

The village also contained a number of tourist guesthouses, all of which were cheap by American standards, but still too much for my budget and the budgets of my traveling companions as well. We made our arrangements: "Floor space only," we were told.

Darkness fell. It had been a long day on a chicken bus since leaving Antigua in the morning. A thought popped into my mind as we prepared for slumber. By unzipping our sleeping bags and spreading them out, Ana and I could sleep on top of one and cover ourselves with the other. In a whisper so no one else could hear in case I met rejection, I put forth my suggestion. She agreed without hesitation.

It didn't take long before we were all over each other, on the cement floor, locked in a fiery intensity until we fell

## Chapter Seven

asleep, which must have come about during a pause. I don't remember who fell asleep first. It seems no one ever does.

At the crack of dawn the four of us headed out for our first glimpse of Guatemala's magnificent Lake Atitlan, deemed by many a seasoned traveler as one of the most beautiful lakes on the planet.

In the crispy cool mist of an early mountain morning, a mile high in the sky we stood, on the banks of Lake Atitlan. As if painted upon a divine canvas, truly touched by the hand of God, we gazed upon the celestial masterpiece appearing before us across the vast horizon, encircled by three majestic volcanoes silhouetting the heavens at ten thousand feet above the windswept, crystalline waters of a pure mountain lake.

Our first mind blowing journey to Lake Atitlan came to a close. We walked back into town and ate breakfast at a health food restaurant run by three hippie girls from California located in a small hut sitting on top of a hill.

Images of rugged self reliant pioneer women on the edges of the old frontier came to mind when I first saw these three adventurous California girls. And they could cook. Their simple, healthy, vegetarian cuisine was my kind of food. I felt a bit of ambivalence at first, though, thinking they were taking money out of the hands of poor Guatemalans. My quandary would find resolution when I became aware of the following facts: Everything required for their small business venture they would still need to purchase from Guatemalans in the marketplace, and they paid rent to the Guatemalan who owned the hut, which also served as their home; hence, most of the money they earned went right back out into the local economy. And it wasn't as if people were lining up around the corner. The local eateries were doing fine.

All they desired out of their smart, admirable, and daring endeavor was a place to live, a means of feeding themselves, and the opportunity to join an expatriate community of gringos who had taken up residence in the idyllic mountain setting in the heart of the ancient Mayan nation.

Thank goodness my moral dilemma had found resolution. I would have been in quite a pickle had it not, because, principles notwithstanding, in all likelihood I would've eaten there anyway. The food was way too good and healthy to pass up.

After breakfast we enjoyed spectacular panoramic views as we hiked into the hills. Sweet Mayan women, perpetually smiling, clad in beautiful handmade traditional tribal garments of rich and vivid hues, carrying baskets on their heads, stepped alongside us on our trek up the winding mountain road while others passed us on their way down. I don't think I saw one over five feet.

Families of Guatemalan Indians farmed stair step terraced plots of land, miraculously, and one would certainly think impossibly, carved out upon the edges of the scenic mountain cliffs.

Ana and Isabella stayed for another three days. After watching their bus pull away, I embarked upon a solitary hike. I walked several miles into the hills before stopping to rest by a lovely mountain stream. I sat awhile, listening to the water's mellow tune as it flowed over small rocks and broken branches. With cupped hands I leaned into the stream and drank several scoops of water.

October through May is the best time to visit Guatemala. Summer is the rainy season. I thought about Ana. She had given me her phone number in Mexico City. I tried to keep my mind in the moment, but fantasies of Ana and what I hoped would finally take place when we met again made concentrating on the picturesque surroundings and breathtaking view as I trekked back to the village impossible, no matter how much of an effort I made, so distracted had my mind become.

## Chapter Seven

Back at the hostel I found a crowd of budget backpackers, American, European, Canadian, and even a few Australians, congregating in the grassy courtyard and milling about on the old wooden veranda. Only on the road did I meet people who lived as I did, people who understood this wandering life. There were those with lesser degrees of wanderlust, and there were those driven by the same mad degree of wanderlust as myself.

Another day came to an end. I crawled inside of my sleeping bag on the cement floor, but I didn't stay long. Excruciating stomach cramps soon sent me running to the bathroom, doubled up and barely making it as Montezuma's revenge struck.

The mountain air turned chilly and cold as I ran through the night to the hostel's filthy bathroom. Every time I crawled back inside of my warm sleeping bag I had to get up and go again. Everyone in the room was sound asleep. No one knew of my misery. I wondered what could have done this to me. I couldn't think of anything bad I had eaten and I had heard no talk of dysentery among the other travelers.

The light of dawn finally appeared. Other than a bit of delirious dozing, I had been unable to sleep. I was miserable. I was sick as a dog, but I couldn't lie on the cement floor all day, even though I didn't feel as if I could do much else. I climbed out of my sleeping bag one more time, rolled it up, put it inside of my backpack and set about looking for an answer.

In desperation I began talking to other travelers. One guy said I may have contracted a parasite known as an amoeba. He told me I might not be able to get rid of it. I freaked out. I wished I hadn't spoken with him. The next person I talked to advised me to buy a drug called Intestopan.

"It's an intestinal antiseptic," he said. "Cures most dysentery. But be careful, it can cause damage to your peripheral vision if you take it for more than two weeks."

A wooden shack resembling a medicine shop on the frontiers of the old West housed the village's sole pharmacy. And one didn't need a prescription. Speaking Spanish, I informed the proprietor of my need. He reached among the many items sitting upon his dusty, cluttered shelves and handed me a package of Intestopan. I read the instructions, which included the warning I had been told about.

It had run out of me all night, and whatever it was wasn't done with me yet. I wondered again what could have made me sick. The mountain stream, I suddenly realized.

I had quenched my thirst from moving mountain streams before. But not in a third world country, I reminded myself. A thought entered my mind: I wondered if the villagers washed their dirty laundry upstream from where I drank the water. Or worse yet: I wondered if the stream served as a dumping ground for sewage. Were the latter the case, and I had begun to believe more and more in its most dreadful and sickening possibility, then only one gruesome, unspeakable, vile, and ghastly detail remained: Good chance I drank water from a sewage dump in Central America. I was horrified!

My intestines had been invaded by an evil army of foul and wicked parasites. With overwhelming worry I posed the following question to myself: What the hell am I going to do if this medicine doesn't work? I'm going to become dehydrated and die, in terror I answered myself.

In the midst of my misery, a wooden bench became available. I would no longer sleep on the cement floor. I awoke the following morning with my condition having noticeably improved. Within seventy-two hours of my first dose of Intestopan my recovery was complete. To this day I shudder to think what would have happened had I not been led in the direction of the miracle drug Intestopan, because a trip on a chicken bus to a place where I could get

## Chapter Seven

serious medical help would have been impossible to make in the shape I was in.

I had only been in Panajachel for three days when Montezuma's revenge struck me down. Now, with those ungodly microbes from the nether regions of hell vanquished and disposed of, I could once again enjoy the magnificent mountain scenery of Guatemala's Western Highlands, its colorful, gentle, captivating inhabitants, and the divine mountain lake around which their lives revolve. It is impossible for the Mayan Indians of Guatemala to do anything less than imprint the most beautiful, everlasting, treasured memories upon those who have been graced by their presence.

Panahachel, the sweet Mayan village in the mountains of Guatemala sitting upon the heavenly shores of Lake Atitlan was everything I had been looking for and all I had hoped it would be. Even Montezuma's revenge couldn't change that.

●

Traveling aboard another chicken bus I continued my journey through the mountains of Guatemala, to the Mayan town of Chichicastenango, sitting at an elevation of close to seven thousand feet. From the neighboring mountain towns and villages the Mayan Indians of Guatemala come pouring into Chichicastenango on market days, held every Thursday and Sunday, to set up shop and sell their wares.

Deemed among the most colorful indigenous markets in the Americas, a festive sea of ramshackle tables, stalls, and stands line the otherwise serene and sleepy streets of the small Mayan village of Chichicastenango on market days.

A display of wool jackets caught my eye as I strolled among the many rows of rickety wooden stalls. I stopped to take a closer look. The proprietor approached, a wrinkled, aged Mayan Indian with a toothless grin, clad in a multi-colored shirt of vibrant hue and a pair of bright multi-colored striped shorts, his bony old legs exposed from the knees down, and a traditional straw hat on his head, completing his eye-catching indigenous outfit. A picture that stays in a traveler's mind forever.

One jacket in particular attracted my interest. The proprietor spoke to me in Spanish and gave me a price. I countered with a lower price.

He responded with another price. We went back and forth. I came up a little, he came down a little, until we agreed upon a final price, which wasn't much lower than his original offer but I accepted it anyway and became the proud owner of a beautiful hand crafted one hundred percent brown wool jacket with colorful images of Quetzel birds, the national bird of Guatemala, embroidered into the fabric.

Perhaps I should have put in more of an effort, played hardball, as I had seen other travelers do. I observed their tough technique on several occasions. They would haggle, walk away, come back, haggle some more, and walk away again. Many times the merchant would go running and yelling after them, desperate to make a sale, the precise effect they were trying to achieve. These travelers were hardcore. To them, bartering was war. I didn't have the heart to take it to such an extreme. These people were so poor. Let them have a few extra quetzals is how I saw it. It hardly amounted to anything in American money.

However, under no circumstances should one ever accept the first offer. One must always make an effort to lower the price, if only the slightest. It is imperative. The game must be played.

The Spanish colonial church, by the mere fact of its existence alone, stands above all else in telling the tale of the

## Chapter Seven

Conquistadores determined efforts to convert the indigenous people of the conquered lands. In substantial quantity in the land of the Maya, these quaint catholic churches present a valuable lesson in Spanish history, colonial architecture, and of Spain's powerful influence in shaping the new world. Also in abundance in Guatemala one finds spirited religious processions as pious Guatemalans march through the streets carrying colorful statues, images, and representations of holy figures and patron Saints.

The Spaniards achieved a high degree of success in their efforts, but an ancient mystical presence still pervades. The ancestral Mayan Gods would not be so easily forgotten. They would find a way to sneak back in, secretly preserving their place in subtle and clever ways and get themselves worshipped as well, bringing even more color and mystique, and countless lit candles, to the rituals and ceremonies in a one of a kind hybrid of exotic worship: mysterious, fascinating, and unknown to outsiders.

In the town of Quetzaltenango, the next stop on the journey through the Western Highlands and the nation's second largest city, in almost every direction one comes across a Spanish colonial church. And I found myself engaging in a most unusual pursuit. At least once a day during my stay in Quetzaltenango I would enter one of the churches and sit in the pew. Each church is a grand museum of colonial history, art, and architecture in and of itself. And from my quiet place in the pew, hands folded in my lap, embraced by mysterious waves of serenity sweeping over me I can neither explain nor to my complete satisfaction describe, precious pictures of the sweet indigenous people of Guatemala, at times entire families, entering the small churches, kneeling before the altar and praying in front of Jesus on the cross would forever be etched into my mind.

From Quetzaltenango I traveled to the town of Huehuetenango, crammed inside of another archaic yet flamboyantly painted American school bus. And as the chicken bus bumped along on the edge of a mountain ridge after another lengthy and tiring journey through the land of the Maya I could see the final town in the Western Highlands of Guatemala come into view.

I met a young Mormon missionary couple in Huehuetenango. They took me home with them, to the small one-story simple wooden house in which they resided in the most austere manner, with the barest of essentials and obsolete plumbing. They fed me a hearty, home cooked dinner and invited me to stay for a few days, which I did, of course, never one to turn down a free meal or place to stay, even in a third world country where a room could be had for under a dollar and a meal for fifty cents.

They ran a missionary school for children. They were kind, big hearted, did good works, were of strong conviction, and preached the book of Mormon.

They didn't preach to me, thank goodness. The difficulty inherent in saving my wayward soul I'm sure they recognized. Thus, the good deed of providing food and shelter would have to suffice. From Huehuetenango I boarded my last chicken bus and headed for the Mexican border. I had heard the busses in Mexico were comfortable coaches with reclining seats and plenty of legroom. I looked forward to it.

I stood at the border crossing. I was deep in Mexico. I couldn't get any deeper. Most people begin their journey in the north and work their way south into the heart of Mexico, but having come up from Guatemala, I was already there.

I put my passport away, threw my pack on my back and commenced to walking the dusty streets of a Mexican border town bearing a close resemblance to the set of a Western movie.

## Chapter Seven

I didn't have to look far for a cheap and shabby hotel; the town had no other kind. In the morning I boarded a bus for the Mexican city of Merida, capital of Yucatan State, my jumping off point into the Yucatan Peninsula.

From Merida I traveled first to the lost Mayan city of Chichen Itza. Images of sun baked bronze skinned scantily clad ancient Mayans appeared in my mind as I stood in the shadow of Chichen Itza's legendary stone built temple pyramid. I imagined hordes of Mayan warriors standing in the same spot where I now stood, millenniums ago, under the same sweltering Yucatan sun. And I visualized them triumphantly waving their spears in the air as Mayan priests sent bodies tumbling down the pyramid's countless stone steps in bloody rituals of sacrifice to their ancient Mayan Gods.

From Chichen Itza I headed for Tulum, at the time an undeveloped location of sand dunes and wild brush on Mexico's magnificent Caribbean Coast in the state of Quintana Roo on the eastern side of the Yucatan Peninsula. I stepped off the bus and with no idea what I might find there, I threw my pack on my back and proceeded to make my way along a desolate sand strewn road. A group of fellow backpackers soon came into view, camped out high on a ridge overlooking the sea with the famous Mayan ruins of Tulum, once a major Mayan seaport, dotting the beaches below.

Several travelers had their hammocks strung up between two trees and I began looking for a place to hang mine. Before leaving the city of Merida I had purchased a green and white double size hammock, otherwise known as the matrimonial size, recommended as the roomiest fit for the average North American male.

Under a star filled Mexican sky I slept soundly through the night in my new hammock. I felt as if I were floating on a cloud. One would have to search far and wide to find the comfort and quality of a hammock equal to those made in Mexico, where the art of hammock making is beyond compare.

The morning skies greeted us with a spectacular Caribbean sunrise and we were soon off to a landing dock from where a small seagoing vessel would transport us to Isla Mujeres, eight miles off the Yucatan Coast.

Isla Mujeres, translated into English as Island of Women, acquired its name from Spanish explorers who discovered the tiny deserted island filled with statues of women once used in ancient Mayan fertility rituals and ceremonies. I followed the crowd, happy to have met some fellow travelers who seemed to know where they were going, because I didn't have a clue.

A kaleidoscope of majestic Caribbean hue glistened upon the water. We cruised into the harbor of the tiny Caribbean island, approximately half a mile wide and not quite five miles long, and headed for the hammock campground, where a rainbow of colorful hammocks, with a backpack sitting next to each one of them, floated above the white sands under a hot Mexican sun.

Low budget travelers filled the ocean front campground, accommodating dozens of hammocks. Each campsite had two poles planted in the ground about six feet apart to hang a hammock, as if between two trees.

I was in hammock heaven. With the ocean at my fingertips I slept under the stars. I woke up each morning to a Caribbean sunrise and spent my days wandering the island's lazy Caribbean village when I wasn't on the beach, in the ocean, or seeking shade under a palm tree during the hottest part of the day. I had landed completely unplanned in a tropical island paradise.

So beautiful and so cheap was Isla Mujeres, a genuine Caribbean island vacation putting scarcely a dent in my wallet. But the time to move on had once again arrived. I

## Chapter Seven

returned to the Mexican mainland and traveled across the Yucatan Peninsula a second time, to the scenic Southern Mexican state of Chiapas, where I again hung my hammock, this time in a jungle campground on the edges of the ancient Mayan city of Palenque.

An ear piercing symphony of crazy, high pitched, roaring, shrieking, screaming, whooping sounds cut through the pitch-black night as I lie in my hammock in the jungles of Southern Mexico and I was scared to death. I had no idea what the lunatic noise could be and I couldn't do anything about it because I had nowhere to go. The outrageous racket became louder and more terrifying as the night wore on. My imagination ran wild. Images of ferocious, gruesome animals, both real and mythical flooded my mind, out there in the hills and forests waiting to attack and have me for dinner. I don't know how I fell asleep, but I thanked all the Gods of every religion when I found myself alive and not chewed to pieces in the morning.

Native to the region, the jungles surrounding Palenque are heavily populated with harmless howler monkeys, a species of monkey ranked among the loudest animals on Earth. The howler monkeys' ridiculous high decibel vocal cords had been the source of my worry. They were talking to each other, sending a non-stop chatter of messages across the jungle and frightening me out of my wits in the process.

The Doors of Perception, the title of a novel by Aldous Huxley, had been carved into the wooden gates leading to the cow pastures where the magic mushrooms, filled with the hallucinogenic agent known as psilocybin, sprouted up each night through piles of cow dung across the road from the hammock campground.

"They'll make mushroom omelets for you in the campground's cantina if you like," a fellow mushroom hunter said.

Into the sprawling cow pastures we stepped, roughly a dozen of us at the crack of dawn, searching for the mushroom sprouting piles of cow poop. Two Mexican cowboys rode by on horseback. Slow and meticulous my eyes scanned the Earth when three large plump mushrooms appeared in my view, standing tall in a fresh pile of cow dung. I leaned over, plucked them out of the manure, continued in my pursuit and soon came upon another fertile pile of cow droppings with a little family of magic mushrooms poking through.

The unpicked mushrooms would soon disappear in the rays of the rising sun. No more than a fleeting window of time existed between the morning dew's moisture that gave the mushrooms their short life and the sunshine that took it away.

"That'll do ya just fine," a fellow mushroom picker said when he saw my harvest.

He seemed knowledgeable on the subject, so I took him at his word and proceeded back to the hammock campground.

Several people gave their mushrooms to the cook at the cantina for him to roll into omelets for breakfast. I decided to eat mine raw.

Considering where they'd been, I rinsed them off extra good before I took a bite. Surprised by the mushrooms' pleasant taste, I finished off all five and headed down the narrow jungle road leading to the ancient Mayan city of Palenque, a short walk from the hammock campground.

Abandoned for centuries, the Spanish discovered the lost city in the 1500s, hidden away, swallowed up by the jungle's unbridled advance.

I entered the grounds of the mystical metropolis, occupying a vast sprawling area encircled by lush tropical rainforest landscapes. With my psilocybin saturated brain now reaching the fully fueled and prepare for take-off

## Chapter Seven

level, I slowly strolled among the lost Mayan City's ancient stone plazas, palaces, and citadels. I stood in the grandeur of Palenque's majestic stone temple pyramid and I gazed upon the many enigmatic stone carvings, sculptures, and statues. Constructed entirely of stone, an aura of otherworldliness permeates Palenque, once a major city-state in the great Mayan empire stretching from Mexico well into Central America. The haunting presence of a powerful, thriving, spiritual, and inspired ancient civilization, vanishing at the pinnacle of its existence, still resonates in every corner, twist and turn of the abandoned city of stone.

I spent the day exploring the world of the ancient Maya and wandering through beautiful rain forest along a gently rambling shallow river where more relics and remnants of the lost city lie. I also ran into most of the travelers I had gone out to the cow pastures with in the morning and all agreed that tripping around the ancient lost Mayan city on freshly picked psilocybin mushrooms was indeed a far out thing to do.

Once again, the howler monkeys bellowed, shrieked, shouted, and screamed. But on this night, my second night in Palenque, I slept without worry, grateful and relieved beyond measure to know what in the hell was going on out there in the jungle between the hours of darkness and morning's first light.

From Palenque I traveled to Aqua Azul, a spectacular series of turquoise tinted cascading waterfalls approximately seventy-five miles from the lost Mayan city. Deemed among the world's most beautiful natural wonders, the resplendent waterfalls flow for miles through dense tropical rainforest in the Sierra Madre de Chiapas Mountains of Southern Mexico, tumbling along their path into sparkling pools of magical blue-green waters where, with caution, one can hop in and cool off amidst the verdant splendor of a thick jungle landscape.

Busses filled with nature lovers arrived and departed several times daily. Most returned to their hotels in the nearby town. The more adventurous camped out for a few days before taking the bus back to civilization. I choose the latter and proceeded to join a small group of backpackers whose colorful hammocks were already hanging in the steamy jungle along the dazzling edges of the gemstone hued cascades when I arrived.

I thought my hammock days had come to an end when I left **Aqua Azul**, until I discovered one can hang a hammock anywhere in Mexico, not only in the great outdoors. In the city of Oaxaca, in the state of the same name, I strung my hammock up on the second floor veranda of an old Spanish hotel overlooking the bustling streets of a crowded and colorful Mexican market town in the depths of the Mexican heartland.

Under open Mexican skies, guitar strumming solo street musicians and costumed quartets singing in harmony sang tender tales of romance, passionate tales of heartbreak, and songs of old Mexico on the spirited streets of Oaxaca and in the festive town square. A love song sung in Spanish, no language does it better. And in Oaxaca's sprawling markets, a vast assortment of foods, delicacies, and desserts share the crowded aisles with the magnificent, internationally acclaimed weaving and handicrafts of the indigenous people of the state of Oaxaca, descendants of the Zapotec and Mixtec Indians, comprising half of the state's population and speaking an estimated sixteen indigenous languages.

By day I wandered the teeming streets and indigenous markets of Oaxaca, pure, timeless Mexico. And in the air of a warm Mexican night I floated, out on the veranda, deep in the perfect slumber only a Mexican hammock can bring.

From Oaxaca I continued north, making no more stops until I reached Mexico City.

*Chapter Seven*

The oddest display of animosity greeted me upon my arrival in Mexico City. A Mexican man threw a pack of matches at me and called me a Gringo as I walked down the street with my backpack on my back looking for a cheap hotel. It would be the one and only act of Gringo hostility I would experience throughout my stay in Latin America.

Ana and I met at noon the following day on her college campus. She seemed pleased to see me, but offered no physical affection, unlike the last time I saw her in Guatemala. We hopped into her car, but instead of taking me to her house, she took me to an elementary school and told me I could sleep on the gymnasium floor. She said she knew the principle and when she informed him of the eventuality of my visit, he had given his okay.

"I'll come back at six o'clock and we'll go out to dinner with my friends," she said.

I surveyed my latest living quarters. There are times in one's life when one is forced to take a hard look at oneself and demand of oneself an explanation to the question: How in the hell did I ever get to as bizarre a place in my life as the one I'm in at this moment? I believe sleeping on the gymnasium floor of an elementary school in Mexico City would qualify as one of those times.

Ana came for me at six, as promised, and brought with her a key to the school's gymnasium for me to use. We walked outside to a waiting car. I climbed in the backseat with Isabella and another girl. Ana sat in the front, cozying up to the driver. "This is Roberto, my fiancé," she said.

And with those words sleeping on the gymnasium floor of a grade school in Mexico City made sense, or made no sense, or made some sense, or made all the sense it was ever going to make. I'm not sure which one it was.

We hadn't driven but a short distance from the elementary school when Roberto pulled over, parked the car and the five of us entered a spacious, festive, beer garden style restaurant filled with large round wooden tables. We took our seats and dined on Mexican cuisine and pitchers of Mexican beer, the latter consumed by all in our group except me. As the evening drew to a close and as if things weren't strange enough already, Roberto asked if I wouldn't mind walking from the restaurant back to the elementary school. I put forth no objection, even though I found it rude of him to make such a request, and the thought of walking the streets of Mexico City alone after dark had me worried.

How could a sophisticated fellow, a law student no less, be so thoughtless and impolite? And I couldn't help but wonder if he had chosen to put me at risk because he suspected his girlfriend had fooled around with me in Guatemala.

A few blocks into my trek back to the elementary school a guy stuck his head out of his car window at a busy intersection while waiting for the light to change and in perfect American English asked me if I needed a lift. I hopped in. The night was about to become a whole lot stranger.

Joseph was bi-lingual. He had grown up in the states with his Mexican mother and American father. He now lived in Mexico City where he operated his own import-export business.

"I can always spot an American," he said.

I told him about Ana and her fiancé who didn't want to drive me back to the elementary school.

"Why don't you stay at my place?" he offered. "I live close by."

I accepted his invitation, even though leaving my backpack for so long a time in a place I wasn't sure of worried me.

## Chapter Seven

"The sofa converts into a bed, you can sleep there," Joseph said as we entered the small, modestly furnished one-bedroom apartment.

We talked into the wee hours before wrapping it up and saying goodnight. I crawled under the covers of the sofa bed and Joseph went to his room, at least I thought he had, until I found him sitting on the edge of the sofa bed with his hand resting on my leg.

I shot to my feet, put on my shoes and made a dash for the door.

"I'm sorry, I made a mistake. Stay here and sleep. I'm so sorry. Nothing more will happen, I promise," Joseph pleaded.

On inexplicable impulse I bolted out the door anyway, but second thoughts came quickly as I found myself walking the streets of Mexico City in the middle of the night, becoming more fearful as each ghostly moment passed.

Two alerts, clear as a bell. How could I have missed them? First, he offered me a ride when I wasn't even looking for one, and second alert, he invited me to spend the night. Had he been up front concerning his preference, I would have had the chance to make sure he knew mine, but he startled me and I freaked out.

He said he thought I had given him a signal. I believe he misinterpreted my customary level of friendliness and openness as an indication of interest and attraction instead, and I, in my naïveté, didn't pick up on it, as I should have, because looking back, it was all too obvious.

I began having feelings of both guilt and stupidity over my hasty exit. Guilt because Joseph was a good guy and I'm sure everything would've worked out fine once he realized the huge error in judgment he had made, and stupidity because of the grave danger I had now brought upon myself with my ridiculous overreaction.

Concerned about my safety, I could still hear the heart-wrenching panic in Joseph's worried voice begging me to stay. Distressed at the thought of me going out into the danger lurking in the Mexico City night, he repeated over and over again: "I'm sorry, I made a mistake," assuring me nothing more would happen. And I will never, until the end of my days, understand why I freaked out and ran as I did.

I cut through the darkness. As if in some bizarre dream I found myself walking through a pitch black alien world. The paranoia became unbearable. Shadows lurked around every corner. The slightest sound made my heart pound so hard I thought it would jump right out of my chest. The word relief took on an entirely new meaning as I marched through the elementary school door and climbed inside of my sleeping bag on the gymnasium floor, putting an end to what had been one of the most screwed up days my memory could recall ever having had.

Ana came for me at noon. "I've arranged for you to stay with Isabella's family for a few days," she said.

I wanted to ask her why Roberto didn't drive me back, and why didn't she intervene and tell him his actions were wrong, but I held my tongue. I also didn't tell her about the rest of my evening. It was way too strange to talk about.

Ana drove me to a lovely home in an affluent area of Mexico City where Isabella lived with her parents and two younger sisters.

Your average Mexicans Ana and Isabella were not, an easy observation I made when I first met them in Guatemala, but little did I know the full extent of the story. I had fallen in with Mexico's elite upper class. In Isabella's house servants did all of the housekeeping and food preparation. The meals were superb, the house was immaculate, and the family couldn't have been kinder.

Sure is strange the way things work out sometimes. In the end, its Isabella's family I stay with during my visit to Mexico City, and its Isabella who goes out of her way to make me feel welcome and at home.

## Chapter Seven

A lesson learned. The girl with the problematic complexion, she's the one I should have turned my attention to instead of falling under the spell of the femme fatal who looked like a young Sophia Loren.

Thanks to Isabella's family taking me in, my stay in Mexico City, although far from meeting my wild anticipation, would end up working out pretty good just the same, in spite of the school gymnasium, the peculiar experience with Joseph, and the situation with Ana, who could have at least told me what to expect when she invited me to visit. A complete waste of mental energy my fantasies of Ana had been, as fantasies no doubt almost always are. But who can control these thoughts? Not me, that's for sure!

From Mexico City I boarded a train heading due north, making no more stops until I reached the American border.

Unwavering in their determination to have me drink Tequila with them, the four young Mexican drunks wouldn't take no for an answer. The situation turned from annoying to intimidating to downright menacing as the four Mexicans gathered close, becoming wild, laughing, and forcing the bottle into my hand. Having no other choice, I took a sip, hoping it would satisfy them, but it didn't.

I was in deep trouble. They had no intention of letting up on me and I soon reached my limit. I have been a devout non-drinker since my teenage years, from the time I discovered how little alcohol it takes to make me throw up.

I had no idea what these crazies might do when I tell them no more, but I had no alternative; otherwise, I'd find myself sick and throwing up on a train rolling through Mexico. In the midst of this impending calamity, a major stroke of luck came my way. Before the bottle reached my hand one more time, the train pulled into a small rural station and the four fools headed for the exit, laughing and hollering adios gringo as they hopped out to the platform.

Darkness fell and as I had hoped, the hard wooden bench I had been sharing with a revolving parade of Mexicans in the third class compartment had emptied out. Using my backpack as my pillow, I stretched out and fell asleep to the rhythm of an old Mexican locomotive, chugging through the night across Northern Mexico, reaching the border town of Nuevo Laredo the following afternoon.

Should I spend the night in a cheap border town hotel and get a fresh start in the morning? With a few hours of daylight remaining I decided against it and headed straight to the checkpoint instead, passing a line of cars with trunks wide open as the border guards made their searches.

My backpack and my pockets were searched, my passport returned to me and I was free to go. No long plane ride, no great ocean to cross. One simple solitary step across an imaginary line is all it took and I found myself standing in the great state of Texas, the one state I swore I would never hitchhike in again.

## Chapter Eight
# NORTH OF THE BORDER

Had it been possible, I would have taken a chicken bus all the way from Mexico to Maryland, to such an extent did I not feel like hitchhiking. But with two thousand miles yet to go and my money close to running out, what other choice did I have?

From the Mexican border I headed for Houston, a distance of approximately three hundred miles. A car pulled over and in I hopped. The driver, a fellow in his early twenties, looked like a Mexican, talked like a Texan, and drove like a maniac at speeds near one hundred miles per hour. Terrified, I could do nothing more than stare at the speedometer, pray, and wonder what the hell was I doing back in Texas?

"Wait here for a moment," Ramon said, bringing the vehicle to a stop in the driveway of a rundown aging farmhouse in a rural border town community. "I'll go inside and ask if you can stay the night."

I was still in shock from the terror of traveling at killer speeds on the back roads of Texas when Ramon returned to the car and told me his family said no.

"I'll just sleep on the floor and be gone in the morning," I said.

"Sorry," Ramon replied. "I tried to tell them, but they wouldn't listen."

Determined to be of assistance in bringing resolution to my dilemma, Ramon drove me to a forested area not far from the house where he said I could safely sleep in the woods.

In route we came upon a small country store. I asked Ramon if he wouldn't mind stopping so I could buy a jar of peanut butter and a loaf of bread. I'd have starved had that little mom and pop store not been there. I wasn't carrying so much as a crumb in my backpack.

We arrived at the forested location. I stepped out of the car and walked a short stretch along a trail through thick woodlands, following Ramon's instructions, until I came upon a tiny meadow hidden away by tall trees and dense foliage.

I strung my hammock up between two trees, slept under the stars, and opened my eyes to the alarming sight of five teenage boys standing over my hammock staring at me when I awoke in the morning.

I crawled out of my sleeping bag, climbed down from my hammock and nervously studied my uninvited quests as I rolled up my gear and packed it away. They look like nice guys, I reassured myself, trying to ease my anxious mind.

They asked what I was doing.

I told them I was hitchhiking home to Maryland after traveling around in Latin America for six months.

I wondered why they had come to this secluded spot so early in the morning, but I didn't pursue my curiosity.

## Chapter Eight

I didn't want to prolong the conversation. Their presence had unnerved me. I wanted nothing more than for them to go.

They asked a few more questions before making their exit. Worried someone else might show up, frightfully aware I might not be so lucky next time, and with paranoid thoughts such as hitchhiker from Baltimore found beaten to death in a small patch of woods in Texas rolling through my brain, I got the hell out of there and headed for the highway as fast as I could.

I made it to Houston nearing day's end. One solitary thought ran through my mind: I need a safe place to sleep. Didn't matter if it meant spending what little money I had left. One more weird experience in the great state of Texas was more than I could tolerate.

I spent the night in a rinky-dink roadside motel, hit the road at daybreak and arrived in the Big Easy in the late afternoon after another full day of hitchhiking through Texas and Louisiana. A thirty minute standing room only bus ride on a local New Orleans transit bus carried me the final distance into the French Quarter.

"Need a place to stay?" a friendly voice inquired as I walked along bustling Bourbon Street with my backpack on my back.

"Sure do," I replied. I thought they were a couple, but I would soon find out different.

I followed Gary and Darlene into a beautiful modern townhome empty of any form of furnishing. Darlene, a cute young Southern girl from the nearby state of Alabama, led me up a flight of steps to a second floor bedroom where I was immediately seduced on top of several blankets spread out upon the polished hardwood floor.

Wow! I couldn't believe it. Out of nowhere my fantasy of having an intimate encounter with a beautiful stranger in the intriguing city of New Orleans became reality.

What more could I ask for? And now, with a place to sleep secured and twilight drawing near, I proceeded to spend the remainder of the day wandering the streets of the famous French Quarter until slumber's call could no longer be ignored. It had been a long and eventful day since pulling out of Houston in the morning.

I hit the road the following day. I thought it best not to spend more than one night in the townhome. Who owned the place remained a mystery, as did the legality of its inhabitants.

Heading in a Northeastern direction, I arrived in Greensboro, North Carolina round about midnight.

How should I proceed at such an inconvenient hour? After considerable contemplation, a most clever thought popped into my mind. How far could I ride a bus heading north and get my sleep along the way for the same amount of money I would spend on a cheap motel?

"Richmond, Virginia, leaving in two hours," the ticket agent said.

I thought about catching another bus from Richmond to Baltimore, a distance of two hundred miles, so tired of hitchhiking had I become, but I decided instead to hang on to my few remaining dollars until I reached Washington, DC.

Hitchhiking across America and back, hitchhiking throughout Europe and Israel, the hitchhiking journey I found myself on at the moment, and the innumerable short excursions, such as the countless times I hitchhiked from Baltimore to the Maryland Shore and back, equaled, I figured, as a pretty good estimate, at least fifteen thousand miles of hitchhiking on three continents in three years.

I boarded the bus out of the nation's capital for the final forty miles of the journey. My hitchhiking days had come to an end. I was burned out!

*Chapter Nine*

# THE BELMONT HOTEL

Tired of sharing living space with the number of roommates needed to afford rent at the beach for the summer, I decided this season to rent a private room instead, but I didn't know where to look until a friend told me to talk to Kate, owner of the Belmont Hotel in downtown Ocean City, the cheesy part of town, where the boardwalk turns into a carnival.

Ocean City, Maryland is a narrow peninsula, ten miles long, with a bay on one side and the Atlantic Ocean on the other. At its narrowest the beach town is only a few blocks wide and at any given point, from oceanside to bayside, one can easily navigate the width of the town on foot. The streets in Ocean City are numbered, all the way to the Delaware line, except the few streets below First Street going south to the inlet, where the ocean meets the bay. The streets in this short stretch of the boardwalk have names instead of numbers, names from Maryland's colonial past.

Seagulls descended upon the beaches of a summer season in early bloom. It was a beautiful morning in the final days of May. I hit the boardwalk and pedaled south, toward the inlet, on my banana seat bike with the high handlebars the owners of the Surf and Sands had kindly allowed me to safely store in their motel through the winter.

The joyful squeals of children filled the air as the carousel, the Ferris wheel, and the bumper cars drew near. I pedaled past the pinball arcade, the lemonade stand, the pizza parlor, and the caramel popcorn stand, made a right turn by the salt water taffy display in the window of the candy shop and came to a stop in front of a three-story yellow shingled hotel resembling an oversized old country house sitting half a block off the boardwalk on Dorchester Street. I locked up my bike and walked up a short flight of steps. Guests of the hotel were relaxing in white wicker rocking chairs on a quaint country porch beneath a wide green awning. I entered the Victorian lobby of the Belmont Hotel, one of Ocean City's few remaining historic hotels, and asked if I could speak to Kate.

Established by Kate's great grandparents, the Belmont Hotel dates back to the early 1900s. I met Kate, a hard working serious minded businesswoman in her late thirties. Kate agreed to rent me a room, but rather than offer me a room in her cheap rooming house, which would have more than met my needs, she offered me a room in the Belmont Hotel instead.

Kate led me up the stairs to a small room on the second floor. A single bed, a dresser, and a sink filled the diminutive space, leaving little area to spare. Toilets and showers were down the hall in the common bathroom, one on each floor. The room had one window from where a narrow slice of the boardwalk and the ocean could be seen.

"Thirty dollars a week," Kate offered.

*Chapter Nine*

"I'll take it," I said, and I would become the one and only person to ever spend the entire season living as a permanent resident in Ocean City's historic Belmont Hotel.

Every summer Kate's rooms filled up with loyal quests returning year after year, decade after decade, to spend their vacation in the old hotel on Dorchester Street.

A room and traditional hearty home cooked meals like your grandma made, an all-inclusive vacation known as the American plan. The Belmont was the last of the historic hotels in the beach resort to offer this vanishing tradition, enjoyed in the cozy atmosphere of the Belmont's original early 1900s dining room.

In the Belmont Hotel, Kate's guests didn't feel as if they were guests at all, but rather as if they were members of Kate's own family. And in the Belmont Hotel Kate's guests felt not as if they were away from home, but rather as if they had come home instead. And at any given time, day, evening, or night, socializing in Kate's old time Victorian lobby, a cast of colorful characters could be found, young and old, guests, friends, and old Ocean City salty dogs, and I became one of them that summer.

I had been staying with a co-worker on Forty-Fifth Street. I couldn't ride my bicycle from Forty-Fifth Street back to Dorchester Street with my backpack on my back and a suitcase in my hand, holding the belongings I had brought for the summer, so I walked instead, over forty-five blocks, collected my possessions, turned right around, walked all the way back to Dorchester Street and moved into my room in the Belmont Hotel. Granted, the beach town's blocks are short, but it was still quite a hike.

A rousing reception greeted me the following afternoon as I left for the job on my first day back waiting tables at the Embers Restaurant, bestowed upon me by a half plastered bunch of characters hanging out in the Belmont's lobby. Watching a guy dressed in full black tuxedo with a white shirt, frills, and a black bow tie come strolling through, walk outside, hop aboard a banana seat bike with high handlebars parked out front and go pedaling up Ocean Highway left them flabbergasted.

The new season took off, and the Belmont, a hop, skip, and a jump from the sandy beach and the bustling boardwalk, buzzed with activity. Many of Kate's guests had been coming to the old hotel for generations, their children and grandchildren carrying the tradition on. Some had even logged as many as fifty summer vacations in the Belmont, and counting, back to when Kate's great grandparents ran the inn. History lived in the Belmont Hotel.

Solitude, tranquility, and not having to negotiate with roommates for private time when in the company of a female companion were a few of the benefits of having my own private room in the Belmont Hotel. And having the resort town's two and a half mile long boardwalk at my doorstep was another.

Every day I would join the endless ocean front carnival parade. A mass of humanity of all ages, shapes, colors, and sizes taking a break from life's monotonous routine, losing themselves for a day or two, or a week or two in the fantasy, desire, adolescent promise, and dreams unfulfilled veiled in the boardwalk's glitter and glitz.

And after my daily ritual of walking the length of the boardwalk, from one end to the other and back again, I would go for a swim and lie on the beach until it came time to return to my room, don the tuxedo, hop aboard my banana seat bike and pedal up ocean highway to the restaurant where I would once again serve drinks, dinner, and dessert to the same hungry strangers in hopes of earning enough money to go wandering off to exotic faraway places by receiving fair and reasonable gratuity in return for my efforts.

High rise condominiums and brand name hotels would one day line the coastal highway all the way north to the

*Chapter Nine*

Delaware line where once only sand dunes lie. Twenty-nine years later, on the old hotel's one hundredth anniversary, an iconic local landmark would fall victim to the inevitable, unrelenting passage of time as the beach town's historic Belmont Hotel closed its doors for the last time. The family owned property would be leveled, three historic blocks, dating back five generations, and a grand state of the art ocean front condominium complex would tower above the boardwalk in its place.

## Chapter Ten
# A WASTED WINTER

On my journey to Europe and Israel I traveled on money earned at the restaurant alone, but I had also been able to live expense free on the kibbutz. For each subsequent trip thereafter, I would find it necessary to work the second job at the motel as I had done for my journey to Latin America. The summer I lived in the Belmont Hotel I decided not to work the second job and to keep my autumn days free instead so I could take maximum pleasure in the months of September and October, my favorite time of year on Maryland's Eastern Shore, when the once crowded summer resort turns into a small seaside village and one can pedal one's bicycle on the boardwalk any time one pleased.

My decision put me in a precarious position. I planned India as my next journey, but when mid-October rolled around and the restaurant closed its doors, I found myself short of the money I would need. India would have to wait until next year. The task of figuring out what to do with myself until the summer season began anew stood in front of me now.

A long, cold, wasted winter lie ahead, frittering away my days in Baltimore, doing nothing but biding my time, waiting for spring to arrive.

●

The month of April finally came around, and in the nick of time. I was broke. Nothing new, of course. I always landed back at the beach destitute. Thank goodness for tips. Instant cash in the pocket. One doesn't need to wait for a paycheck. And this year I didn't have to worry about a place to stay as I had in the past. I knew Kate would have a room for me, even if I couldn't begin paying her right away.

I couldn't wait to get back to work. I would begin the season at the restaurant on opening day, mid-April, giving myself a good head start, and the final two months I would work both jobs, the restaurant and the motel, as I had done two years earlier.

Kate wouldn't let me stay in the Belmont Hotel this year. She gave me a room in her cheap rooming house instead. The Mt. Vernon was a large three-story white shingled structure in a wide ranging yet somehow still functional state of disrepair on the next block over from the Belmont. The Mt. Vernon first opened its doors to guests in 1891, when the ocean front wooden promenade had yet to come off the drawing board and sand dunes covered the Maryland Shore.

No doubt a grand and stately structure in its time, patronized by a refined and stylish clientele, the Mt. Vernon had long since deteriorated into an eight room flophouse, its list of lodgers also having deteriorated into a group of seedy characters, alcoholics, and directionless drifters.

## Chapter Ten

Kate gave me one of only two rooms in the dilapidated dwelling on Talbot Street containing a complete bathroom. Everyone else used the common bathrooms, one on each floor. The price remained the same, thirty dollars per week, and from my window, a narrow view of the boardwalk and the Ocean could be seen.

I needed to keep my expenses at a bare minimum. I had some serious saving to do. I put my system in place. I would not spend one cent on anything but the bare essentials. I invested in a toaster and an electric hot plate. I also acquired several cooking pots and an ice cooler which I refilled with a ten pound bag of ice every couple of days, creating a complete kitchen in my room, enabling me to sustain myself by the cheapest means possible. I would live on peanut butter and jelly toast, and basic dinners of beans, rice, and steamed broccoli, cooked on my little hot plate in my little room by the sea.

The incomparable sweet and delicious Maryland Eastern Shore cantaloupe, boardwalk pizza, delicious lemonade from Love's lemonade stand on the boardwalk, and the best ice cream on the boardwalk, Dumser Dairy's homemade ice cream would also with great prudence be rationed into the budget. One must still be good to oneself, even in the most stringent of times.

I could also sneak baked potatoes out of the kitchen at the restaurant and load them up with butter and sour cream. And the delicious mini loaves of hot bread placed upon each table in small baskets, another easy to sneak out of the kitchen freebie. Pile on the butter and they would simply melt in your mouth. One could make a meal out of those delicacies alone.

Spending the most minuscule amount of money possible was of critical importance in achieving my goal. Through the entire summer season into mid-October I would enforce upon myself a bare bones budget demanding a boatload of discipline and self-control. Under no circumstances could I or would I allow myself to stray. Difficult, painful at times, but I needed, more than anything, to get back on the road.

Mid-October rolled around. The Embers Restaurant and the Surf and Sands ocean front motel closed their doors until next year. I had spent the summer living as frugally as a human being possibly could, I am not ashamed to say, and my goal had been achieved. I was on my way to India, at last.

## Chapter Eleven
# INDIA AND BEYOND

I planned to catch the Icelandic Airways flight to Luxembourg. From Luxembourg I would begin my trek across Europe to Istanbul, the first leg of the overland journey to India. But when I returned home from the beach I received bad news. My mother had taken ill and would need hospitalization. Naturally, I couldn't leave under these conditions, and not until early December did I feel as if I could. The postponement forced me into making a difficult decision. Should I brave the Afghan winter, or should I fly directly to New Delhi instead? I choose the latter. The overland journey to India was put on hold once again.

Clad in beautiful Indian saris, lovely Indian stewardesses welcomed me as I stepped aboard the Air India flight from New York to New Delhi. Flying east into the sunrise on a frosty December night, the jumbo jet sailed over the Atlantic, touching down for its first stop in London's Heathrow Airport. From Frankfurt, Germany, our next stop, the mammoth aircraft coasted high above the snow covered peaks of the Swiss Alps, a magnificent sight to see from the air. The lengthy flight touched down one more time in the small Arab Emirate of Kuwait for refueling, spent a second long night in the air and arrived in New Delhi as dawn was beginning to break. I had purchased the excursion fare, a round trip ticket with a four month expiration date, the only air fare to India I could afford. Both the change in plans and the four month time limit were disappointing, but I knew I had made the right decision.

I passed through security and hopped on a shuttle bus waiting curbside as I walked out of the airport. The bus driver must have had a deal to earn a commission from the New Delhi YMCA because as soon as I boarded he asked me if I wanted to go there, and I, having no idea whatsoever about anything, said yes.

A rambling one-story structure housed the New Delhi YMCA. Known for a host of amenities, this YMCA had none, unless one considers cleanliness an amenity. Not a far-fetched assumption, I would soon realize, as my tour of India's cut-rate hotels began, an eye-opening adventure in its own right. A thick bearded purple turbaned Sikh held the door open for me as I walked inside. My room consisted of nothing more than a well-worn mattress on a shabby wooden frame and one tiny tattered wooden table. A ceiling fan whirled above my head.

The twelve hour time difference had turned my circadian rhythms upside down and I had only managed to sleep a few hours on the plane. I was in desperate need of slumber, but I headed out anyway, jet lag and sleep deprivation be damned, so eager was I to see where my crazy wanderlust had taken me this time around. Besides, how can one sleep when one has just arrived in India?

A legion of motor scooters, three wheel taxis, bicycles, and bicycle rickshaws zipped in and out of heavy traffic,

## Chapter Eleven

narrowly missing the busses, automobiles, and beasts of burden lumbering through the crowded streets, hauling heavy loads under the hot Asian sun. A cacophony of beeping horns filled the air. And nowhere had I seen so many vehicles with either holes in their exhaust systems or no exhaust systems at all.

Stunning in their artistry and multihued brilliance, mystical pictures depicting the Hindu Gods and Goddesses and the heavenly abodes in which they dwell covered the walls of endless ramshackle shops, restaurants, and chai stalls lining the streets of New Delhi.

I chose one open air restaurant in the crowded bazaar and stepped inside. Sweating, shouting cooks stood in cramped quarters over steaming pots of food. The choices seemed infinite and hardly any item on the menu did I recognize. I randomly selected several curried vegetable dishes along with a bowl of rice and a couple of chapattis. A bit of time it would take, but highly proficient would my knowledge of the vast world of Indian cuisine in due course become. And in India I would have no trouble fitting into my budget three full course meals a day, including deserts, snacks, and endless cups of chai.

My eyes began to water, my nose began to run, and my mouth felt as if it were on fire. A grandfatherly fellow with an amused look upon his face, speaking the Queens's English in the perfect manner of an upper caste educated Indian gentleman took a seat at my table.

"I see you are not accustomed to our spicy food," he said.

He gave out a holler in Hindi and a tall glass with a white drink soon appeared before me.

"This drink is called a lassi. It is made of yogurt. It will stop the burning," he said.

And he was right, to a point. It didn't altogether put out the fire, but I would say it toned it down a fair amount. And

I learned another valuable lesson on my first day in India. Bananas will do the same.

My friend began bombarding me with questions, about myself and about America. I tried my best to satisfy his curiosity. But when asked why I had come to India, I could only answer: "Sir, I don't have a clue."

On my second day in India I checked out of the YMCA and moved into a cheap hotel in the middle of the street bazaar for one third of the price. Both offered more or less the same. Granted, the YMCA met much higher standards of cleanliness, but as I had already learned in Istanbul, as long as I could save money, the filth, stench, decrepitude, and decay of a cheap hotel in Asia didn't bother me one bit.

A boy about eight or nine years of age carrying a tray filled with hot cups of chai in reddish-brown sun hardened disposable clay cups came to my door. "Chai garam," (hot tea) he said in Hindi. I bought a cup for what amounted to three or four cents in American money. He also asked if I wished to have my laundry done. Not sure about giving him my clothes, I declined his offer. I would in time learn I had nothing to worry about. One might question where and how they do the washing, but the laundry always comes back clean and folded. I sat on the edge of the bed with my cup of chai, fascinated by the sun hardened disposable clay cup I held in my hand.

As in much of the Eastern world, the toilets in India are squatters with footrests on each side to place ones feet upon while squatting over the bowl. A faucet sits to the left of the squatter for the purpose of washing one's butt after a bowel movement. A container to splash water upon one's butt is required. I bought a little brass bowl in the street bazaar which I kept in my side bag, along with a bar of soap. Both items reserved solely for this purpose. Toilet paper is expensive in India and not always easy to find, so I decided to take care of nature's business the Eastern

## Chapter Eleven

way. It also makes for a much more complete Indian experience.

There is no flushing mechanism. Flushing occurs by pouring water down the squatter instead. Toilet paper will clog the system if flushed down the squatter, so for the Western travelers who prefer to continue taking care of business the Western way, a small waste container for the purpose of collecting the used toilet paper is provided. As a curious by-product of the latter, employment is created, as it becomes some poor wretched soul's job to take the used toilet paper away, bringing into existence yet another one of those odd occupations found only in the Eastern world.

I needed to make a currency exchange. I carried my money in the form of insured American Express travelers checks, as all travelers did in the days before bank cards and ATM machines. I carried mine in amounts of ten and twenty dollar checks.

Every major city in the world had an American Express Office. One could also cash travelers checks at most banks. On this day I decided to cash mine at the New Delhi American Express Office in Connaught Place. A young Indian fellow clad in baggy white pajama pants and a long white kurta approached me on the street. He asked where I was going.

"Connaught Place," I told him.

"I will be your guide," he said.

"I'm fine. I can find my own way. I don't need a guide," I replied.

He spoke poor and broken English in an awful grating voice and he walked alongside of me all the way to my destination talking non-stop. I was sick of him by the time we arrived.

"Good Sir, would you kindly pay me five rupees for showing you the way."

"That's ridiculous," I said, staring at him in disbelief.

I took care of my currency exchange, and when I walked back out of the American Express Office, he had disappeared.

I wondered how many tourists he manages to sucker in a day. If he pestered enough foreigners between sunup and sundown, as outlandish as it may sound, it's possible he could in fact accumulate enough rupees to survive. Wow! I marveled. In India a guy can earn a living pestering people. What an incredible country!

I began to notice the number of Western travelers clad in native garb. There's the answer, I no sooner realized; otherwise, these pestering guys will never leave me alone. I had new tourist written all over me in my tee-shirt and blue jeans.

Connaught Place is an area in the heart of New Delhi made up of multiple blocks of upscale shops and restaurants. I strolled the circle several times, walking in and out of stylish shops filled with a myriad of magnificent handcrafted art and artifacts, prized and priceless collectibles in the Western world, and a treasure of gemstones and jewelry, all at prices a fraction of the cost one would pay in a Western nation.

I stepped into a restaurant. Multiple ceiling fans whirled above a spacious dining room. Unlike the dilapidated open air restaurants with tattered furnishings one finds in the street bazaar, this restaurant had a front door, solid walls, unscathed polished wooden tables and chairs, and elegant décor. And the kitchen was hidden from view, as opposed to the street bazaar where all of the cooking is done out in the open.

A Frenchman, a German, and an American couple invited me to join them at their table. The American couple, Vince and Gloria, had grown a large crop of Marijuana in the middle of a cornfield in Ohio. Their harvest had brought

## Chapter Eleven

them enough money for a journey to India. All four were dining on a South Indian dish known as masala dosa, a mixture of potatoes, onions, and peas wrapped in a thin layer of dough, resembling a large crepe.

I followed suit and ordered a masala dosa. Cheap, nourishing, tasty, and filling, the masala dosa would become a favorite. Restaurant workers would come around carrying buckets filled with a fiery curried sauce known as sambar, slopping generous amounts of the mouth burning sauce over the masala dosas. In India, one could not avoid feeling as if one's mouth had burst into flames at almost every meal, regardless of one's request to keep it mild.

"Accha," they would say with a smile, a versatile Hindi word meaning: yes; good; I acknowledge; I understand; okay. But nothing would change. The word mild, it seemed, simply didn't exist in their vocabulary. A lost cause for sure, I soon realized, and so I began playing a challenging game with myself; namely, how blazing burning hot can I take it? And there seemed no limits to the scorching infernos of India's native cuisine.

Back on the streets of New Delhi, I set about purchasing my new wardrobe of native garb. In America I would walk into a clothing shop and pull garments off the racks. Not so in India. In India my new wardrobe would be custom made by my own personal tailor, as it has been done since ancient times.

In the West, the personal tailor has been lost to mass production, but in India, the age-old art of the personal tailor has never ceased to flourish. Tailoring is one of India's major professions, an irreplaceable source of income for millions of families. In the bazaar, countless labyrinthine blocks of narrow lanes and winding pathways are devoted to the tailoring craft.

At random, I chose one tailoring shop and stepped inside. Thrilled to have a customer from the Western world come into their shop, an ecstatic crew of fathers, uncles, brothers, sons, and cousins greeted me with overwhelming enthusiasm. I told them of my wishes. They in turn wasted no time breaking out the measuring tools and measuring me from head to foot. Next, I was shown innumerable rolls of pure cotton fabric in a multitude of colors and textures. I made my selections and left them to their labor, returning several hours later to pick up my new Indian wardrobe.

I had ordered four loose fitting collarless Indian shirts, two white, and the others light shades of brown and green, with three buttons at the top, and three pairs of white baggy drawstring pants, all one hundred percent cotton of the finest cloth, and the entire purchase had cost me the equivalent of five American dollars.

On my third day in India, clad in baggy white drawstring pajama pants, a white kurta, and flip-flops, I walked along a street in New Delhi wondering when the culture shock would strike. God knows it should have by now, and in droves, considering I had seen almost nothing recognizable to the Western mind since I arrived and now I'm strolling down a street in New Delhi wearing white pajamas.

What occurred next is indeed unexplainable. Without warning, my mind became seized by a bizarre gripping sensation, and in the next second I saw myself, clear as a bell, walking through an Eastern bazaar wearing white pajamas, as if I had become two people. A genuine out of body experience had taken place. This uncanny phenomenon in all likelihood didn't last more than a couple of seconds, but it felt like an eternity. Distorted time always seems to accompany an extreme culture shock occurrence. A momentary hallucinatory episode, the severe culture shock I had been expecting, and well deserved. Walking down a street in New Delhi wearing white pajamas finally tipped me over the edge.

## Chapter Eleven

I came upon a street lined with beggars. They were the filthiest, most suffering, diseased humans imaginable. Passing desperate outstretched hands, I strolled down the line, through a sea of inconceivable misery and overwhelming despair, dropping coins in their begging bowls until I had no more coins in my pocket to give. From this day forward giving to the beggars would become part of my daily routine.

A bullock cart had come to a halt in the middle of the street. Captivated, I stopped for a moment to take a good look at this amazing beast. A castrated bull, also known as the ox, the bullock is India's most vital and trusted beast of burden since time immemorial. And I also fixed my attention on the man holding the reins, whose destiny it was to toil his entire time on Earth commanding a bullock cart, from morning till night, as in all likelihood his father and his father before him had done.

Back at the hotel, I headed past the front desk and up the steps to my room. Several guys were milling about in the hotel's lobby, bugging me to sell them my blue jeans and any other possessions I might consider letting go of at a fair price. American blue jeans were at the top of the list, next came radios, rock and roll tapes, and cassette players, as was the technology of the day. I had already sold them the bottle of Johnnie Walker Black Label Scotch whiskey and the carton of Marlboro cigarettes I brought in from London's duty free shop, and I made a fair profit, as I had been told I would on the traveler's grapevine. I had nothing more to sell, I told them, but they would still bug me, every time they saw me.

The shower water ran out like a faucet, not a spray. One slow thin line of freezing water. On a budget such as mine, taking care of one's hygiene needs in India would more often than not prove a challenging task. Following my shower I stretched out on the bed, watching the ceiling fan spin, taking great pleasure in its manufactured breeze after walking around all day in the muggy Asian air. Without fail, and it will forever be a mystery to me, but no matter what shape a building in India might be in, crumbling, decaying, the walls could be falling down, a fully functioning ceiling fan would still hang overhead. I fell asleep watching a trail of ants climbing up the wall. Reality as I knew it was nowhere in sight.

"Chai garam, chai garam," the chai boy yelled as he came marching through, his tray filled with the sun hardened disposable clay cups of hot chai. I bought a cup and settled in, ready to take a ride on the great Indian railroad, the first of hundreds of hours I would spend over the next two years riding the rails across the sub-continent. The whistles blew, the chai boy hopped off, and the old steam engine locomotive rambled out of Delhi station.

Porters served breakfast, distinguished and stately in their trim and tidy button down colonial uniforms, speaking the Queen's English with eloquence, ease, and perfection. Fried eggs and jelly toast, as I had ordered, and a cup of chai with real cup and saucer, served with surprising efficiency and a politeness one rarely sees in this world anymore.

Five hours later I arrived in the city of Agra, home of the Taj Mahal, passing within a few miles of the birthplace of Lord Krishna along the way. An onslaught of bicycle rickshaw drivers greeted me as I walked out of Agra station. I made a random choice, climbed aboard and instructed the driver to take me to a cheap hotel near the Taj Mahal.

Strong as an ox, with stick thin legs of steel, the dark skinned, sarong clad rickshaw driver peddled his rickshaw through the crowded streets. The sun beat down upon us

## Chapter Eleven

and sweat dripped from his brow. At one point he stepped down to walk his bicycle rickshaw up a hill. I hopped off with him to lighten his load and climbed back in when we reached the top. The rickshaw drivers toiled from morning till night, hauling their human cargo, earning scarcely enough money to survive. He peddled on, his focus unflinching. His work seemed humanly impossible.

My hotel room in Agra contained nothing more than a bare wooden bench and a ceiling fan, no mattress this time, and no showers, only bucket baths. But at fifty cents a night, who's complaining?

The hotel employed a crew of young men, half a dozen, more or less; although I don't recall seeing them do much more than heat up buckets of hot water for bucket baths and make pots of chai. These guys also slept in the hotel. Some slept in the hallways and some slept on the roof of the dilapidated one story structure, where the motley group of budget backpackers from the Western world hung-out, getting stoned and drinking cups of chai.

I wanted to look and feel my best when my eyes first gazed upon the Taj Mahal. I should have asked the hotel guys to heat me up a bucket of hot water, they only charged one rupee, but I didn't want to wait. I proceeded to take a freezing bucket bath instead.

I stood in the dungeon-like concrete walled bathroom naked except for the rubber flip-flops on my feet. After a few moments of mental preparation for the inevitable shock I would soon experience, I took a deep breath, as deep as I could, held it as tight as I could and poured the bucket of freezing water over my head.

There is a science to taking a freezing shower or bucket bath. First, one must control the breath by filling the lungs deep. Next, one must hold the breath in, as tight as possible, and when the shock of the icy water hits, one must exhale, pronto, and without delay take another deep breath. If these steps are not followed and the breathing is not controlled, the initial shock of the freezing water will be far worse and what air you do have in your lungs will be knocked right out of you and you'll find yourself clamoring to catch your breath. Although sometimes the water's so damn freezing cold it knocks the breath right out of you anyway, no matter what you do.

Shivering, I soaped up from head to foot. To rinse off, I dumped two more buckets of freezing water over myself. In these torturous moments I gave myself a severe scolding for not allowing the hotel guys to heat me up a bucket of hot water and I vowed it would never happen again. The process goes as follows: Two buckets are brought in. One bucket is filled with hot water. The other bucket is empty. One fills the empty bucket two-thirds with cold water and the remaining one-third with hot water. In doing so, one can stretch one bucket of hot water into several buckets of warm water and a nice warm bucket bath is to be had. Chilled to the bone, I dried off, got dressed and hit the streets of Agra, warming up quickly in the noonday Asian sun.

Sacred cows strolled about town, free and unfettered. Cows are given divine status in Hinduism. As providers of milk, they symbolize life and sustenance. Horse drawn carriages with passengers in tow clippity-clopped along ancient, dusty streets. Rickshaws rolled and the jingling of bicycle bells filled the air. Clad in my new Indian garb, I strolled through the crowded bazaar, bustling with ramshackle shops and steaming pots of curry.

Tourists from all corners of the planet make journeys to the Indian city of Agra to behold the Taj Mahal. Construction of the celebrated architectural wonder took twenty-two years to complete, from 1631 until 1653, upon orders of the Mughal Emperor Shah Jahan. Within the marble walls of the world's most notable mausoleum the

*Chapter Eleven*

Queen is laid to rest. The Shah's beloved wife Mumtaz Mahal died giving birth to their fourteenth child.

I walked through the entranceway, an impressive structure in its own right, made of red sandstone and white marble, inlayed in beautiful gemstone motif. From there one continues into a verdant, manicured landscape adorned with fountains, flower gardens, and narrow water channels. It is here one's eyes first cast a wondrous gaze upon the Taj Mahal, built of the finest white marble, with its magical domed roof flanked by four majestic minarets, sitting in splendor upon the banks of the Yamuna River. I could do nothing more than stand, stare, and wonder if I was dreaming.

One must witness the Taj Mahal from sunrise until the night has fallen, for each new hour of the day, in the passage of the sun and in the light of the moon, brings to the Taj Mahal an unrivaled multiplicity of shifting and changing hues, tints, tones, shapes, and shadows, dancing and silhouetting upon the mystical monument's gorgeous white marble. And inside of the royal chamber, dazzling multi-hued gemstone inlays adorn the resplendent white marble walls encircling the Queen's eternal abode, immeasurable in their number, incalculable in their worth, stunning in their beauty and design.

The Taj Mahal would be my only planned destination, owing, of course, to the historic attraction's familiar name. Where I should go from here I hadn't a clue. But I knew the traveler's grapevine would see me through. And it did. Three days later I left Agra and headed deep into the sub-continent's interior.

The great Indian railroad and India's postal system, parliamentary democracy, and the English language, the latter unifying a land with over thirty languages and three hundred dialects, this is Britain's legacy to India. There is much negative to say about colonialism, but the infrastructure put in place by the British enabling India to come into the modern world, in my humble opinion I would consider worthy of exclusion from the list.

The whistles blew. "Chai garam, chai garam," the chai boy yelled, marching through with his tray full of hot cups of chai. I settled back, cup of chai in hand, my eyes following a herd of water buffalo roaming the banks of a small riverbed as the old steam engine locomotive rolled out of Agra station, steam hissing, whistles wailing, black clouds of smoke billowing into the mystical mist of an Indian daybreak. I was on my way to the sacred city of Varanasi, also known as Banares, on the banks of the Ganges River.

A most fascinating raggedy street musician came on board several stops into the journey. Hoping for a few coins in return, he walked through the train car singing an exotic tune in an ancient language, an otherworldly combination of both painful sorrow and spiritual ecstasy is the best I can do in describing his song, sung in an anguished high-pitched voice, musical scale and melody unknown to my Western ears.

Equally otherworldly, exotic, and unfamiliar musical notes cried out from the unknown small stringed instrument he played. Wow! I love this place. What a country! My inner dialogue spoke in awe. One guy earns a living pestering people and another earns a living riding the trains all day singing mysterious mystical melodies.

Chai boys came on board at every station, hopping off in the nick of time as the whistles blew and the old steam engine locomotive began rolling, their trays emptied of the sun hardened clay cups of chai. Another street musician came on board, a young boy about ten years of age, playing an exotic Eastern melody on a wooden flute, his blind father walking behind him, one hand on the boys shoulder, a begging bowl in the other. I would fall in love with the sounds and sights of India's street music, its colorful array

## Chapter Eleven

of musicians displaying a soul stirring exoticism, mystery, mysticism, and authenticity I would find nowhere else outside of the sub-continent.

The journey from Agra to Varanasi took twenty-four hours, requiring me to prepare for an overnight voyage. I reserved a third tier berth. The third tier is best, I had been told by fellow travelers, because no one can sit on your bench during the day and no one is above you at night while you sleep.

The great Indian railroad is a world entirely unto itself, a remarkable journey in its own right, filled with untold color, unimaginable character, and an extraordinary assortment of humanity at the highest level of fascination. A railway system like no other. In India, everyone rides the rails: Hindus, Muslims, bearded Sikhs wearing colorful turbans; the young, the old, the infirm; the rich, the poor unwashed masses in rags; businessmen and holy men; merchants and monks; farmers with chickens in cages; men clad in dhotis, sarongs, and long kurtas; women clad in saris, rings in their noses, red dots on their foreheads, half naked children sitting on their laps. One might even find oneself sitting beside a sadhu with matted hair and face covered in ash. A mind blowing microcosm of every fascinating face and facet of this inexpressible land will pass before one's eyes when riding the rails of India.

Darkness fell. I climbed up to my third tier berth and fell asleep to the rhythm of an antique steam engine locomotive rolling across the sub-continent.

I awoke at daybreak, hopped down from my berth and peered out the window. The train had slowed to a crawl, rambling its last few miles past fields of tattered tents and shanties and shadowy figures squatting by tiny fires in the ethereal mist of an Asian dawn. I had arrived in the holiest place in all of India, the ancient city of Varanasi, sitting upon the banks of the sacred river Ganges. I rolled up my sleeping bag, put it inside of my backpack and prepared to disembark. An assortment of languages and dialects filled the air as sleepy families from all over India began waking up, their hallowed pilgrimage to Varanasi nearing its completion, the blessings they wished to receive from Mother Ganges about to begin.

Whistles blowing, steel wheels screeching, the archaic locomotive closed in on its final approach, belched one last cloud of black smoke, groaned its final breath of hissing steam and came to a halt in Varanasi station. I grabbed my pack, hopped off the train and joined a cavalcade of men and sari clad women scrambling down the crowded platform and out to the street, coolies scurrying behind carrying heavy trunks and suitcases on their heads.

I randomly choose one rickshaw out of a crowd of frenzied bicycle rickshaw drivers waiting outside the train station, clamoring for my business.

"Cheap hotel near river," I instructed the driver.

"Aacha, Aacha," he responded.

"How much rupee?" I asked.

"Twelve," he said.

Well, I may not have known my exact location in relation to the river but I had a damn good idea a major attempt to rip me off was in progress. I had learned the art of bartering in Guatemala and Mexico. Child's play, I would say, in comparison to this place. In India, learning the true price of life's necessities, what a native would pay, is crucial to a traveler's economic survival. Big merchant, little merchant, didn't matter. Everyone in this country I would no sooner discover was determined to overcharge me. The rickshaw driver and I agreed on a price of ten rupees and I climbed aboard. Six rupees should have been tops, I would in time learn.

The three wheel bicycle rickshaw rolled toward the river along a street the likes of which I had never before witnessed. It appeared as if the town's entire population of over a million and a half people were all walking around in the middle of the street and it seemed as if half of them were sadhus, many in loincloths, in addition to the rickshaws, motor scooters, bicycles, sacred cows wandering to their heart's content, and beasts of burden trudging in their toil. Dilapidated shops and chai stalls, some no larger than closets, ramshackle open-air restaurants, rows of beggars, and an army of street peddlers and pushcart vendors also lined the teeming dusty path.

Of bone, muscle, and sinew were the rickshaw driver's powerful legs. Through the tangled maze of the mind-blowing ancient Hindu city of Varanasi I was pedaled and to the Central Hotel I was delivered, suitably named for the hotel's convenient location, about a five minute walk from the river.

Lodging at the Central Hotel cost five rupees, somewhere in the vicinity of forty cents. My room consisted of nothing more than a wooden bench and a ceiling fan, same as the hotel in Agra. A bit cleaner, though, everything being relative, of course. And the Central Hotel had freezing showers instead of freezing bucket baths. I had been given a room on the ground floor of the two-story building. Like most structures in Varanasi, the Central Hotel was old and in varying degrees of dilapidation and decay. The rooms ran in a circular direction surrounding a crumbling courtyard and the individual components making up a bathroom were scattered in various places throughout the courtyard. Shower stalls in one location, squatters in another, but the sinks presented the oddest sight, free standing, sitting out in the open by themselves.

I dropped off my backpack, locked my door with my trusty American combination lock and headed out for my first glimpse of the holy river, when a young smooth talking Indian fellow of slim and delicate physique, clad in fashionable European pants and shirt, called out to me from a small kiosk located in the hotel's lobby.

"Surely good sir, you will want to have a couple of these beautiful shirts, they will look so nice on you," he said, speaking the Queens English with impeccable excellence.

I stopped and made eye contact. Big mistake! As soon as he had my attention he proceeded to unfold dozens of shirts for my viewing pleasure.

"Good sir, these shirts are a combination of the finest silk and cotton India has to offer. Feel the cloth, sir," he said.

I did as he asked. The shirts were ultra soft and velvety to the touch.

I could have simply walked away, but I didn't have the heart after watching him unfold countless shirts, knowing he would have to fold every one right back up again. A planned strategy, of course, and he saw a sucker coming. I would end up buying two shirts, one a deep green and the other a light tan, with elegant hand embroidered multi-colored flower designs across the shoulders, along the collarless top, and on each side of the three buttons in the front.

"Thank you good sir, thank you good sir," the slick shopkeeper repeated as we finalized the purchase.

I had fallen victim to the unparalleled psychological salesmanship of the East, walked head on into a classic Indian ambush and thirty-five of my precious rupees did a disappearing act when I had no intention of spending anything in the first place.

But all was not lost, for two valuable lessons had been taught. First valuable lesson: One must develop a thick skin in this country. These people have an uncanny ability to persuade. And second valuable lesson: Keep walking before the unfolding begins. There was so much to learn in India.

## Chapter Eleven

Without further interruption, I proceeded to make my way along the remaining stretch of unimaginable road leading to the sacred river Ganges. I came upon a cow standing in the middle of the street in front of a restaurant scraping the remains out of a large pot brought out to her by one of the restaurant's workers. Determined to dig out every last morsel, the cow scrubbed the pot spotless with her tongue. Wow! I marveled. They gain merit in the spiritual realms and good karma in their present and future lives by feeding the sacred cows and they get their pots cleaned in the process. The resourcefulness I would encounter in this country never ceased to amaze me.

Continuing to walk toward the river, I came upon an old woman carrying a pile of cow dung in her bare hands. I followed her and watched her make cow dung patties, putting the small dung pies out to dry and harden in the sun. Dried and hardened cow dung has been used in India since time immemorial as a source of cooking fuel. Its slow burning properties create a level of heat that is perfect for the cooking of rice and curries. In India, nothing is wasted. The old women supported herself by selling dried and hardened cow dung patties, another one of those odd occupations found only in the Eastern world.

Never had I seen, nor could I have imagined a more wretched bunch of suffering souls as the beggars of India, and in Varanasi their numbers staggered the mind. Blind, crippled, deformed, social outcasts, destitute widows, and lepers with noses, fingers, and toes eaten away by the disease of leprosy, reaching out with their begging bowls as I walked past.

Also lining the route were the relatives of the dead, those who couldn't afford the expense of having their loved ones cremated, begging for money to cover the costs. To die in Varanasi and have one's ashes scattered in the holy river is the wish of every Hindu. This, according to Hindu belief, assures one of their place in heaven.

By a hair's breadth my foot missed colliding with a pile of cow dung sitting in the middle of the road, a near mishap leading to yet another valuable lesson learned: The importance of developing what is known among Western travelers as cow dung radar, an essential survival skill in India, and even more so when wearing flip-flops.

I arrived upon the legendary ghats, short flights of ancient stone steps leading down to the water's edge. A skyline of domes, minarets, maharaja palaces, ashrams, mosques, and Hindu temples lined the riverfront as far as the eye could see. Sadhus abounded. These wandering mendicants have given up all material possessions and worldly attachment and devote themselves entirely to the service and glorification of God. Homeless, penniless, and celibate, by choice, they live on alms provided by the community. Indian society puts great value on the spiritual life. A good re-birth awaits those who support the sadhus in their quest. Some sadhus are clad in robes of white, others in saffron, and others merely in loincloths. Many have long matted hair coiled up on top of their heads, their bodies and bearded faces covered in ash, lines painted on their foreheads in colors of clay from the banks of the sacred river.

Many of the sadhus in Varanasi are Shaivites, worshippers of Shiva, as the holy river has its origins in the mystical mythology surrounding Lord Shiva. Others are worshippers of Rama, an incarnation of God whose time on Earth, according to Vedic scripture, directly preceded the advent of Lord Krishna. Lord Rama's life on Earth spent teaching the highest principles of Dharma by example and selfless sacrifice is detailed in the beloved Ramayana, an epic masterpiece of ancient Sanskrit literature.

On occasion, one will bear witness to the Naga Baba sect. These sadhus don't even wear loincloths, so serious

## Chapter Eleven

are they in their efforts to give up all attachment to the material world. When one's eyes fall upon a naked Naga Baba one will never forget it. A naked matted haired Naga Baba covered in ash is a sight to behold. It will change your life, as will so much of what one sees and experiences in India. Nobody, I believe, can travel this land and remain unchanged.

Water buffalo roamed the river's edge. Street barbers cut hair. Men received massage and rubdowns, practiced yoga, and meditated under the blissful watch of Mother Ganges in the ancient city of Varanasi, among the oldest cities in the world. Varanasi was an established city before the Roman Empire existed, and with the exception of a few modern conveniences, not much has changed since then.

It begins at sunrise and is a scene like no other. Holding the belief that bathing in the Ganges will wash away the sins of many lifetimes, untold masses of devout Hindus descend upon the river with palms pressed together in prayer position. Women in elegant saris of silk and fine cotton immerse themselves fully clothed and fill brass pots with the sacred water. Men run the gamut from fully clothed to loincloths. Offerings are made. Rice and grains are tossed into the river. Marigolds, pink lotuses, water lilies, and small oil lamps float upon the water, and from a small Hindu shrine close to where I stood, the mystical sounds of kirtan sprang forth as a group of skinny bearded sadhus, absorbed in continuous hypnotic harmony, chanted the holy names, while an exotic drum beat played, providing a spiritual soundtrack to the ancient life along the holy river.

As the story is told, Lord Brahma commanded the Goddess Ganges to descend from heaven. Lord Brahma's demand made her unhappy. In retaliation, she threatened to tumble down with haste and tremendous force. Her threat caused alarm bells to ring out in the godly realms out of fear her forceful fall would flood the earth and wash it away. Lord Shiva stepped forward, and as she began her plunge, Lord Shiva captured her in the matted locks of his hair, and there, for untold time in celestial years, she would wander until Lord Shiva gradually lowered her down in small slow moving streams. This, of course, is an explanation in the simplest of terms possible as the full account of what took place in the godly realms is yet another colorful ancient tale of enormous complexity taking up innumerable pages of sacred Vedic texts.

There are over one hundred ghats in Varanasi, but Manikarnika Ghat, the main burning ghat, is the most sacred of them all, and from where I stood I could see Manikarnika Ghat, and I could see the funeral pyres burning. The fires burn day and night and the ashes of the dead are scattered upon the river.

I wished to get an up close look at the burning of the bodies. Into an ancient labyrinth of unknowable narrow lanes, twisting pathways, and mysterious winding backstreets I ventured, a shadowy maze of squalor and decay guiding me to the cremation grounds. And there I stood, in morbid fascination, watching the bodies burning to the crackling sounds of flesh and bones melting away. The cremations have been controlled since ancient times by the Dom Rajas, a secretive untouchable caste. Spread out on the ground nearby I caught sight of the shroud wrapped bodies, covered in flowers, waiting their turn as the Dom Rajas poked and prodded, keeping the fires going, the sacred river's steady currents carrying the ashes away.

I came upon a small Hindu temple while navigating back from the cremation grounds along the narrow corridors, some ancient footpaths so skinny two people could barely pass without grazing shoulders. I slipped out of my flip-flops and stepped inside. But the greeting I received was not what I had come to expect. Rather than the usual

## Chapter Eleven

welcoming namaste, I was met instead by an alarmed bunch of holy men standing in the doorway, freaking out, waving their hands in the air, telling me to stop, communicating to me that a non-Hindu shall not enter, such was the holiness of this temple. Startled and bewildered, and feeling bad I had upset the holy men, in haste I stepped out.

"Namaste," I said with palms pressed together in prayer position and a slight bow as I backed away, and they in turn, having calmed down, with a bow and palms also pressed together in prayer position, replied in kind.

I wondered about the meaning of namaste. The divine in me recognizes the divine in you, I would soon learn. It is a common salutation in India and Nepal and would become second nature to me. It also carries the same meaning when performed in silence, using only the gestures of palms pressed together and a slight bow.

Arriving back at the hotel, I stood studying the street, a street like none I could have in my wildest imagination envisioned. Monkeys skirted rooftops. A sacred cow with a garland of yellow marigolds dangling round her neck came close, stopped, looked me in the eye for a moment, then turned around and moseyed on her way. Dilapidated shops and open air restaurants, rickety chai stalls and push cart vendors, beggars and bullock carts, rickshaws and bicycles, holy men in robes and loincloths, and an endless steaming stream of humanity filled every inch of Varanasi. The intensity of the holy city of Varanasi defied description. The entire town was one massive ancient Eastern bazaar. And the fact that Lord Shiva's earthly abode ranked among the filthiest places in India didn't bother me one bit. In my mind, it only added to its character.

I watched a colorful religious procession march past my hotel, heading toward the river, led by an elephant decorated in flamboyant attire and adorned in jewels, followed by a brass band and people carrying statues of Lord Shiva's beloved son, Ganesh, remover of obstacles, God of wisdom and learning, and God of beginnings. And how the head of an elephant came to sit upon the shoulders of Lord Shiva's son is yet another fabulous ancient Sanskrit tale.

It had been a long day since arriving in Varanasi with much seen and much learned and dinner time drew near. I walked into a restaurant and ordered servings of rice, dal, vegetable korma, malai kofta, a couple of chapattis, and a lassi. A full course dinner for approximately thirty-five cents. Who could ask for more? A cow meandered into the restaurant. A worker slapped it on the rump, yelled, and the holy cow walked back out to the street.

Evening approached and the temperature began to drop. But wearing my American zip-up jacket, I no sooner realized, would look awful odd with my baggy drawstring pajama pants, and even more so as I saw not one soul wearing a jacket. To keep warm in the cool evening air, everyone, including Western travelers, wore either a blanket or a shawl draped around their shoulders.

The city of Varanasi is world renowned as a major center in the manufacturing of textiles. An infinite assortment of superb garments made of the finest materials and dyes are hand crafted in Varanasi. Upper caste Indian women from every corner of the sub-continent come to Varanasi on family pilgrimages. Their purpose, first and foremost, is to worship Mother Ganges and receive her blessings, but never do they go home without having purchased a trunk load of new Varanasi saris. Out of the many textile shops lining the streets of Varanasi, I choose one at random, ventured inside and purchased an exquisite blue and silver wrap-around hand embroidered shawl, made of the highest quality wool, silk, and cotton.

Enveloped in flowing fabric, a stranger to myself, I walked down to the ghats and in a moment almost too

## Chapter Eleven

intense to bear, with my new Indian shawl wrapped around my head and shoulders, I stood upon the ancient stone steps, gazing out upon the Ganges at sunset while in the background, a group of sadhus giving praise to Lord Rama in a kirtan of slow and mellow drum beats, rhythmic bells, and the mystical chanting of Sri Ram, jai Ram, jai jai Ram, serenaded the holy river from a small Hindu temple adjacent to where I stood.

An Asian city at daybreak never fails to fascinate. I awoke in the early hour of dawn and in the brisk and refreshing air of first light I wrapped myself up in my beautiful new Indian shawl and headed for the river. Along the way I bought a bowl of yogurt and bartered for a couple of bananas from a street vendor sitting crossed-legged on the side of the road with a basket of bananas in his lap. A banana-wallah, his lot in life to sit from dawn to dusk with one aspiration in mind: To find his basket of bananas empty by day's end.

With breakfast in hand I seated myself upon the ancient stone steps. A delicate veil shrouded the sacred waters in an ethereal morning mist, casting a pensive mood upon me. Small row boats floated by, giving tourists views of ancient life on the waterfront at sunrise from a different vantage point, and the slapping sounds of washer-men could be heard, beating wet clothes upon the rocks, nature's washing machine, as it has been done for thousands of years.

I took my camping knife out of my side-bag and sliced a banana into my disposable sun hardened clay bowl of yogurt as dozens of pious Hindus with hands in prayer position poured past, descending into the river to perform their ablutions, accompanied by the mystical rhythm of continuous kirtan emanating from a nearby riverfront shrine.

I finished slicing my banana into my bowl of yogurt, put my knife back in my side-bag, took out my spoon and dug in. Slow and deliberate I proceeded, delighting in every bite, each spoonful almost too rich to swallow, so delicious, thick, and creamy was this yogurt. Downright blissful, I would say, its qualities so rich and delectable, I would soon learn, because it is made from the milk of the water buffalo.

"Sixty paise," the chai-wallah said, handing me the cup of chai I had requested.

"Why sixty?" I asked. "I paid thirty yesterday."

"I made yours with cardamom this morning, special for you," he said.

It only amounted to a few pennies more, but that wasn't the point. I hadn't asked for cardamom. I had been bushwhacked and hoodwinked once again and it made me mad. But how can one stay angry at a chai-wallah? And his cardamom spiced chai tasted so delicious.

For the remainder of my stay in Varanasi and each subsequent stay thereafter, I would pay double the cost of a regular cup of chai. I couldn't help myself. The devious chai-wallah knew what he was doing. He got me hooked on cardamom.

I spent the morning wandering the river's edge. At one point I found myself face to face with a humongous water buffalo as I walked along the lower steps of the ghat. I tried to move out of his way but the lumbering beast wouldn't let me pass. I wasn't sure what to do as we both stood motionless, staring into each other's eyes. I tried not to freak out. I had never been in such intimate proximity to a creature of such immense measure and strength. I had no idea what he wanted or what he might do. A long moment passed. And as we continued standing motionless, staring into each other's eyes, the two ton animal, in a surprising gesture, lowered his snout and gently nudged me in my chest with the top of his head. He then took a few steps backwards, swayed his monstrous body to my

## Chapter Eleven

left and moseyed on his way. Was he giving me a love tap? Was he saying hello? Was he welcoming me to India? Or was he telling me: "You're in my world now foreigner, so watch yourself." I'll never know, but one detail of this most unusual encounter remains indisputable: Had the beast so desired, he could have crushed my bones.

I set about walking to Sarnath, among Buddhism's most sacred sites, seven kilometers from my location in Varanasi.

I munched from the street vendors along the way, knowing full well the risk I was taking by breaking the fundamental rule of not eating from the street vendors' push carts. But the deep fried samosas, pooris, and pakoras were hard to resist, so tasty were they, and unbelievably cheap. In India, one must at all times be on the lookout against those evil microscopic critters who wreak such misery upon one's intestines, known in the scientific community as dysentery. Although I had to believe even they couldn't survive the blistering temperatures of the push cart vendors' pots of bubbling oil.

The Buddha attained enlightenment sitting under the Bodhi tree in the village of Bodh Gaya in the year 530 BC. Upon accomplishing this most venerated feat, he picked himself up and walked to Sarnath, two hundred fifty-eight kilometers from Bodh Gaya. Having lived as a wandering sadhu for a number of years, he had grown accustomed to walking long distances.

In the ancient village of Sarnath the Buddha spoke the words of Dhamma for the very first time, and in the ancient village of Sarnath, the Sangha, the Buddhist monastic order, came into existence.

I wandered through the serene village. Buddhist monks walked in silence, circling the ancient stupas. Monasteries sat upon hallowed ground. The religion's mysterious quietude and the stillness permeating Sarnath struck a chord deep within, igniting in me a desire to learn all I could about Buddhism. But where does one go to learn the true meditative path the Buddha taught, in its original purity? I would find that place, but not until my second journey to India.

Every new day in India seemed to bring a stranger sight than the strangest sight I had seen the day before. And one of the strangest sights I had ever seen was the street corner dentist. He sat on the street waiting to work on some poor soul's teeth with a host of tools spread out before him on a piece of cloth covering the ground, including pliers, wires, small picks, tiny hammers, and more, a horrifying hodgepodge collection of odd instruments with which to pick, poke, probe, and yank out, as well as a jumble of false teeth, made of various materials, including wood, and not a drop of disinfectant or numbing agent in sight. As I stood studying the tools of this man's trade an unfortunate fellow with no other choice but to seek out this dude's help in his time of dental need came along. In awe I watched as he sat on the ground and allowed the medieval tooth worker to examine his mouth with ungloved and unwashed hands. A few words were spoken, to which the patient paid close attention before getting back on his feet and walking away. A consultation perhaps, or could it have been a six month check up?

The Indian men with blood-red mouths created yet another bizarre sight. At first, the grotesque appearance of these men had me alarmed. I thought perhaps they had a terrible mouth disease and I worried it might be contagious, until I learned the reason behind the mysterious red mouthed men. These men were all in the habit of chewing on a palate cleanser known as paan, beetle nuts wrapped in a green leaf. This popular practice would leave their mouths looking as if they were drenched in blood. And they would spit the stuff out in the street.

## Chapter Eleven

The government dope shop resembled a dusty old grain and feed store on the frontiers of the Wild West. Marijuana, known in India as ganga, sat in small barrels on the floor inside. Only by the generosity of others would I partake of intoxicating substances, a decision I made several years earlier. In other words, I had reached a point where I could take it or leave it, and if it meant spending my own money, I would leave it. But now I find myself standing in front of a legal dope shop in India. It was a no brainer. I had to do it, at least once. I asked the clerk to give me five rupees worth of ganga. He reached into one of the barrels, took out a small amount, weighed it on the most intriguing tiny medieval cast iron balancing scale made for the most minuscule of weights, an antique dealers dream, and wrapped it in newspaper. I paid him, he handed me the package and I headed back to my hotel, nimbly dodging a pile of cow dung parked in the middle of the street.

I stopped to buy a couple of loose cigarettes from a street vendor. Once back in my room I emptied the tobacco out of one of the cigarettes and filled it with the marijuana I had purchased from the government shop.

I lit up, got stoned and walked down to the river, and as I sat on the banks of the Ganges drinking a cup of cardamom spiced chai, a young, barrel-chested dwarf about three feet tall seated himself beside me.

"Good sir, may I be allowed to introduce myself?" he said.

"By all means," I replied.

"My name is Mukesh. I am from Bangladesh. And if you would be so kind, good sir, may I ask your name and the reason you have come to India?"

Mukesh was clad in a yellow button down collared shirt tidily tucked into a pair of light brown trousers which he wore high on his waist, a stylish European outfit. I ordered two cups of chai, another for myself and one for the smartly dressed midget sitting beside me who I believe had just chosen me as his new best friend. The tiny fellow grinned from ear to ear as I attempted to answer his many questions.

Mukesh had no job. He spent his days walking around town socializing. He knew everyone, and he spoke three languages: English, Hindi, and his native Bengali.

I would run into the mysterious little man every day, standing at a height of barely three feet, with his barrel chest and no neck to speak of, and his oversized head, although I think perhaps his head only appeared oversized in proportion to his body. Through the jam packed streets of Varanasi my eyes would find him, with a big smile on his face, a twinkle in his eye, his shirt tucked in and his pants pulled high above his waist. We would sit on the water's edge, drink cardamom spiced chai and talk. The pleasure of my company overjoyed him.

An American girl occupied one of the rooms across from mine. I had spoken to her on several occasions and she seemed pleasant and responsive, so I decided to pay her a visit. I stuck my head inside of her open door and said hello.

"Come in," she said.

I walked inside and sat on the edge of her wooden bench. We talked and the visit seemed to be going well. The last thing I expected to see was a young long haired bearded sadhu clad in a full length white robe stroll in and take a seat cross-legged on the floor.

He asked if I had any ganga to put in his chillum. Smoking ganga is part of the religious practices of many sadhus. I walked across the courtyard to my room and retrieved my stash. We filled the chillum, passed it back and forth, everybody got stoned, and then, to my utmost shock and bewilderment, point blank, in the most degrading fashion, she demanded I leave.

## Chapter Eleven

"Please go!" she rudely said to me.

I couldn't believe it. She's banging an Indian holy man. Having been jolted into an enormously disturbed state of mind, utterly unnerved by this crazy American girl, I walked out of the room.

In millenniums, since the first sadhu walked the land, these dudes hadn't seen anything like the middle class white girls from the Western world that began showing up in the late 1960s. How many have seen their vows to God go flying right out the window since then? More than a few I would in time discover.

An eye-opening pile of naïve illusions would my innocent belief in the infallibility of those who walk the path of renunciation suddenly become. I was stunned, but I was learning.

I walked down to the river and with a delicious cup of cardamom spiced chai in hand I seated myself upon the ancient stone steps along the water's edge and let the Goddess Ganges soothe my naïve, humiliated soul.

Passengers barreled down the platform looking for their assigned train cars. I joined the crowd and in the chaos I found mine. I can think of no other place on Earth where chaos and order live side by side as they do in India, both fully functioning simultaneously within the same space.

I climbed aboard, took my seat, and the old steam engine locomotive rolled out of Varanasi station. I was on my way to the small Indian town of Ruxaul, on the Nepali border, where a bus waiting to take me to the ancient city of Katmandu in the Himalayan kingdom of Nepal would depart shortly past dawn.

The reclusive Himalayan kingdom, home of Mt. Everest, opened its borders to the outside world in the 1950s. By the late 1960s, Nepal had become a hippie haven as Western budget backpackers, with one eye on the breathtaking snow-capped Himalayan Mountain peaks and the other on the legendary Nepali hashish, began turning up in droves, many arriving via the magic busses traveling overland from Amsterdam to Katmandu.

I spent the night in a cheap hotel on the Indian side of the Nepali border. This is where I first ate the Indian dessert gulab jamon. A huge vat sat on the street in front of a restaurant next to my hotel filled with bubbling oil and deep fried gulab jamon balls floating on top.

I arrived on a chilly night in the Katmandu Valley after an all day bus ride from the Indian border. One of several questionable characters hanging around the bus depot waiting for the bus from India to pull in approached as I disembarked.

"I have good cheap room," he said.

I put my backpack on my back, wrapped my shawl around my shoulders and without a clue I followed him into the Himalayan night. We soon entered a decaying two-story concrete building with no centralized location of any kind, such as a front desk or lobby, as one would expect to find in a hotel or guesthouse. My host led me up a flight of steps to a tiny room containing nothing more than a narrow wooden platform which took up the majority of the room's minuscule amount of space.

The bathroom pipes were exposed and rusted over. Moisture covered the floor. The shower froze me to the bone and an odor emanating from the squatter escaped into the hallway outside of my room. But at forty cents a night, who's complaining?

It was mid-December in the Katmandu Valley, sitting at an altitude of forty-five hundred feet. The mornings and nights were cold, but the days were comfortable, warming up nicely in the afternoon sun.

## Chapter Eleven

I deposited my backpack upon the wooden platform where I would sleep, wrapped my new Varanasi shawl around my head and shoulders and set about exploring the mysterious city of Katmandu.

Katmandu is a living museum of Buddhist and Hindu architectural design. Known for centuries as the forbidden city, Katmandu is packed like no other place on Earth with ancient Hindu and Buddhist temples, shrines, palaces, and pagodas. And using the term packed like no other place on Earth is not simply an expression, but an actual fact. Practically the entire city is a UNESCO World Heritage site.

I strolled along Katmandu's legendary Freak Street. Hippiedom had traveled to the other side of the planet and it had its own street. Freak Street of course had an official Nepali name, but everyone, including the locals, called it Freak Street. A street sign had even been placed at the intersection displaying the words Freak Street.

In those days the term freak had become synonymous with hippie. I never thought of myself as either. I figured I would have been the way I was regardless of the time period I found myself living in. Coming of age when I did only made it a whole lot easier to be me.

Young Western travelers packed Freak Street and almost all were clad in the colorful native attire of the Eastern world.

Exquisite Nepali and Tibetan jewelry, including rings, bracelets, and necklaces with authentic gemstones encased in pure silver, hand crafted with striking intricacy of detail and design, inimitable in all aspects, and hand crafted clothing, including baggy cotton pants, native shirts, native hats, jackets made of yak wool, and for the lady Western travelers, beautiful Nepali and Tibetan blouses, scarves, shawls, and skirts, colorful and splendid, hand embroidered, and my favorite item, beautiful and rare rice paper prints portraying complex and mystical ancient Buddhist art, and everything at costs undreamed of, filled the shops lining Freak Street.

I'm walking through an ancient city hidden away in a valley between India and China, open to the world for only twenty years, and what do I hear? Rock and roll music booming out of chai and pie cafés filled with travelers from the Western world. Jimi Hendrix came blaring out of one café as I walked past and Led Zeppelin came blasting out of another.

In response to the opportunities brought about by the Western world's fast growing interest in their country, the shrewd Nepali people, in an exceptional display of entrepreneurship, had fashioned on Freak Street, in menu, ambiance, and décor, an ingenious cultural hybrid of charming restaurants and quaint cafés serving Nepali, Tibetan, and Indian cuisine, and European and American pastries, including delicious pies and cakes to satisfy the palates of hippies with munchies, stoned on Nepali hashish.

Slumber soon called. It had been a long day since leaving India in the morning. At daybreak I hit the streets of Katmandu again, snug and warm in my new jacket made from the wool of the yak, a species of bovine native to the Nepali and Tibetan regions of the Himalayas. Many consider yak wool far superior to all other animal fibers.

Back on Freak Street, I slipped between hanging strings of multicolored beads layering the entranceway of the tiny restaurant I had randomly chosen as the place where I would eat breakfast.

Under a low ceiling the soft and cozy hues of yellow and blue pastel warmly welcomed me. One long wooden table filled the dining room's diminutive space. A beautiful artistic hand crafted Nepali carpet covered the floor.

A young Nepali couple owned the restaurant. The wife did nearly all of the cooking and not once did I see her without the sweetest smile upon her beautiful Nepali face.

## Chapter Eleven

"The banana porridge is delicious," an Australian named Spencer said as I joined a group of Western travelers sitting at the long wooden table.

Spencer was the straightest budget backpacking traveler I had seen since arriving in Asia. Spencer wasn't interested in wearing native garb, he wasn't interested in Eastern spirituality, and he wasn't interested in hashish. Spencer came to Nepal strictly to see the mountains, and with his mission accomplished, he would soon return to the coast of Malaysia, to a small Chinese fishing village called Batu Ferringhi, a few miles outside of the Malaysian city of Penang.

"Where do I go to see the snow capped Himalayan peaks?" I asked Spencer. "As of yet, I haven't seen anything."

"The town of Pokhora is where everyone goes to see the mountains. It's only a day's bus ride from here," he said.

Situated on the banks of a majestic Himalayan mountain lake, the town of Pokhara offered breathtaking views of the snowcapped peaks of the Annapurna range, reaching altitudes of twenty-six thousand feet. I finished my bowl of banana porridge, bid my new friend Spencer farewell and walked back out to the streets of Katmandu.

I sat in Durbar square at the top of Freak Street, surrounded by ancient pagodas. A leper approached, filthy, in rags, his nose, fingers, and toes eaten away by the disease of leprosy. I dropped a few coins in his begging bowl, which he held with hands wrapped in soiled bandages.

To my surprise, Gloria, whom I had met in New Delhi with her boyfriend Vince, came strolling in my direction, by herself. A kind, friendly, and good-natured girl, Gloria was also the only obese human I had thus far seen in this part of the world.

India should be a good place for her I thought when I first met her in New Delhi. Indian cuisine certainly doesn't lend itself to bulk. She should lose weight over here, most people do. Unfortunately, it didn't look as if she had lost one ounce. But her weight would be the least of Gloria's problems.

I asked Gloria about Vince. In reply, Gloria proceeded to unload a truckload of woe upon me. Vince had descended into out of control opium use and Gloria had slid into despair.

"Vince has become addicted to opium and I don't know what to do. I can't get him to stop," she said, tears welling up in her eyes.

Instead of spending their days together taking in the sights, Gloria now found herself walking around alone, in misery and hopelessness, while Vince spent his days nodding off in a world of opium dreams. Gloria took me back to their hotel room to see Vince. A polite and personable mid-Western guy, Vince graciously welcomed me. But he kept nodding off as we spoke. There wasn't much I could do.

Everyday I'd see the poor girl walking around in a state of anguish.

"He'll come out of it soon, after all, how long can someone stay strung out on opium in Katmandu?" I said, trying to give her support and reassurance.

A long time, in response to my question my inner voice pointed out, but I didn't reveal to Gloria what my inner voice had told me.

Horrible, putrid tasting belches and severe abdominal cramps woke me up in the wee hours of the morning on the day I planned to leave for Pokhara, and I so looked forward to seeing those magnificent snow capped Himalayan peaks. I held my knees firmly pinned to my chest for the remainder of the night, but it gave little relief.

## Chapter Eleven

As soon as the first rays of dawn's early light came peeking over the horizon, I put on my new yak wool jacket and set about Katmandu in search of an answer. The pain became unbearable. I couldn't stand up straight. My stomach became hard and bloated and the repeated burps continued bringing up the vilest taste into my mouth.

In dire need of immediate medical attention, I walked into the Katmandu hospital. The medical staff placed me upon a surgical table and instructed me to take off my pants and position myself on my side. Next, they inserted a hose into my butt, an invasive medical procedure in a country rated by the world health organization as one of the filthiest places on the planet. With the hose in place, they pumped my belly full of water to the point where I felt as if I would explode. Upon completion of the ghastly procedure, the medical staff instructed me to put my pants back on and head for the squatter. In untold agony, hunched over, I drug myself down a long hallway. The place resembled an infirmary circa the 1800s. Modern medical equipment was scarce. Suffering souls lying upon narrow cots lined the hallways and packed the bedrooms. I reached the squatter and not a minute too soon.

My next move, with my belly now emptied of the God knows how many gallons of water they had pumped into me, was to lug my ravaged body over to the restaurant where I had eaten breakfast on my first day in Katmandu. The proprietor and his wife were such nurturing and compassionate souls, showing genuine kindness and concern for the Western backpackers coming in and out of their lives.

I had no energy. The mere act of walking a few blocks from the hospital to the restaurant wiped me out.

I was terrified. They had no answers for me at the hospital and the medical treatment I received did nothing more than provide temporary relief, which caused me even more alarm.

My Australian friend Spencer and several other travelers were sitting at the long wooden table and all had become concerned about my deteriorating health. The proprietor's wife brought me a cup of plain tea. I tried to take a sip, but all I could do was rest my head upon the table, so sick did I feel.

"You must see Dr. Manna without delay!" the proprietor said, his voice stern and uncompromising.

I left the restaurant and followed the directions I had been given. Does he know what he's talking about? I could only hope. I felt so horrible I gave serious thought to going home and having an ambulance waiting for me at the airport in New York when I arrived. But making the trip would have been impossible. I was too sick, which scared me even more, to be so sick and ten thousand miles from home.

A one room stand alone shack served as Dr. Manna's home and office. I knocked on the door. A middle-aged man with a shaven head, wearing the robes of a Tibetan monk invited me inside. Jars containing herbal remedies took up much of the space in the tiny ramshackle house. Dr. Manna, a venerated Tibetan Buddhist monk and practitioner of Tibetan medicine took one look at me and said: "It's your liver, you're jaundiced. The whites of your eyes are yellow and so is your skin. You have infectious Hepatitis."

"What do I do now?" I asked, growing more distressed by the minute.

"Don't worry, I have the cure," he said.

Dr. Manna prepared two packets of herbal remedies. One packet contained tiny dried tea leaves. He said my friend at the restaurant would prepare the tea for me. Chewy dark brown balls about the size of peas filled the other packet. Dr. Manna prescribed time and dose, told me not to worry and sent me on my way.

I walked back to the restaurant. I told the restaurant owner what Dr. Manna had said and I showed him the remedies I had been given. His wife prepared a cup of Dr. Manna's tea for me. I forced myself to drink it and I swallowed the chewy pea sized balls before returning to my room.

"Hey, did you hear about the American guy? He's got Hepatitis," a booming voice in the hallway outside of my room said to whoever else was out there with him as I lie in my sleeping bag unable to move. The voice was that of another American guy, the annoying big-mouth who walked around in a full length white robe and made a point of letting everyone know he attended the Buddhist University in Bangkok. But I felt too sick to allow him to irritate me, as he had done from the moment I laid eyes on him.

I hauled myself back to the restaurant in the evening. I swallowed my chewy little tar balls and drank my medicinal tea, so caringly prepared for me by the proprietor's sweet Nepali wife.

I couldn't sleep. I lie in my sleeping bag moving in and out of a restless delirium all night. How screwed up is this? I need serious medical attention and I'm not getting it. Instead, I'm drinking tea and taking little brown tar balls prescribed to me by a Tibetan monk. How am I supposed to get better? Fear, panic, and hopelessness swept over me.

In the morning I lumbered back to the restaurant. As usual, I found my Aussie friend Spencer sitting at the long wooden table.

"You should come with me to the beach in Malaysia. I'm leaving in a week. The sun and surf will do you good," Spencer said.

"Sounds great," I replied, "but right now I can barely walk."

"Don't worry. You'll be healthy by then. The Tibetans know what they're doing," Spencer said, giving me support and reassurance.

Once again I swallowed my tiny tar balls and drank my tea. On the way back to my room I stopped in to see Dr. Manna.

I walked into Dr. Manna's house, seated myself, and with tears in my eyes I told him how horrible I felt and of the frightening weakness I experienced throughout my body and the awful putrid tasting belches I continued having. Luckily, the excruciating stomach cramps had decreased to a tolerable level and remained so following the horrendous enema ordeal at the hospital.

"Three days, you must give the regimen three complete days," the mysterious monk said.

"As bad as I feel right now," I responded, "how is it possible I'm going to be fine in only two more days?"

"You'll see," Dr. Manna said with a fatherly smile and the light of the Buddha's compassion in his eyes.

I walked out of Dr. Manna's house. Desperate thoughts rolled through my mind: My life is in this guy's hands. He wouldn't steer me wrong. The guy's entire purpose on Earth is the personification of truth and compassion. I have to believe him.

Another two days passed. I still felt horrible. Engulfed in gloom, I once again drug myself over to the restaurant. In route, severe stomach cramps struck with an urgency requiring immediate action. I had no choice but to slip into an alley behind a building and in broad daylight I put myself in a full squatting position in full view of anyone who may have been passing by. I was thankful no one saw me during my moments of exposure, although I doubt it would have mattered. Nature takes on a whole new meaning in this part of the world.

Upon experiencing one massive explosion, of which I will give no further detail, other than to say my full recovery began the instant the explosion occurred, precisely three days after my first dose of Tibetan medicine, exactly as the mysterious Dr. Manna had predicted. A miracle had

## Chapter Eleven

taken place. I had been cured of Hepatitis-A in only three days, an illness routinely requiring weeks of treatment and oftentimes hospitalization in the Western world.

I decided to take Spencer up on his suggestion and travel to Southeast Asia with him. I would leave Nepal without seeing the breathtaking snow capped Himalayan peaks, the very reason I came to the Himalayan Kingdom. A difficult decision, and I cannot express how disappointing, but I couldn't deny my Aussie friend's advice when he said the tropical sunshine and the salty ocean air would provide the best environment to complete my recovery and regain my full strength in as little time as possible.

I tried to look at the positive side of the experience and what I had learned. I had developed a life threatening illness ten thousand miles from home and there's no telling how it would have turned out had it not been for the compassion of strangers and one Tibetan monk's wondrous ancient herbal remedies. I had truly received a gift.

I came so close to experiencing majestic views of the snow capped Himalayan peaks of the Annapurna range. Only a day's bus ride from Katmandu. But what I received instead, albeit through grave misfortune, could in many respects be said to have been of greater value, and I will be the first to admit I say this with more than a fair degree of self-pitying regret. But I knew how lucky I had been, and the mountains will still be there if I ever make it back.

Spencer and I shared a taxi from the airport into Bangkok with two young American guys who had come to Bangkok for the sole purpose of engaging in Thailand's legal sex industry. Spencer had been to Bangkok several times. He knew where the low budget hotels were and directed the taxi driver to the one he preferred.

We pulled up to the entrance. A group of young Thai women were standing around in front. More were in the lobby.

Even the cheapest hotels in Bangkok were clean, modern, and westernized, equipped with real beds, real bathtubs, European toilets, and water at comfortable temperatures. I much preferred to room alone, but to cut costs, as Thailand is more expensive than India and Nepal, I agreed to share a room with Spencer, cutting the cost for each of us in half to around two dollars apiece.

A short time later the two American guys with whom we shared the taxi came bursting into our room with an excitement bordering on madness. They couldn't wait to tell us what had happened. Within an hour of arriving in Bangkok they had both been serviced by the same prostitute for what amounted to a couple of dollars between the two of them.

A knock came to our door. "It's her," one of the American guys said, and sure enough, into our room strolled the prostitute. She was small and thin, and older than the other girls I had seen hanging around in front of the hotel and in the lobby, all of whom were in their late teens and twenties. She could have been forty. And while the younger girls were delicate and pretty, she, on the other hand, was tough looking, her face reflecting the many years of street life she had lived. And while the others wore tight sexy mini-skirts, she wore funny baggy cotton pants coming down a little below her knees. I imagined they would all look like her in twenty years. The downward cycle can't be avoided. They're all stuck. They're all doomed. They have no way out.

She reached into her bag and pulled out a package of Thai sticks. Wow! I was taken aback. Of tremendous value in the states, Thai sticks contained powerful concentrations of THC and had become almost impossible to come

*Chapter Eleven*

by since the American military presence in Southeast Asia had ended.

The two American guys paid her for the Thai sticks and everyone except Spencer partook. Spencer and the American guys then decided to hit the streets of Bangkok. I stayed back. I was still recovering and the day of travel from Katmandu had been fatiguing for me. The prostitute also stayed back, with the intention, I assumed, of drumming up another customer. "I'm not interested," I told her, but she wouldn't leave.

Listening to her chattering away in her high pitched sing-song voice with her heavy Thai accent and awful broken English and staring at her face, which had begun to appear misshapen to me as the effects of the Thai stick reached its peak, filled me with anxiety and I began to feel as if I would go crazy. I began to have paranoid thoughts of her slitting my throat and stealing my stuff. Of course, if she slit my throat I wouldn't need my stuff anymore. I was desperate for her to go, but she kept hanging around, her mindless chatter pushing me closer and closer to the edge, when at last she gave up and left, and not a minute too soon, because I had reached my limit and I didn't know how much longer I could hold on.

Tropical sun beams burst through our window. Morning had arrived. Spencer and I headed out for breakfast, passing a group of girls in miniskirts and tight short-shorts hanging around in front of the hotel. Waves of temptation rippled through my imagination as I cast my gaze upon these curvaceous, sexy young Thai women. Thailand's sex industry made it so easy. But for the sake of my soul I thought it best to abstain.

The following morning Spencer and I boarded the train to Malaysia. What class we were traveling in I found impossible to determine because the seats were so uncomfortable I don't think they could even be classified.

Constructed of solid wood, they had no padding, were low to the floor, and were half the size of normal seats, as if they had been made for children.

We arrived in the Malaysian city of Penang after a twenty-four hour, seven hundred mile journey from Bangkok leaving me with a stiff neck because there had been no place to rest my head while I slept, and as every seasoned traveler knows, sleep's gonna take over, regardless of the position one's head is in.

From the train station we boarded a bus for the short ride to Batu Ferringhi on the Malaysian Coast a few miles outside of Penang. Living simple lives in huts along the shoreline, humble Chinese families inhabited the sleepy backwater fishing village. In time, Batu Ferringhi would grow into a popular seaside vacation spot with a host of fashionable resort hotels. But in the 1970s, Batu Ferringhi was still an isolated, lazy Southeast Asian village by the sea, well off the beaten path, its sole visitors the budget backpackers from the Western world.

The sun, the salt air, and delicious heaping platefuls of prawns over rice, a specialty prepared by the small food stall sitting a few steps from our hut, provided the perfect formula to complete my recovery. Push cart vendors sold a sweet and delicious white drink made of soy. I couldn't get enough of it. Good thing it only cost the equivalent of a nickel a glass.

Most of the travelers in the village were Australians and New Zealanders, a smaller number were Europeans, and three were American, myself included. One was a girl from California and the other a guy from New York City. The girl from California had made an unusual journey. Traveling alone, she crossed the Pacific, spending time in Tahiti and Samoa. I had never met anyone who had been in those two countries, nor would I again.

The New Yorker was an incessant talker and wrote long drawn out stream of consciousness narratives. I believe he

## Chapter Eleven

saw himself as the second coming of Jack Kerouac. He would read his works out loud to Spencer. This behavior annoyed me, as did his personality in general. Spencer, on the other hand, couldn't have been more impressed. I don't think he'd ever met anyone from New York before.

Spencer and I shared a hut. The bed consisted of a huge sheet of black rubber, an inch or so thick, sitting about two feet off the ground, stretched out and connected to four corner posts. I had by this point in my wandering life experienced a fair number of unusual and unique sleeping apparatus and arrangements, but this one took the cake. The few times I found myself forced to share sleeping space with another guy I hadn't been able to sleep well. But by staying on the edges, this area would prove spacious enough as to provide plenty of room between us.

The waters in Batu Ferringhi were cloudy, unlike the pristine waters of so many of the other Southeast Asian coastal areas. Tiny thatched fisherman sleeping huts dotted the shoreline.

The nation's theatres would often show English language movies. Malaysia had been under British rule through many generations and for much of the population English is spoken with the perfection of a native tongue.

The movie about the troubled life of Lenny Bruce, starring Dustin Hoffman, was playing in a theatre in Penang. The ground breaking comedian had been repeatedly harassed, arrested, and hauled off to jail on obscenity charges in the 1960s and every comedian who came after owes Lenny Bruce a debt of gratitude for the freedom of expression they now possess.

Spencer knew nothing of Lenny Bruce. The New Yorker, who considered himself an all knowing pundit on pop culture, couldn't bear the thought of our Aussie friend remaining uninformed on the subject. The three of us shall attend the cinema, it was thus decided.

We rode the bus into Penang. While walking from the bus stop to the movie theatre we came across an opium den located in a tin shanty in an alley. Malaysia has ultra strict anti-drug laws, foreigners beware, but their immigrant Chinese citizens had been given special permission to continue operating their opium dens. The double standard puzzled me. I could only assume the government didn't want to deal with untold numbers of old Chinese guys going cold turkey and getting sick all at the same time.

I had no interest in opium; otherwise, I would have tried it in India or Nepal. But how could I turn down the rare experience of smoking opium in a genuine Chinese opium den in Malaysia? There are some experiences one simply can't walk away from.

The New Yorker and I were on board but Spencer would have nothing to do with it. The proprietor, a wizened old Chinese man, toothless and frail, a few straggling white hairs remaining on his head, his ancient eyes and timeless face telling a thousand stories, had me position myself on my side on a hard wooden platform. He did the same, facing me on another wooden platform parallel to mine. Next, he extended to me the unusually long stem of a pipe reaching across the distance between us. In his hand he held the bowl, filled it with opium and lit up. I wondered why the stem should be so long, but I didn't ask because the proprietor and several of his aging cronies who were sitting around in opium stupors only spoke Chinese.

I expected pleasant feelings from the opium. Instead, I spent the remainder of the day suffering from an awful nagging nausea. The New Yorker did fine. Some get sick and some don't. For those that do, I heard the nausea stops as your body becomes accustomed to the drug. I didn't plan on finding out. But the priceless picture of our Chinese host forever etched and imprinted upon my brain as I stared into his ancient face while puffing from the strange long stemmed pipe he held in his hand made it all worthwhile, I have since convinced myself, despite the dreadful queasiness and the non-stop series of bizarre opium dreams disturbing my sleep all night.

Every so often the Malaysian authorities would raid the Chinese villages. The government, controlled by the indigenous Malays, didn't much care for the scruffy budget backpacking Western travelers, and the immigrant Chinese generating income by providing them with inexpensive shelter didn't sit well with the government either. On these raids, Malaysian authorities would take the Western travelers' passports and stamp the letters S-H-I-T in them, an acronym for suspected hippie in transit. Those with SHIT stamped in their passports would have twenty-four hours to get out of the country.

A substantial amount of time had passed since a raid occurred and rumors began circulating. Best not to take chances, I decided. I had been in Batu Ferringhi for over a week and it would soon be time to move on anyway. I packed up, bid farewell to my Aussie friend Spencer and checked into the cheapest hotel I could find in the Malaysian Peninsula's intriguing city of Penang. I shared a room with two strangers, an Australian girl and a guy from New Zealand. The three of us slept on one large wooden platform covered with a straw mat. A ceiling fan spun overhead. The girl slept in the middle. I couldn't do it any other way. I imagine the New Zealand guy felt the same as I did.

In the morning I boarded the train to Bangkok. The same train with the tiny wooden seats. My neck would be spared this time, though, because I wasn't going all the way back just yet. I disembarked at the Malaysia-Thailand border. From there I rode a bus to the shores of Phuket, Southern Thailand's tropical paradise. Pristine ocean waters sparkling in heavenly hues of turquoise and crimson, dazzling coral reefs, breathtaking sunsets, and undreamed of palm fringed shorelines welcomed me with unrivaled beauty.

Southern Thailand had yet to become the popular international vacation resort it would over time grow into, and Phuket, in the 1970s, was still an isolated Southeast Asian beach destination.

I shared a hut with three Australians, two girls and a guy named Albert. The hut had one double bed and all four of us slept in it with the two girls in the middle. I could barely budge. It's a wonder I didn't fall out of bed. A few dollars and a hearty dose of austerity went a long way in Phuket, affording me a healthy measure of time to linger and enjoy the incomparable majestic coastal splendor of Southern Thailand.

When the time came to return to Bangkok I choose to travel the remaining distance by bus. In route the bus made a dinner stop. I ordered squid. I found it delectable. I had never eaten squid before, nor have I eaten it since.

I had been back in Bangkok for two days when Albert appeared at my door. Before leaving Phuket I had given him the name of the hotel where I planned to stay. To save money, the two of us moved into a double room together. But Albert was no Spencer and it didn't take long to realize what a big mistake I had made.

Round about three in the morning, in the deepest part of my sleep, I awoke to a most disturbing sight. Albert had brought a prostitute back to the room. The noise of the squeaking bed woke me up. He was really going to town on her, and she, spread out like a wet washrag, obviously couldn't wait for it to end. I lay my head back down on the pillow and fell asleep for the remainder of the night.

## Chapter Eleven

Images of the sight I had seen in the middle of the night began flooding my mind when I awoke in the morning. Needless to say, these were not visions I wished to carry in my head.

I walked into the bathroom and found myself confronted by another disturbing sight. The sex worker had cleaned herself with my towel, which now lie on the floor, crumpled and soaked. I wouldn't touch the damn thing. I wouldn't even kick it to the side with my shoe on. I left it right where I found it. Words cannot describe how foul and offensive I found the entire episode. I told Albert his prostitute ruined my towel.

"Sorry," is all he could say. I believe he should have at least offered to buy me a new towel.

I would spend the better part of the morning on a towel hunting expedition. Upon finding and purchasing a satisfactory replacement I walked to the bus station and booked a seat on a bus leaving the following morning for the city of Chang Mai in Northern Thailand. If Albert wanted to spend money on a prostitute, he had the right. But his degenerate behavior not only forced me to squander my precious time looking for a new towel, it also cost me money, and as a final consequence to Albert's decadent deed, I could not break out of a pissed-off state of mind until the following day. On my final night rooming with Albert I made sure my new towel was nowhere to be found by anyone but me.

The quintessential allure of the Orient is perfectly embodied in the Thai city of Chang Mai. The ancient walled city is home to over three hundred Buddhist temples, all of which present superb examples of the exquisite ancient Thai temple design, a distinctive architectural style of unequaled splendor, dating back to the thirteenth and fourteenth centuries. Gold plated shrines to the Buddha, places of pilgrimage, and home to countless Buddhist monks clad in flowing robes of orange.

## An Extraordinary Tale of Travel

In the picturesque Thai town of Chang Mai I found accommodation in a lovely family run lodge. Lush and secluded grounds gave sanctuary to a delightful one-story wooden framed villa. The spotless modern rooms ran in a connecting circle around a beautiful open air wooden porch where travelers gathered and socialized. Within walking distance one found colorful outdoor markets and outstanding restaurants, authentic Thai of course. Pushcart vendors sold my favorite Thai snack, sticky rice with mango, served on banana leaves.

While in Chang Mai I booked a guided tour of the hill tribe country. The hill tribes migrated from Southern China into Thailand, Laos, Burma, and Vietnam countless generations ago and each tribe has maintained its original tribal culture, religion, dress, and language. I would venture to say no other place on the planet have I seen such eye catching charm filled faces as I would see among the hill tribes of Northern Thailand.

A young Thai dude driving a jeep came for me at dawn. He would also serve as our guide. Four Australians comprised the remainder of our group. We shot out of Chang Mai, and through captivating scenes of jungle villages, houses on stilts, and women working in rice paddies wearing conical hats, we journeyed, until we arrived on the banks of a jungle river in the far reaches of Northern Thailand. Next, we boarded a small boat transporting us to another landing dock several hours up river. Upon reaching our final destination we disembarked and spent the next three days dwelling among the hill tribes of Northern Thailand, hiking from village to village. The tribal women prepared our meals for us and we camped in a different village every night.

At times I found remarkable similarities to the American Indians of the old American West reflected in the hill tribes' appearance and village architecture. To my

## Chapter Eleven

disappointment, my Aussie companions showed no interest and I wished there had been at least one other American in the group with whom I could have shared my startling observation.

The hill tribe adventure came to an end. We returned to Chang Mai, and several days later I was back in Bangkok booking my return flight to India.

I would visit one more Southeast Asian nation before returning to India. The Thai Air flight from Bangkok to Calcutta offered a seven day stopover in the nation of Burma, the maximum amount of time the reclusive nation, now known as Myanmar, allowed visitors to stay.

The flight from Bangkok to neighboring Rangoon, capital of Burma, took no time at all. A bus waiting at the airport carried the Western travelers to a hostel in Rangoon located in an abandoned colonial government building.

Australians and New Zealanders comprised the majority of Western world travelers I would meet in Southeast Asia, and I must say, a nicer, friendlier, more likeable group of people I had yet to come across, including Albert, the towel episode notwithstanding.

Narrow wooden platforms minus mattresses sitting bumper to bumper filled with low budget travelers packed one enormous room on the first floor of the aging colonial structure. I sold the bottle of Johnnie Walker Black Label and the carton of Marlboro cigarettes I had purchased in the duty free shop in Thailand for a reasonable profit, same as I had done in New Delhi.

Feelings of guilt over my actions would eventually ensue, for two reasons: First, the detrimental effect these two substances have on one's overall well being, and second, the unworthy position I had put myself in by selling an intoxicant for profit in one of Buddhism's most hallowed lands, although I would not become aware of Burma's sacred history until my second journey to India.

A fascinating antique car show of British automobiles rolled along the streets of the Burmese capital. Time seemed to have stood still in Burma since the end of British colonial rule nearly thirty years earlier. And as their Indian neighbors had done, the Burmese too had become experts at keeping anything on wheels functioning decades beyond any logical expectation.

The exquisite three hundred twenty-five foot tall gold plated Shwedagon Pagoda dominates the Rangoon skyline. The towering gilded Pagoda, said to contain eight strands of the Buddha's hair, is the largest and most sacred of the estimated four thousand stupas in the land. The Shwedagon Pagoda is also believed to be the oldest Buddhist Stupa in the world.

The Burmese people couldn't have been more gracious and welcoming. And the Queen's English is widely spoken throughout the nation as Burma too had been a British outpost for over a century.

Aboard an antique steam engine locomotive I traveled north to the city of Mandalay, Burma's ancient royal capital. Small Burmese villages and scenic Southeast Asian jungle landscapes rolled past as I sat on a hard wooden bench for the all day journey to Mandalay.

The jade mines of Burma serve as a major source of imperial jade, the most valued form of the prized stone in the world. In Mandalay, a major trading center for jade, many travelers were buying quantities of imperial jade to sell back home. But as seemed to repeatedly be the case for me when such opportunities arose, I would have no money to invest.

There is a great deal to see in this historic nation, but a seven day visa doesn't give one much time to veer off the beaten path. Although I believe simply setting foot in

## Chapter Eleven

the country of Burma is in and of itself a journey far and wide off anybody's beaten path, and I will forever thank the traveling Gods for giving me the rare and unforeseen opportunity, if only in the tiniest amount, to experience the beautiful, enigmatic, ancient land of Burma.

The Thai Air flight from Rangoon carried me to the Indian city of Calcutta. I walked out of Calcutta's airport and hopped into a taxi, once again putting myself at the mercy of an Indian taxi driver.

"I take you to good hotel," the driver said.

"Cheap hotel," I instructed him.

"Yes, yes, good, good, cheap," He responded.

I would make my stay in Calcutta brief. I wished to spend as much time as possible in the small Himalayan village of Rishikesh before my four month round trip air fare expired in one month.

To break up the journey from Calcutta to New Delhi, I would make a quick stop in Varanasi. Rarely would I visit a place more than once. In India, this would change.

Ready to ride the rails of India once again, I hurried down the crowded platform on the day of my departure, passing mighty rows of forged steel, rolling out again, and again, and again on never-ending journeys to the far corners of the sub-continent.

I located my train car and climbed aboard. The whistles blew, steam hissed, and black smoke poured into the Calcutta sky. I settled back with cup of chai in hand, the following thoughts of the great Indian railroad running through my mind: How do these old steam engines keep going? Their weary locomotive souls should be put to rest, for eternity, and much deservedly so, after the many decades of service they have put in, all the hard travelling they have done, and all the incredible history they have witnessed, through the days of the Raj to independence and beyond.

India is the most alien place imaginable to a person born in the Western world, and yet in India I felt more at one with myself than I ever had at any time or place in my life. What kind of an odd individual am I? One who loves being a foreigner. One who loves being a stranger in a strange land. And the more unfamiliar my surroundings, the better I felt. An uncanny phenomenon is the only way to describe how at home I felt from the moment I set foot in this land.

In route to Rishikesh one must pass through the sacred city of Hardwar, where the Ganges River makes its initial descent out from the mountains, sending its precious waters flowing across the vast plains of Northern India.

I spent one night in New Delhi and boarded the train to Hardwar in the morning.

Several hours into the all day journey from New Delhi to Hardwar a young Indian fellow by the name of Ashok took a seat on the bench opposite mine. He began bombarding me with questions. He wanted to know everything about me. I had seen other Western travelers brush off the curious and not respond. This would appear rude, but also perfectly understandable. These impromptu street interviews are capable of causing severe tiring of one's mind as question after question is hurled one's way. But I always seemed to get pulled in. Ashok invited me to have dinner with him when we arrived in Hardwar. He also said he would like to arrange for me to spend the night in the Sikh temple. I knew he meant well, extending hospitality to a guest in his country, but truth be told, I didn't feel like spending one minute with this guy, on the train or off, so intense, wired up, and long winded was he. Nevertheless, I agreed.

*Chapter Eleven*

The train pulled into the city of Hardwar. We disembarked, exited out of Hardwar station and proceeded to walk across the main thoroughfare.

Ashok, reckless and aggressive in his movement through traffic, cut right in front of a motor scooter. I followed a few feet behind. The driver scarcely grazed him from a near standstill as he desperately tried to veer out of his way. I will never forget what happened next. Ashok became enraged and began yelling. The scooter driver attempted to apologize, but Ashok went nuts, shoved the guy off his scooter onto the ground and proceeded to kick him without pause. He must have kicked him at least a dozen times, in his back, front, head, legs, everywhere as the poor fellow doubled up on the ground in a fetal position with his hands covering his face trying to shield himself against this crazy guy's vicious assault. I could do nothing more than stand in place, stunned and in utter disbelief. And when satisfied with the beating he had unleashed upon this unfortunate soul, a fellow who didn't deserve any of it, Ashok finished crossing the street with an air of calm and casualness I found astonishing.

We seated ourselves in Ashok's favorite restaurant and a marvelous feast soon sat before me. Delicious servings of aloo gobi, malai kofta, vegetable korma, saffron rice, and dal, with mouth-watering hot and fresh nann to wrap everything up in and lip smacking mango lassi to wash it down. And Ashok paid for it all.

We finished our meal and headed over to the small Sikh temple where I would spend the night as Ashok had insisted upon. Along the way I talked to God. I don't do it often, but I needed to ask him to please not let anything else bizarre happen before this day ends, because once again I refused to listen to my own better judgment and allowed myself to get mixed up with a nutcase instead.

Upon entering the temple, a small, thin, humble, devout aged Sikh with a heavy white beard who spoke not a word of English greeted us. He was clad in baggy white cotton pajama pants and a long white kurta. He wore a blue turban on his head and he had a miniature sword strapped across his chest. The Kirpan, a decorative ceremonial sword or dagger represents a Sikh's commitment to do battle against the forces of evil and injustice.

I found myself captivated by the old Sikh. He radiated an inner peace I believe to have been in no small way directly related to the ornamental symbolic weapon he so proudly displayed. Here in front of me stood a man who knew exactly what he lived for. I envied that. A spiritual warrior for Guru Nanak is the only purpose his life could ever have. The devout disciple agreed to allow me to take refuge for one night in the holy shrine of India's Sikh religion.

Ever so respectful, the old Sikh led me to my sleeping quarters, a small empty room with concrete walls and cement floor. Next, he showed me the location of the squatter and handed me a bucket in case I wished to take a bath. As much as I needed a good scrubbing I decided to let it go until I could check into a hotel where I could get a freezing shower instead of a freezing bucket bath.

In the morning I gave thanks to my kind and compassionate host for the honor he had bestowed upon me by allowing a stranger to spend the night in the sacred house of the righteous fifteenth century sage Guru Nanak.

"Namaste," I said with hands folded in prayer position, giving a slight bow.

In humble response the old Sikh reciprocated. "Namaste," he said with hands folded in prayer position and a slight bow as we bid each other farewell.

I checked into a hotel, took that much needed freezing shower and proceeded to spend the day exploring the North Indian town of Hardwar. Both Hardwar and Rishikesh are hallowed places of pilgrimage along the Ganges River.

## Chapter Eleven

In Hardwar, at the end of each day, multitudes of Hindus gather to participate in the Ganga Aarti ceremony on the Ganges River at the spot where Lord Vishnu is believed to have left his footprint. Prayers and offerings are made and what a miraculous sight it is watching a parade of floating glowing flower decorated miniature oil lamps light up the night as darkness descends upon the holy river.

Tumbling down from the icy Himalayan peaks of the Gangotri Glacier, the Ganges springs forth, its hallowed waters soon reaching the serene village of Rishikesh, the river's final Himalayan sanctuary before the sacred stream that fell from heaven begins its journey to the sea, a journey of fifteen hundred miles, across India and Bangladesh, where she at long last takes her own well deserved refuge, first in the Bay of Bengal, prelude to her final resting place in the infinite waters of the Indian Ocean.

The near empty train from Hardwar to Rishikesh ran a slow and lazy country mile, taking no more than an hour, the usual teeming commotion one is accustomed to when riding the rails of India strikingly absent.

A pleasing aura of tranquility welcomed me as I strolled out of Rishikesh station. Fresh mountain waters flowed with smooth and steady currents. Ashrams and temples dotted the green hills on each side of the river. The essence of spiritual India emanated throughout the small village resting in the foothills of the Himalayas.

I continued walking along the gravel strewn river road. Refreshingly absent were the multitudes of humanity so often found packing the streets of India.

One could reach all points in Rishikesh on foot, presenting an abundance of opportunities for vigorous and enjoyable walks and jungle hikes offering scenic river views. And in Rishikesh one could sit in solitude on a rock on the banks of the Ganges and meditate with no one else in sight, surrounded by the peaceful sounds of Himalayan waters rushing past.

I wondered how one crossed over to the other side. The answer came when I saw a small open boat, public transportation freely provided by the municipality, carrying people back and forth across the Ganges. And further up the road one finds the Lakshman Jhula iron rope suspension bridge, an astonishing feat of construction designed for foot traffic only. Prince Lakshman, as legend has it, crossed the river on an ancient bridge made of jute rope, thus, the present day bridge is named after him. Lakshman was the brother of the avatar Lord Rama.

Passed down without change for thousands of years, the rich multi-layered tales of the Gods and Goddesses of Hindu mythology symbolize all aspects, descriptions, and clarifications of the mystery of creation and existence, woven with a depth and intricacy of moral messages, wisdom, and complex cosmic explanations providing a moral compass and a spiritual foundation upon which Indian culture and civilization has been built. In India, the religion and the culture are one, they are inseparable, and it is this fact, be it mythical or not, that makes India the most colorful, mysterious, mystical, spiritual, and unique place on Earth.

Sadhus abound in Rishikesh, clad in flowing robes of saffron color. Every where one looked in the Himalayan village one saw a sadhu. A number of them are yogis, as Rishikesh is the yoga capital of the world, and many hold the title of swami, a title given out quite liberally in Rishikesh, I would discover.

An aged, white bearded sadhu stood on the path. He approached as I walked past. In his outstretched hand he held a chillum. "Ganga," he said, inquiring if I might have some ganga in my possession and if so would I please be willing to put some of it in his chillum.

*Chapter Eleven*

In the Western world the majority would consider these dudes bums. In India, they're holy men, and today just happened to be this holy man's lucky day. I had once again made a purchase in the government shop in Varanasi. I'm not sure why. The best reason I can give is because I could. It blew my mind to purchase marijuana legally in the days when legalization in America was unthinkable.

Allowing myself to fall into the old sadhu's orbit, I followed him to a nearby spot where we sat together on a large rock in a field filled with impoverished people living in tiny tents.

I reached into my backpack, pulled out the ganga wrapped in newspaper and handed the small package to my new friend. He lit up, took a strong draw off the chillum and handed it to me. On a Himalayan rock on the banks of the Ganges River I sat with the old sadhu passing the chillum back and forth. When sharing with others smoking from a chillum is best because no one's lips touch the mouthpiece. As a result of the special way one shapes one's hands around the chillum, one's lips touch the tiny opening one makes with one's own hands instead.

As I prepared to move on I decided to give away my entire stash to the old sadhu. He became overwhelmed with happiness. He couldn't stop smiling and bowing with hands in prayer position.

"Namaste," I said with my hands also in prayer position and a slight bow.

"Namaste," he replied, his hands remaining in prayer position and still bowing for several minutes after I walked away, so humbled and filled with gratitude was he.

I found affordable accommodation in a compound comprised of one small two-story guesthouse, several concrete huts, and a courtyard where travelers gathered and socialized. Showers and squatters were outside. The list of lodgers included budget backpackers from a variety of Western nations. A well liked middle-aged Indian man known as Swami owned the property. On a curious note, nothing indicated he was anything other than a businessman, but everyone called him Swami, nonetheless. Swami's guesthouse ranked among the more popular places to stay in Rishikesh. Lucky for me, one of the small concrete huts had recently been vacated.

Out of morbid curiosity, I would stroll past the Rishikesh leper colony several times during my stay. The miserable souls with noses, fingers, and toes eaten away by this dreadful disease would stand outside of their decrepit compound and stare at me as I walked past. But they weren't begging. They had no need. These lepers had fallen under the care of an international charity organization. They were the lucky ones.

I came across a sadhu sitting cross-legged on a bed of nails. This holy man had chosen extreme penance as his path to achieving enlightenment. He motioned for me to come close. He asked if I had a cigarette. Surprised by his request, I walked into the village, purchased several cigarettes from a street vendor, walked back to where he sat on his bed of nails and handed him the cigarettes.

Murals of the Gods and Goddesses and of their mystical dwelling places in the heavenly realms, in vibrant hue and brilliant animation, adorned the exterior walls of Hindu temples. Sacred cows lounged on temple steps.

I spent my days hiking along the river and visiting ashrams and temples on both sides of the Ganges. At times I would ride the small open boat, packed at each crossing with ancient holy men clad in robed garments of flowing cloth. At other times I would traverse the river by way of the Lakshman Jhula suspension bridge, a nerve racking experience at first, but it would soon gain my confidence. Offering spectacular views of the river and of the enchanting Himalayan village below, this most remarkable of foot

## Chapter Eleven

bridges spans four hundred and fifty feet with only two supports, one at each end, and towers an intimidating seventy feet above the Ganges.

It is imperative to note one more important fact about Rishikesh. And although this vital historical event is not part of ancient history, overlooking it would, nonetheless, be utter sacrilege of the highest order and downright unforgiveable, for this was an occasion of the greatest magnitude. Rishikesh is where John, Paul, George, and Ringo stayed as guests of Maharishi Mahesh Yogi, famous guru of transcendental meditation, when the Beatles made their legendary pilgrimage to India in the landmark year of 1968.

Such an impression did hearing the Beatles for the very first time make upon me in 1963 at the age of fifteen that for the remainder of my life I would have a precise and vivid picture permanently imprinted upon my brain of where I was and what I was doing in the exact moment the song, "I Want to Hold Your Hand," their first hit in America, came on the air.

Little could I have imagined what my ears were about to witness. A seismic blast of inconceivable historic consequence suddenly came exploding through my trusty little transistor radio, which I always kept by my side, tuned to WCAO, 60 on the AM dial, the only station in Baltimore that played Rock & Roll music. I felt as if I had been hit in the head by a speeding locomotive. Everyone was talking about it in school the next day. They had heard it too, and no one had ever heard anything like it. From that moment forward, everything changed. Nothing would ever be the same again.

My four month excursion fare neared expiration. I would spend my final days in India immersing my mind and tiring out my feet in the natural beauty and ethereal mystique of the Himalayan village of Rishikesh.

## An Extraordinary Tale of Travel

I sat in the Air India Airline office in New Delhi booking my ticket home when the words Hare Krishna rang in my ear. I turned to my right, and to my unimaginable utmost astonishment I saw my second grade friend Stewart, clad in the saffron robes of a Hindu monk, one thick tuft of hair sprouting from the back of his clean shaven head.

"Hare Krishna," I said in stunned reply, taking a moment to get my bearings straight. I had run into my childhood friend on the other side of the planet and I was blown away.

Stewart had followed our other grade school friend Marty into the Hare Krishna movement. The number of childhood friends from our neighborhood in Baltimore to surrender their lives to the blue skinned God of ancient India now totaled five.

Stewart's annual pilgrimage to the sacred sites where Lord Krishna took birth and spent his childhood had come to an end and he too was booking his flight home. We wrapped up our business in the airline office and walked back out to the streets of New Delhi. Several of Stewart's saffron robed bald headed companions stood outside waiting for him.

Stewart and I agreed to meet in front of the Air India airline office on the day of our departure. From there we would share a taxi to the airport.

Visibly irritated, shaking his head in blunt disapproval, the ticket attendant spoke harshly to Stewart as we boarded the plane.

"You are American! You are not Indian! Why do you dress like this?" he yelled in resounding annoyance.

"Vaishnava! I'm a Vaishnava!" Stewart fired back, explaining his status as a member of the Vaishnava sect, a much venerated tradition in India.

## Chapter Eleven

Stewart's unadulterated embrace and surrender to the customs, worship, and dress of one of India's oldest religious traditions did not impress the airline attendant in the least bit.

"Why would an American want to become a Vaishnava?" he blurted out, targeting Stewart with one more verbal attack as we handed him our boarding passes and disappeared from his view.

Taking refuge in Lord Krishna after having been so rudely insulted and disrespected, Stewart began chanting the Hare Krishna Mantra in a whisper to himself as we walked down the aisle to our seats, repeating God's names as much and as fast as he could.

The long flight home made its routine stops in Kuwait, Frankfurt, and London. I looked over at my childhood friend sitting next to me. Could it get any more surreal than this? And I couldn't help but wonder, in uneasy contemplation, if our encounter wasn't in fact a karmic signal telling me I should join the International Society for Krishna Consciousness after all. I mean, what were the odds? A billion to one, I would say. Uncertainty had me in its clutches once again.

Stewardesses clad in beautiful Indian saris handed out headphones for a movie about to begin as we coasted over the Atlantic on the final leg of the journey. Stewart didn't take a set, but I did.

I sat back with the large bar of Swiss chocolate I had purchased in the duty free shop in London and watched a Western starring John Wayne as a terminally ill aging gunman in the final days of his life and Lauren Bacall as a widow and owner of a rooming house where the gunman had come to die. A young Ron Howard, of Opie and Happy Day's fame, played Lauren Bacall's son. The movie was called the Shootist and I enjoyed it, my bar of Swiss chocolate making it all the more better.

Stewart shot me a hardnosed look of critical displeasure. "Any activity other than serving Krishna is meaningless, mindless, and a complete waste of time. Come to the temple with me and get out of the material world," he said.

Stewart loved having his boyhood friends with him in Krishna land and he would have been thrilled to have had me there too.

The jumbo jet reached its final destination and touched down on American soil.

I must admit I envied them for the camaraderie of communal life they experienced on a daily basis and for the peace of mind their strong religious convictions had brought them, while my mind remained in a perpetual state of restlessness and uncertainty. But I also knew I couldn't live the life of a devotee.

Stewart made one more attempt to persuade me before we parted ways, and I once again declined, feeling the pressure as I always did when declining my boyhood friends' sincere efforts to bring me along with them to Krishna Consciousness and save their childhood buddy's wayward soul.

Kate gave me the same room I had the previous season in the Mt. Vernon rooming house. My cooking supplies and my bicycle had been safely stored away courtesy of the kind owners of the Surf and Sands Motel. I was all set for another summer at the beach.

When I came off the road, the people I met, and the many intense, enlightening, emotional moments I experienced ceased to exist, except in a place I could only revisit in my mind.

When I tried talking to my co-workers at the restaurant about what I had done over the winter, I may as well have been telling them I had gone to Mars and back.

## Chapter Eleven

In an instant, my world shrank from a world of exotic faraway places and the company of vagabonds, rucksack warriors, and people seeking answers to life's questions to a world where all anyone seemed interested in was what bars they were going to spend their time in after work and how drunk they were going to get.

But I would be fine just the same, living in my little room by the sea, saving every penny so I could get back on the road, for only on the road did I feel as if I had found myself in this world, moving from one unfamiliar place to another, with a backpack on my back.

## Chapter Twelve
# OVERLAND TO INDIA

The time to visit London had at long last arrived. I had wanted to visit England on my first trip to Europe, but the Icelandic Airways one hundred dollar one-way flight to Luxembourg had been too good of a deal to pass up. Since then a new budget airline had come into existence offering flights between New York and London comparable in price to the Icelandic Airways flight to Luxembourg, and making it even more affordable was an invitation of a place to stay from an Australian couple I had met on my first trip to Asia.

Aaron and Lois had taken up residence in a run-down rooming house in London. They had both secured employment and planned to stay in London for a year, saving their money so they too could get back on the road.

A sign in the window of a small travel office caught my eye as I strolled along a busy British boulevard on my third day in London, still looking for the cheapest way in God's creation to cross the English Channel and get to France. I ventured inside and for the bargain price of only thirty-five dollars I booked passage on a bus traveling all the way from London to Thessaloniki in Northern Greece, from where I would once again catch the train to Istanbul.

I roamed the streets of London every day until dusk, observing life in the Kingdom of the English. On my final day in London I arrived back at Aaron and Lois's rooming house past midnight. My hosts wondered where I had been so far into the night.

"You'll never believe what happened to me. It's the most incredible stroke of luck I've ever had," I said.

I proceeded to tell them about the beautiful French girl attending university in London. She approached me as I walked out of the metro station. We hung out awhile, sat in a park and talked, and she invited me home, sneaking me into her room with caution because the rooming house rules didn't allow her to have guests and she wouldn't let me stay the night for fear her landlord would see me leaving in the morning.

I crawled inside of my sleeping bag on the floor at the foot of Aaron and Lois's conjugal bed and drifted off to sleep, hopelessly wishing I could have met the French girl on my first day in London instead of my last.

My day of departure arrived. I packed up, bid Aaron and Lois a grateful farewell and headed for the metro, the subway in America, also known to the British as the tube. I took a seat opposite a group of punks. Punk was huge in England at the time. They were in their late teens, dressed head to foot in black, piercings, garish makeup, pink and purple colored hair. So serious were they in whatever it was they were making their big statement about.

A thought crossed my mind: Perhaps we're not so different after all. Although I'm sure they would have begged to differ, seeing me in my flannel shirt, blue jeans, and tennis shoes. But alienation was no stranger to me either. I just didn't wear it.

## Chapter Twelve

I arrived at my station, stepped off the tube, walked out of the underground and made my way to the journey's departure point, the same travel office where I had booked my ticket. An Italian company ran the operation and three Italian guys shared the driving, making regular runs from Athens to London and back. I peeked inside of the bus parked on the street in front of the travel office. An uncomfortable rattletrap vintage 1950s with hard non-reclining seats, but the price couldn't be beat and I had ridden worse, just not for three days straight.

Backpacks were placed in the luggage compartment and the passengers piled on board, filling every seat. The American girl whom I had been talking to in the waiting room motioned for me to sit beside her. Marla was traveling to Athens, from where she would catch a boat to the Greek Islands. I imagined most of the passengers on this bus had similar plans.

We rolled out of London and cruised through the English countryside, to the town of Dover, where a ferryboat taking us from the white cliffs of Dover to the coast of France awaited our arrival.

We reached our destination and boarded the ferry. Darkness had fallen. Marla and I took seats on a wooden bench on the lower deck. The horns sounded and the huge boat drifted out to sea.

I began to feel bad in my stomach. Marla suggested we leave the enclosed area and go to the upper deck.

"The fresh ocean breeze will help," she said.

But for me it was already too late as I grabbed my vomit bag and joined the chorus of seasick passengers. I made several attempts to get up and go with her, but I found it impossible. I couldn't move. I was caught in the nightmarish throes of seasick hell and all I could do was vomit.

Up and down, back and forth, side to side, the ferryboat bounced like a helpless toy upon the rough waters of the

English Channel. I couldn't stand it anymore. I wanted to die. I began talking to God.

"Please God, end this misery," I pleaded. Had God offered to beam me back to Baltimore and cancel my trip, I would have said go ahead. I would have done anything to make the vomiting stop.

The chorus continued, and I was too sick to get away from the gruesome sounds of scores of people vomiting together, which only made me vomit more. I don't recall how long the hellish journey lasted, but the torturous ordeal stopped the minute we docked in the French port of Calais. Marla came down from the upper deck to retrieve me and we walked back to the bus together.

Our bus rolled off the ferryboat, passengers returned to their seats and we traveled into the night. Marla and I slept taking turns resting our heads upon each other's shoulders until a voice awakened us in the early light of dawn.

"One hour," the driver hollered as a busload of bleary-eyed passengers piled out to a boulevard in Paris.

Marla and I sat at a table for two at a sidewalk café on a crisp autumn morning in Paris, enjoying croissants for breakfast and drinking bottles of sparkling water. An hour in Paris, what a tease, but this trip wasn't about Paris or Venice or Rome. This trip was about traveling, by land, from London to New Delhi.

We traveled all day through the beautiful French countryside and across the Italian border. The passengers had begun showing signs of restlessness on the second day of the journey and a bit of drama began to unfold. The American girl sitting opposite us had been rude to Marla. Marla said she was jealous. She may have been right, but I thought perhaps twenty-four hours on the bus had gotten to her and we still had another two days to go. And the Australian girl, whining and crying over missing her children whom she had left in the care of her mother back

## Chapter Twelve

home in Australia while she ran all over the world. She and one of the Italian drivers had begun passionately kissing, their public display of affection so intense as to cause embarrassment among the passengers sitting closest to them. And the American couple, also on their way to India, as I was, but not sure what to do after finding out she was pregnant. Everyone on the bus tried to convince them to go home. I agreed. Having already been to India, knowing the conditions they would be facing, and thinking perhaps I should throw my two cents worth in as well, I told them India was no place for a pregnant tourist.

They resisted all advice at first, but in the end they decided to catch a flight home from Athens, disappointed, I'm sure, to have been forced to cancel their adventure of a lifetime.

We cruised across Northern Italy, into the hours of darkness, stopping at two o'clock in the morning in front of the train station in the Italian town of Bologna. Marla went inside of the train station and stretched out on the floor, keeping her head upright and off the ground by using her side bag as a pillow. I decided to walk around a bit, enjoying the refreshing night air, when I came upon a scene I will never forget. A man and a woman were having sex standing up against a wall.

I stood and watched from a short distance. I have never been one to engage in perverted behavior, but at this moment I couldn't help myself; it's not a sight one comes across every day. The road, as it has so much throughout my traveling years, chose once again to teach me something new about myself; namely, if you're gonna do it on the sidewalk and I just happen to come strolling along, then for sure, buddy, right or wrong, perverted or not, you're gonna have an audience. And then I joined Marla on the train station floor, using my side bag as a pillow.

At dawn our Italian drivers ushered everyone back onto the bus. Marla and I made an early breakfast out of my loaf of hearty French bread and my block of high quality European cheese, both freshly purchased during our stop in Paris. After breakfast I slept with my head in Marla's lap all the way to Venice.

"One hour," we were once again told as we stepped off the bus in Venice, our first break of the day.

A cute brown eyed fair complexioned girl in her mid-twenties, Marla stood not much over five feet. She had curly bushy black hair, a lively, good-natured personality, and a kind and thoughtful disposition. Small boats, water taxis, and gondolas drifted past as we stood on a medieval foot bridge in Venice, our eyes fixed upon the eternally enchanting Grand Canal.

Motoring out of Venice, we crossed the border from Italy into Yugoslavia, a federation of small Slavic states living under Communist rule, locked behind the iron curtain since the end of World War Two. We rode all day through Yugoslavia, watching Western Europe disappear into dreary shades of gray as we traveled through the Communist world. Everything seemed old and forgotten in Russian controlled Eastern Europe, as if frozen in some distant era. I asked Marla if she would like to accompany me as far east as Istanbul. She agreed without hesitation.

It was a long haul through Yugoslavia, and even more so being our third day on a bus with hard uncomfortable seats and not enough legroom. Marla was short. The legroom part didn't bother her. We rolled across the Greek border and cruised into Thessaloniki as darkness fell. We had told our drivers to drop us off in Thessaloniki and to my astonishment, I found myself coasting down a surprisingly recognizable boulevard.

"I know this place," I said to Marla.

And sure enough, there it was, the same neon sign, lighting up the night, spelling out the word hotel in bright colorful neon letters, still dangling precariously over the

## Chapter Twelve

same narrow recessed doorway of the same shabby hotel where I had stayed four years earlier, tucked away between rows of smoky shish kabob restaurants.

We took much needed showers and crawled into bed, although it would be awhile before we fell asleep, needless to say. In the morning we boarded the train to Istanbul.

I told Marla of my previous experience on the same train from Thessaloniki to Istanbul and not to worry when our passports disappear into the hands of border guards while we sit stranded for hours in the middle of nowhere in the middle of the night on the border between Greece and Turkey.

Upon arriving in Istanbul the following afternoon, we walked from the train station to the ancient Sultanahmet district and checked into the same dilapidated, mouse-infested hotel I had also stayed in four years earlier. It was still only sixty cents a night.

We sat in the pudding shop, enjoying Turkish desserts and drinking cups of hot tea. We took luxurious Turkish baths and toured the four hundred-year-old sultan's palace. We wandered the Grand Bazaar and strolled along Istanbul's internationally celebrated harbor on the Bosporus Strait. A week passed. The time had come for me to move on. I had stayed in Istanbul longer than I had planned, but we were having such a wonderful time together. Why I never looked her up when I returned home makes no sense to me at all.

I obtained my visa from the Iranian embassy and booked my bus ticket to Iran. Marla accompanied me to the bus depot on the morning of my departure. A modern comfortable coach designed for long distance traveling sat waiting to carry me to the Iranian city of Tehran.

An Italian girl sat beside me. The same Italian girl Marla and I had met on the train from Thessaloniki to Istanbul and who kept asking, every time we ran into her, in an obvious attempt to annoy Marla, if I had booked my bus ticket to Iran yet and on what day would I be leaving.

Between the French girl, Marla, and now the Italian girl, I had become a pretty popular guy all of a sudden. Luck comes in bunches, and a dry spell always seems to follow.

The bus filled up, the Turkish drivers came on board and the three day journey from Istanbul to Tehran began. Four Italians sat among the passengers, including my seatmate, and all four began having loud conversations with each other, shouting in Italian across rows of seats from one end of the bus to the other.

We rolled over the Bosporus Strait, crossed the bridge between two continents and headed east. Several hours into the trip I fell asleep, until a jokester Turkish driver held a lit cigarette to my mustache. I opened my eyes to a burning sensation above my upper lip and the disturbing sight of the Turkish driver hovering over me. I jerked my head away in sudden, stinging pain. Everyone laughed. I didn't see anything funny about it. The Turk stood beaming in his stupid moment of glory for several minutes before returning to his seat at the front of the bus, where he sat laughing with the other drivers. I tried not to think about stories I had heard of busses lying in ravines, having gone over narrow, winding cliffs in the mountains of Eastern Turkey, and about the fact that my life for the next three days was in the hands of the crazy fool who had burned my mustache and two others who didn't seem much different.

By day's end we arrived in Turkey's capital city of Ankara. We stopped for a dinner break and continued traveling through the night. I had hoped to sleep with my head on the Italian girl's shoulder, but I awoke in the morning with a sore neck instead. She and her compatriots had decided to disembark in Ankara, spend the night in a hotel

## Chapter Twelve

and hop on a train in the morning, for a roomier journey, I assumed, the remaining distance to Tehran.

Several loaves of hearty bread, baked in earthen ovens and a sufficient quantity of nuts and raisins I had purchased in Istanbul before boarding the bus to Iran sustained me throughout the journey. I would not eat prepared meals at the roadside stops we made in remote Turkish villages, nor would I drink the water. To hydrate myself, I bought strange brands of sodas and I drank cups of hot tea, making sure I could see the water boiling. I was taking no chances. To be stricken with diarrhea while stuck on a bus across Turkey for three days would be a nightmare.

In the distance, as we rolled across Eastern Turkey, the snow-capped peaks of Mt. Arahat came into view, rising to an altitude of sixteen thousand feet. A sizeable segment of biblical historians and theorists, as well as the area's local population, believe Mt. Arahat to be the final resting place of Noah's Ark.

Approaching the Iranian border, we passed through a small Kurdish village. No more pranks had been or would be perpetrated by the Turkish drivers. I was to have been their only victim.

As scheduled, we pulled into Tehran seventy-two hours after leaving Istanbul. From the bus depot I hopped into a taxicab with as many Western travelers as the driver could humanly squeeze in. We were taken to a hotel where all of us slept in the same room on a floor covered with gymnastic mats.

Springing forth from the mosque's towering minaret, as it does five times a day, the Muezzin's haunting mystical melody calling the faithful to prayer echoed across the metropolis.

The Shah of Iran, a friend to the West, still held the power, but a change was brewing, a change that would shake the world. No one could have foreseen what little time remained before it all came crashing down. The Islamic revolution was on the horizon. In two years time the American Embassy in Tehran would be overrun and held hostage, the king would be overthrown, the ayatollah would take charge, and the days when a Western traveler could travel freely and safely throughout the Islamic world would come to an end.

Wandering the streets of Tehran, I soon fell victim to a masterful hoodwinking at the hands of a child huckster about ten years of age whose powers of persuasion were the equivalent of twenty used car salesmen, an eerie but not uncommon trait found in children born in the Eastern world. He led me into a small shop stocked with jewelry and gemstones. I should have known better, but greed clouded my judgment and I allowed him to talk me into buying a packet containing twenty beautiful turquoise stones, convinced I could make a good profit back home.

Several months later, while showing my collection of what I had been led to believe were valuable turquoise stones to a jeweler in India, I would make a shocking discovery. I had been ripped off. The stones, although appearing perfect and authentic by every means, were in reality plastic fakes, and I had wasted twenty dollars, practically a week's living expenses in this part of the world. I had been bamboozled, duped, and deceived by a slick talking child and I couldn't stop obsessing about it for three days, so angry at myself and feeling stupid had I become.

But all was not lost, for in the midst of this yet unknown calamity I had purchased a small quantity of dates, leading me to an incredible discovery: Iran produced the sweetest most succulent dates I had ever tasted. As a connoisseur of dates, I had experienced a revelation.

Iran's restaurants offered a scarcity of choices for a non-meat eater. But with ancient Persia having the most

## Chapter Twelve

delicious dates in the world, I had found the answer. My diet, I thus decided, would consist of three foods: The best dates ever in the history of dates, wonderful fresh baked naan, and substantial quantities of nuts. And per my peculiar talent for subsisting on the strangest of diets, I would be satisfied and sustained eating nothing else during the entirety of my stay in Iran. And my food budget would be ungodly cheap.

So far, my latest crazy little adventure had taken me on one gruesome sea sick boat ride, a three day bus ride, one thirty hour train ride, another three day bus ride, and now another thirty-six hour bus ride across the deserts of Northeastern Iran, to the ancient city of Mashad, Iran's holiest city. Mashad would also be my final stop before reaching Afghanistan.

The heart of Shiite Iran, the Imam Reza shrine, a mosque unequaled in splendor, serves as the centerpiece of Mashad. A destination of profound pilgrimage, under the mosque's golden dome the eighth Imam is laid to rest.

I didn't stay long in Iran, only passing through, but I will forever thank the traveling Gods for allowing me the rarest of opportunities to experience this historic land, its rich culture and roots stretching back millenniums, and its people, who were always kind to me. Ancient Persia, a place of great kings, lost kingdoms, biblical tales, and glorious mosques, the latter an unparalleled display of the finest in classic Islamic art and architecture. I had traveled into the far depths of the Islamic world, and I loved it, and in the world of 1977, not once did I fear for my safety.

I arrived upon the Iran-Afghanistan border. My passport was stamped, my backpack searched, and into the Afghan night I marched on a cold, dark desert night in Central

Asia, accompanied by two Canadian guys, a Dutch girl, a Canadian girl who went by the name, Sierra Nevada, and a Brazilian couple, Paulo and Maria. A bus taking us to the Afghan town of Herat will arrive shortly, we were told. What shortly meant was anybody's guess. Time, as I had long since discovered, has an altogether different meaning in the East.

Seven Western travelers stood bundled up and shivering, wondering if we might be stranded through the freezing Afghan desert night, when at last a glimmer of headlights appeared on the moonlit horizon and the outline of a minibus came into view. The mini bus pulled up, we piled in, and through the darkness speedily carried along an international aid built highway were we. A narrow strip of benevolence. One lone two-lane blacktop across a land time forgot.

We entered Herat. The exact age of Herat is not known. Alexander the Great conquered and rebuilt the town in 330 BC. This piece of information historians seem sure of. And by my own eyes I can say not much had changed since then. Little one-horse buggies, the local taxi service, greeted us upon our arrival.

Harness bells and the clippity-clop, clippity-clop of the one-horse buggies stepping along on an ancient dirt road were the only sounds we heard in the eerie silence of an Afghan night. The Brazilian couple and I were carried to a mud walled guesthouse not far from where the mini-bus had dropped us off. The Canadian guys, Sierra Nevada, and the Dutch girl were taken elsewhere by the bearded turbaned drivers of the little one-horse buggies they had hopped into.

Paulo, Maria, and I shared a one-room mud walled hut containing two beds at a cost of forty cents a night per person. The tidy condition of our mud walled hut surprised me. The outhouses were a different story. Nothing but holes in the ground and the stench could be searing.

## Chapter Twelve

Our Afghan host wasted no time bringing us a block of Afghan hashish so large we knew we wouldn't be able to finish it off before we left the country, no matter how hard we tried, but it only amounted to a couple of dollars so we bought the entire block anyway. We paid him for the room, the hashish, and three heaping platefuls of rice and potatoes.

I had heard the legendary tales of dysentery in Afghanistan. But I had been living on nothing but bread, nuts, raisins, and dates since leaving Istanbul and I believed the time for a change had come. The food is piping hot. It must be freshly boiled, I reassured myself. And with those thoughts in mind, weighing the odds, I chowed down. We used our hands, as they do in Afghanistan, scooping up the rice and potatoes and shoveling the food into our mouths. Only make sure you don't use the left hand.

Paulo emptied the tobacco out of a cigarette, mixed the tobacco with hashish, and like a vacuum, inhaled the mixture back into the cigarette and we had ourselves a joint. He lit up and the three of us had our first smoke of hashish in Afghanistan, freshly pressed, we were at the source, and it blew us away.

A deep slumber soon took charge after another hard traveling day. I rose at first light and ventured outside, enjoying the brisk refreshing air of a November morning in Afghanistan.

I seated myself at a table in the courtyard, joined by Paulo, Maria, and a German guy named Klaus. Klaus broke out a chillum, filled it with hashish and tobacco and passed it around, and he rolled a joint, European style, the size of a cigar, and passed it around as well.

Our eager to please bearded Afghan host, his shoulders wrapped in blankets and a turban round his head, delivered to our table a most satisfying breakfast of fried eggs, delicious fresh baked naan, and a steaming pot of tea.

With our mud walled huts to our backs and the ancient dirt road in our direct line of vision, we sat in the courtyard, hypnotized by a continuous caravan of small donkeys, in timeless motion slowly drifting past, carrying young boys and bearded, turbaned old men upon their backs.

Paulo and Klaus continued taking turns filling the chillum. I thought about getting out of my seat and taking a walk, but I couldn't move, and before I knew it, hours had passed. We had been sitting in the courtyard all morning. Time, it seemed, had taken an Afghan hashish vacation and those little donkeys continued drifting by, carrying ancient little boys and ancient old men upon their backs.

I finally forced myself to get up. I took a freezing bucket bath, after which I took a walk, finding few signs of the twentieth century in the streets of Herat. Horse drawn carts and carriages clippity-clopped along the corridors of a place frozen in time. Camels laden with goods sauntered through the dusty streets, medieval merchants leading the way. Many buildings were one-story mud-brick structures. Streets had open sewers running through them.

Men wore baggy Afghan pants with blankets and shawls wrapped around their shoulders. All had beards on their faces and turbans on their heads. Women wore the burqa, covered from head to foot, with a tiny spot of mesh over the eyes allowing them to see. Ancient looms spun cotton cloth and Afghan men squatted over fired up earthen clay ovens, baking delicious flatbread naan.

In the evening Paulo, Maria, and I found ourselves invited by four bearded, turbaned guys to come inside of their tiny textile shop. We sat on the floor next to an ancient spinning wheel. Their usual dinner of meat and bread simmered in a large pot over a wood fire. They spoke one language, we spoke another, and yet it all seemed so natural, sitting round a pot of simmering chunks of mutton and naan on a chilly autumn evening in Afghanistan. Tin

## Chapter Twelve

bowls filled with hot soup were passed around. We tried to say no, we didn't want to eat their food, they were so poor, meat and bread, their dinner night after night, but they insisted. And so the soup I sipped and the bread I ate, but the meat I left, hoping they wouldn't notice until after we had gone.

We sat awhile, enjoying the legendary Afghan hospitality. They were so humble, sharing their meager portions with us. And when we left my companions and I agreed that full communication had somehow magically taken place, even though neither side understood one word of what the other side said.

One would think already having been to India would have made this trip anticlimactic. But no matter how deep into the Eastern world my travels had already taken me, every step along the overland trail would still leave me awestruck, for this trip was no ordinary journey through exotic faraway lands. The overland journey to India was a once in a lifetime, mind blowing voyage into the far and untouched depths of the Islamic world.

These were days when a traveler could wander off into any area of Afghanistan, even the remotest parts, and find themselves welcomed with the utmost of hospitality and respect. Not once did I feel unsafe or threatened in any way.

Little could anyone have known the final days of a timeless and beautiful, one of a kind culture and civilization hovered on the horizon. Soon, Afghanistan would become a pawn in the chess game of international power and politics, leaving the nation shattered beyond any foreseeable hope of repair.

Few foreigners, other than the hippie wanderers, remember Afghanistan as one of the most peaceful and welcoming places on the face of the earth. And I believe in the accuracy of my observation because I saw no other tourists in Afghanistan during the entirety of my stay other than the budget backpackers traveling overland to India.

From Herat I traveled by bus to the Afghan town of Kandahar, the next stop on the overland trail, accompanied by Paulo, Maria, the Dutch girl, and Sierra Nevada, her unusual name bestowed upon her by her Canadian Indian grandfather we were told. She had the Canadian flag sewn onto her backpack. She didn't want anyone to mistake her for an American, a common dilemma plaguing Canadian travelers. The Dutch girl was having bouts of tearfulness. Her boyfriend had left for India a month earlier. She hoped to catch up with him in Katmandu. Sierra Nevada, who blamed all of the world's troubles on America despite my presence, tried to comfort her. Although as I observed it, her manner of comforting seemed to suspiciously involve a bit more usage of her hands and arms than the act of consoling actually called for. Paulo remained the caretaker of our block of hashish. The five of us became traveling companions and would remain so until we reached India.

We pulled into Kandahar after an all day journey from Herat, stopping several times in route so the Afghans could roll their prayer mats out on the desert floor, face Mecca and pray. Mid-sized busses carried us across Afghanistan. Crowded and dusty, but well within a budget traveler's reasonable expectation of comfort, or discomfort, depending on how one looks at it, and I had ridden worse. The overland journey, via public transportation, had thus far gone much smoother than I had anticipated and would continue to do so all the way to the Indian border.

In Kandahar the five of us stayed in the same hotel. The guys who ran the hotel, an exceptionally friendly bunch, insisted we take their pictures, alone and with ourselves included. When I returned home I sent them copies, and I have often wondered if a photo of me with a bunch of

## Chapter Twelve

bearded, turbaned, smiling Afghan guys could still be floating around somewhere in Afghanistan.

As global change and modernization began taking place throughout the world, the Afghans, an ancient tribal culture, continued living as they had for centuries past. But sometime in the 1960s an unforeseen event took place. Strangers from another world began showing up, a tribe of a different kind, carrying their belongings in packs they wore on their backs. Some hitchhiked. Some came by public transportation, and others rode the magic busses from Amsterdam to Katmandu. Hippiedom came face to face with the first century.

In a land appearing in every timeless corner as a living page straight out of the Old Testament, the isolated Afghans, shrewd and resourceful, developed an ingenious system to meet the needs of Western wanderers.

Seeing the unexpected opportunities popping up in front of them, the Afghans fashioned a brilliant fusion of East meets West, complete with food, lodging, transportation, and hashish to make the overland traveler's journey across Afghanistan a pleasant and memorable one. All in the name of capitalism, of course, and it couldn't have worked out better for both.

In the unlikeliest of cultural collaboration, from Herat to Kabul, the Afghans had shaped a network of folksy restaurants and quaint cafés pulsing with the beat of rock and roll music smack-dab in the heart of the Islamic world, serving Afghan, European, and American cuisine, and European and American style bakeries, offering an abundance of delicious cookies, cakes, pastries, donuts, and pies, all of which the clever and industrious Afghans had learned to create to satisfy the palates of stoned hippies with munchies, steadily rolling through, heading east to India.

Istanbul and Afghanistan were the milestones of the journey: Istanbul, where the overland wanderers got their first taste of the East, and Afghanistan, where the Western world vanished, as if it had never existed at all.

For a brief moment in time Western travelers could roam, free, safe, and unrestricted throughout this historic, ancient land. There was no place on earth, and may never be again, like the Afghanistan I had the good fortune to see before the Russian invasion and the Islamic revolution slammed the door shut on the overland journey to India.

From Kandahar we headed for Kabul, the nation's capital, its largest city, and the final stop before reaching the Pakistani border.

Kabul sits at an elevation of six thousand feet. We arrived in early December. Winter had also arrived in Kabul and the only heat our guesthouse had came from one corroding woodstove resting in the center of a small dusty sitting room. And around this woodstove bundled up overland travelers would gather to keep warm, socialize, and get stoned, and I don't recall one moment where a chillum or a joint filled with hashish and tobacco wasn't traveling around the room.

In Kabul, two notable locations awaited the India bound traveler: The famed bazaar on Chicken Street and Siggi's Restaurant, the renowned gathering place for overland travelers.

Siggi's was to Kabul what the Pudding Shop was to Istanbul. Both would become legendary in the history of the overland journey to India.

A German named Siegfried owned Siggi's. In Siggi's Restaurant a traveler could take pleasure in a variety of Asian, European, and American cuisine. In the heart of Central Asia, Western wanderers would sit in the charm and intrigue of an expat café, shades of Casablanca, exchanging information and sharing stories of the road while savoring dishes as far ranging as American apple pie is to wiener schnitzel. And Siggi's served both and much

## Chapter Twelve

more. The psychedelic chessboard in Siggi's garden with chess pieces three feet tall sitting on twelve by twelve inch squares is an image I have always carried in my mind.

We tried to finish off the large block of hashish we had bought when we first arrived in Afghanistan. To no avail, though. God knows we gave it our best, the remainder of which we gave to another traveler on our day of departure before boarding the bus to Pakistan. And I was relieved. I needed a break. I had been smoking too much. But how could I not take advantage of the opportunity to over indulge myself in the best hashish on the planet, at its source? After all, it's not every day one finds oneself in Afghanistan.

Both beautiful and treacherous, reaching an elevation of thirty-five hundred feet, the Khyber Pass is a steep and narrow twenty-eight mile long winding mountain passage of carved and jagged rocky terrain connecting Central Asia to the sub-continent. Many powerful forces sweeping across Asia marched through the historic passageway, among them the ancient armies of Genghis Khan and Alexander the Great.

We boarded the bus, rolled out of Kabul, and traveled through the Khyber Pass, arriving in the Pakistani frontier town of Peshawar, where proud Pushtun tribesmen rule the wild and lawless edges of Afghanistan, their rugged faces, captivating in every detail, reflecting an unforgettable eye-catching blend of the great Asian expanse. Timeless tribal horsemen stepped along Peshawar's dusty streets and the crowded bazaar bustled with a colorful range of traders and merchants, from near and afar; coming, going, and staying; buying, trading, and selling everything from camels to Kashmiri carpets, at the crossroads, where Central Asia ends and South Asia begins, depending of course on which direction one is coming from.

Shades of brown under a blue sky were the colors of Afghanistan, mud-brick houses and desert sands. In Pakistan the colors changed, becoming bright and abundant as India approached.

Several days later we booked passage on the Pakistani railroad. Across the whole of Pakistan, clouds of black smoke belched, steam hissed, and whistles sounded as the old steam engine locomotive delivered us to the city of Lahore, the final stop before reaching the Indian border.

Ramshackle shops and rickety open-air restaurants, their steaming stovetops crammed with boiling pots of curried dishes, lined the bustling streets of Lahore. Pakistani women with faces uncovered wore multihued flowing cloth of the finest cotton. The air in every direction burst with symphonies of sound, color, chaos, and beeping horns as cars, busses, three wheel taxis, bicycles, bicycle rickshaws, motor scooters, horse drawn wagons, and bullock carts rolled along the crowded streets.

Apart from the absence of Hindu temples, sadhus, and holy cows, Pakistan, from Peshawar to Lahore, sure sounded, looked, felt, and smelled like India to me. And that's exactly what it was, before the British decided to give away a chunk in 1947, thus creating the state of Pakistan, the colonial masters' final act before handing the nation back to the natives.

India's Hindu population became outraged and a horrifying bloodbath ensued during the final stages of the struggle for independence as Hindus and Muslims butchered each other, much to the dismay, sorrow, and untold grief of their beloved leader, Mahatma Ghandi, father of non-violent revolution. And for the most part, the non-violent revolution had been successful, until the British took it upon themselves to give away a piece of the motherland.

In Lahore, in the middle of the madness of Asian traffic, I saw a sight I will never forget. A bicycle rickshaw had

## Chapter Twelve

a miniature yellow school bus filled with children attached to it, adding an unimaginable dimension to the already punishing labor of peddling a bicycle rickshaw.

A few days spent in the Pakistani city of Lahore and we were off to the Indian-Pakistani border, where the overland trail explodes into infinite possibilities upon ending its straight run from Istanbul. Now, one can head in a multitude of directions. One can travel into the breathtaking Himalayas, to Dharamsala, home of the Dalai Lama, to Kashmir, Kulu-Manali, and Katmandu. One can travel the ancient cities along the Ganges River, Rishikesh, Hardwar, and Varanasi. One can visit ancient temples and ashrams, the Taj Mahal, and Jaipur, the pink city, and one can travel throughout exotic South India, to the beaches of Goa and the lush tropical beauty of Kerala state. Sharing a tremendous sense of accomplishment, the five of us crossed the border. We had traveled from Europe to India by land, the Brazilian couple, Sierra Nevada, the Dutch girl, and I.

We traveled next by bus to the Indian city of Amritsar, capital of Punjab Province, homeland of the tidily turbaned Sikhs and their sacred Golden Temple. A taxi carried us from the bus depot to a beautiful Sikh owned and operated two-story hotel, permeating in colonial era ambience, architecture, and décor.

Paulo and Maria took a private room. The price of our luxurious lodging proved expensive compared to the decrepit accommodations I had become accustomed to. To cut my costs, I would share space in a dormitory room with Sierra Nevada, the Dutch girl, and a German girl named Frieda. Frieda was a pretty girl with a wonderful fair complexion and beautiful long blond hair. She was also the skinniest girl I had ever laid eyes upon. Below the neck, Frieda bordered on skeletal.

Frieda had also traveled overland to India, but she took an unusual route. For reasons I could not imagine, she had bypassed Afghanistan and traveled through Iraq and Iran to the Pakistani border instead, and she had made the entire journey solo, all the way from Germany.

I'm not sure why, because I don't usually do it, but I gave Frieda a rundown of my family's fate under the Nazi regime. Frieda's father, she would in turn reveal, had served in a Gestapo unit responsible for rounding up Jews and sending them to the death camps.

"I've always hated him for what he did during the war," she said.

This surprising bit of information planted a morbid yet fascinating thought into my mind: That this girl's father could have been a direct participant in bringing members of my own family to slaughter might be a bit of a long shot, but it certainly falls within the realm of possibility. The beauty of the road: eerie connections, uncanny encounters, mystifying meetings. One never knows what's around the next corner.

Amritsar is home to the landmark four hundred-year-old Golden Temple, the holiest place in Sikhism. The gilded shrine honoring Guru Nanak is an exquisite combination of Hindu and Islamic architecture casting golden hues shimmering upon the waters of a gentle forest lake. A sight to behold and a sight not to be missed, its position well earned among India's impressive list of majestic architectural wonders.

Paulo and Maria left for Dharamsala. I advised them to wait until spring before going into the mountains, but their minds were made up. The Dutch girl made a hasty exit for Katmandu looking for her boyfriend, and I'm not sure what Sierra Nevada had on her agenda, but I would run into her one more time in Varanasi.

## Chapter Twelve

I planned to make stops in Rishikesh and Varanasi before heading south to Goa, and as it turned out, Frieda and I were traveling in the same direction. I told Frieda I had been to Rishikesh and I knew of a good place to stay called Swami's guesthouse.

We arrived in Hardwar station after an overnight journey from Punjab Province. From Hardwar we took the short train ride to Rishikesh and to our good fortune, Swami found a spot for us in his already crowded guesthouse. Frieda and I were to share floor space with two other travelers in a large tent similar to a tee-pee Swami had constructed since I was last there, situated in the middle of the courtyard.

On our third day in Rishikesh Frieda came down with the runs. It would turn into the worst case of dysentery I had ever seen, progressing with frightening speed to the point where she could barely make it to the squatter.

Winter drew near and I didn't intend to hang around Rishikesh too long. I would return in the spring. But how could I leave now with Frieda in the shape she was in? She was so skinny to begin with. One would think she could very well disappear if she lost anymore weight. I advised her to take Intestopan, the medicine that had cured me of dysentery in Guatemala, and which I had been forced to use on several occasions in India as well. But Frieda insisted on trying Ayurvedic treatments instead, in abundant supply in the land of Ayurveda.

Three days passed since the onset of Frieda's dysentery and she showed no signs of improvement. Frieda couldn't comprehend why a stranger would be so concerned about her well being, and she couldn't comprehend why I insisted on staying with her, as I had been ready to move on when she took ill.

"Someone's got to," I said, shocked she would even ask.

Finally coming to realize what a dangerous situation she was in, that such a serious case of dysentery could lead to dehydration and death, Frieda agreed to take my advice. In time, perhaps, the Ayurvedic medicine may have done the job, but Frieda didn't have the time. She was already on her way to dehydration and the issue of her weight had become alarming.

As much as I would prefer to avoid pharmaceuticals and go the natural route, when it comes to dysentery I don't believe in messing around. I'm convinced taking a chemical drug to rid oneself as quickly as possible of those horrifying parasitic invaders is by far the wisest treatment choice to make.

It took three days of treatment with Intestopan for Frieda to complete her recovery. I thought at least a small gesture of appreciation would have been in order. Didn't happen. Not one word of acknowledgment or gratitude would come out of Frieda's mouth for what I had done for her. She didn't even offer to reimburse me the rupees I spent on her medicine. And to top it off, she made a point of letting me know she thought I was the strangest person she had ever met.

From Rishikesh, Frieda and I headed for the sacred city of Varanasi, although I hadn't a clue why I continued traveling with this girl.

Upon arriving in Varanasi we hopped into a bicycle rickshaw outside of the train station and had the driver take us straight to the river, upon Frieda's insistence, rather than check into a hotel first.

We walked along the river's edge with our backpacks on our backs until we came upon a section of the river lined with houseboats.

"I want to stay in a houseboat," Frieda said.

We began taking closer examination of each houseboat when a young Indian fellow came running toward us,

## Chapter Twelve

waving his arms and yelling at the top of his lungs: "You want houseboat? You want houseboat?"

We bartered, settling on a price of five rupees a day, half the cost of two individual rooms in a cheap hotel. The price greatly pleased Frieda, since she was even cheaper than I was.

Living on the houseboat allowed me to observe ancient life along the banks of the Ganges without pause from dawn till dark. I could see the funeral pyres burning, and in every direction, temples, mosques, domes, minarets, and maharaja palaces, hundreds of years old, lined the riverfront. I fell asleep under the stars on a houseboat on the Ganges River while the funeral pyres burned and a melodic kirtan, emanating from a small Hindu shrine a few yards from where I slept, echoed with a steady spiritual drumbeat and the mystical sounds of Hindu holy men chanting the sacred names.

Sunrise saw a steady flow of worshippers, hands folded in prayer position, marching down to the ghats and into the water to bathe and worship Mother Ganges. Women clad in beautiful saris, men ranging from fully clothed to loincloths, joyfully filling brass containers and pouring the sacred water over their heads while offerings of miniature oil lamps, rice, grains, and aromatic flower petals were made to the holy river. I watched this remarkable scene unfold as I had so many times before. But this time would be different. The houseboat offered no means of washing oneself; hence, I decided to join them.

Dirty laundry is washed in the river and the bodies of those whose families can't afford cremation are dumped into the river and I had even seen a dead cow float past my houseboat. But I joined the pious masses of India in their ablutions anyway and jumped into the nippy waters at sunrise, with my bar of soap, and took a bath in the sacred river Ganges.

My friend Mukesh the dwarf would visit and we would sit on the ancient stone steps with our cups of cardamom spiced chai and talk. My undivided attention made him so happy.

On my previous two visits to Varanasi home for me had been the Central Hotel, and after one week on the houseboat I decided the time had come. I desperately needed a good scrubbing with fresh water. Frieda would soon follow. She hadn't bathed at all while on the houseboat.

Traveling solo again felt great. I'm sure Frieda felt the same relief to have unloaded me as I did of her. So why did I spend over two weeks with this girl? It wasn't about the possibility of intimacy. The thought never entered my mind, not even in the beginning. It simply wasn't there. And her obvious dislike of me began within twenty-four hours of traveling together, reaching a point where not one word was shared between us. Without a doubt, Frieda and I were the oddest traveling companions in the history of travel.

I could come up with no logical explanation for the two weeks I spent with Frieda. What I will say is if it hadn't been for Frieda I wouldn't have stayed on the houseboat, and if I hadn't stayed on the houseboat I wouldn't have bathed in the river, and who knows, maybe I did wash away the sins of many lifetimes by bathing in the Ganges, and if so, I would owe Frieda a debt of gratitude. And who knows what would have become of the Nazi storm trooper's daughter had I not been there to help her when poo water was pouring out of her behind in Rishikesh from the worst case of dysentery imaginable.

Sometimes events happen in our lives for reasons impossible to understand and for reasons far greater than ourselves. As hard as I tried, no other explanation for the time I spent with Frieda made any sense to me at all.

## Chapter Twelve

The train to Bombay, a forty hour journey across half of India, rolled out of Varanasi station in the morning hour and arrived in Bombay's historic Victoria station, a world heritage site, near the end of the following day. A wonder to cast one's gaze upon, Victoria Station, in service since 1887, is a masterpiece of Victorian gothic architecture on the grandest of scales.

Krishna's Guest House had nothing to do with Lord Krishna, but rather with the proprietor, a pot bellied middle-aged sarong clad Indian fellow named Krishna. In Krishna's one-story sprawling Bombay guest house showers were limited to certain times of the day, but one could take bucket baths any time one pleased in a dimly lit cob webbed corner of the hotel out of large tanks filled with stored water that more often than not had dead bugs floating on top. I would make use of both. And I didn't mind the bucket baths. The sitting water's tepid temperature proved quite comfortable in comparison to the freezing shower. And as far as the dead bugs were concerned, I had been traveling in the Eastern world way too long to allow a few dead bugs floating in my bucket bath to bother me.

"Sir, good sir," I heard a voice calling after me. I turned around to find a young Indian gentleman dressed in a stylish suit and necktie requesting my attention. "Good sir, did you just take a roll of toilet paper out of the hotel's bathroom?"

I stood dead in my tracks. I had been caught red handed stealing a roll of toilet paper out of the bathroom of one of Bombay's luxurious five star hotels overlooking the harbor on the Arabian Sea. Toilet paper is an expensive item in India. I had become accustomed to taking care of nature's business the Eastern way, but it was at all times good to have a roll of toilet paper on hand for insurance.

Embarrassed to no end, my guilt impossible to deny, I took the roll of toilet paper out of my side bag and with all the politeness and humility I could muster, I handed it back to him.

"Thank you, good sir. You really shouldn't do this kind of thing," he said.

"I know," I meekly responded.

I was lucky. He was a kind fellow. Had he been so inclined he could have threatened to call the police and no telling how many rupees in bribe money I would have been forced to shell out to keep him from doing so.

Not once had I seen a roll of toilet paper in a bathroom in India. One either takes care of business the Eastern way, or brings their own. I didn't think Bombay's magnificent Intercontinental Hotel would miss one roll of toilet paper.

It was wrong of me, I know. I don't know what got into me. But how could they have known one roll of toilet paper had gone missing? It must be someone's job to keep a precise toilet paper roll count. How bizarre is that? Another one of those odd occupations found only in the Eastern world.

This person reported the missing roll to the manager, who must have been watching me, knowing full well I didn't belong inside of the elegant hotel, and he went running after me.

I walked down to the waterfront and stood looking out upon the historic gateway to India. The arched monument is the centerpiece of Bombay's harbor, built by the British in 1911 to commemorate King George and Queen Mary's visit to the crown jewel of the British Empire. I felt like an idiot, and I could only hope the overwhelming feelings of embarrassment sweeping over me weren't going to stay with me too long.

## Chapter Twelve

The horns sounded and the boat to the former Portuguese colony of Goa floated out to sea. Setting sail every day at ten o'clock in the morning, the boat from Bombay to Goa arrived in the Goan port of Panjim early in the morning of the following day. The still undeveloped beaches of the Indian state of Goa had become a legendary counterculture destination.

I couldn't help but take notice of a certain fellow traveler. He carried himself with an extraordinary air of calm, and while most of the young Western travelers in India dressed in native garb, myself included, he was clad in European style conservative slacks and a tucked in button down collared shirt.

I struck up a conversation. A native of New Zealand, Ivan had been invited to stay in Panjim for a few days as the guest of an Indian family. He told me he had been living for the past two years in a meditation center in the tiny village of Igatpuri, a short train ride from Bombay. My curiosity had been sparked.

Ivan addressed my interest. He said a Buddhist meditation technique known as Vipassana is taught at the meditation center by a man named Goenka. The duration of the course is ten days and the student must commit to staying the entire time.

He also explained the manner in which the meditation center operates. Only well established students live at the center, under special permission from the teacher. These students are responsible for managing the courses and maintaining the center, and do so on a voluntary basis. All others stay only for the course, and leave when the course ends.

What Ivan told me gave me a good feeling. The Vipassana meditators were called students, not devotees or disciples. This I found especially to my liking. I asked Ivan how I could go about signing up. He gave me the meditation center's address and told me to write a letter to them as soon as possible in order to reserve a spot for myself on the next English language course.

Refreshing salty breezes swept over me. Picturesque scenes of life in small coastal fishing villages captured my fascination throughout the daylight hours of the near twenty-four hour journey. Wearing colorful South Indian sarongs, dark skinned fishermen moved about in small fishing boats and children waved to us from the lush tropical tree line.

The boat from Bombay to Goa pulled into the port of Panjim in the early morning hour. The well preserved Portuguese architecture dating back to the fifteenth century, the cobbled streets and the quaint colonial Catholic churches gave the capital of the Indian state of Goa a distinct Latin ambience.

I checked into a hotel sitting opposite the boat landing. My room faced the water, offering a beautiful view of the harbor. I figured I could look for a place on the beach later, depending on how long I decided to stay.

The following day I took the short bus ride to Calangute Beach, the most popular of the Goan beaches. It started in Haight Ashbury. From there it traveled all the way to the beaches of Southern India.

"See you in Goa," became the overland traveler's catchphrase.

The Indian state of Goa had become a hippie haven, populated by an international community of youthful wanderers from the Western world and would become legendary in the archives of hippie history. Many stayed through the entire winter, some stayed for years, and some are still there. The dream realized? Many thought so. A legend in its own mind? Certainly a conceivable notion. Overly romanticized? Sure, but then again, isn't everything?

## Chapter Twelve

I stepped down from the bus, stood on the shoreline, took off my flip-flops and let the surf of the Arabian Sea roll over my feet. Thatched roof open-air restaurants, thatched roof huts, small houses, and tropical fruit drink stalls dotted the beach front landscape. Dark skinned Goan fishermen, sarong clad, wiry and strong, pulled their boats ashore and hauled their salt water catch to market. Motor scooters driven by young Goan men zipped about, transporting Western travelers between Calangute and Anjuna Beach.

In isolated Anjuna Beach, travelers from the Western world, among them beautiful young Western women, skinny dipped in the ocean and sunned themselves in the nude upon sparkling Asian sands. Calangute Beach and the adjacent secluded Anjuna Beach were the heart of hippie Goa.

I had signed up for the Vipassana meditation course, which left me with a self-imposed time constraint. If I wished to have adequate time to explore South India, I would need to cut my stay in Goa short. For this reason, rather than find a place to stay on the beach, I chose to remain in the hotel in the beautiful Port of Panjim and take day trips to Calangute Beach and Anjuna Beach instead. A simple plan it should have been, but complicated it would become, because Maya, Goddess of the material world, on the day before my planned departure, decided to put a fork in my road.

I met an Australian girl while enjoying a delicious fresh mango juice in a tiny tropical fruit drink stall on Calangute Beach. A guy from Spain passed a joint around. This joint gave me a terrible case of cotton mouth, forcing me to keep sipping on tropical fruit drinks one after the other until my mouth stopped sticking together. The Australian girl invited me back to her small beachfront hut. She had been living in Goa for several months and she invited me to stay with her.

### An Extraordinary Tale of Travel

A not so bad looking Australian girl invites me to move into a hut with her on a beautiful South Indian beach. My self-imposed time constraint now hung over me. My instincts told me I should attend the meditation course. I also wanted to explore the Southern half of the sub-continent. I would have no time for both if I took the Australian girl up on her offer.

Maya had thrown a monkey wrench into my plans, as is the Goddess of illusion's goal, to distract us and lure us away from our search for truth and meaning. With my mind hurled into a confusing and all too familiar state of ambivalence and indecision, I returned to my hotel room in Panjim, thinking long and hard about the Australian girl's offer. In the morning I boarded the bus for the South Indian city of Bangalore. By noon I was kicking myself in the head as I added one more to my list of missed opportunities.

The Indian city of Bangalore is in the state of Karnataka, roughly five hundred kilometers south of Goa. Bangalore is India's third largest city. Tamil Nadu and Kerala, the nation's southern most states, sit below Karnataka state, adjacent to each other and span the width of the nation, from the Arabian Sea to the Indian Ocean. I would focus first and foremost on Kerala state, known as God's own country, and as I would discover, it is a title not given lightly.

The masala dosa and the idli, the latter a small rice patty also eaten with fiery sambar sauce and both already favorites, and new favorites, upma and sheera, exotically spiced delicacies prepared with semolina flour, eaten as either breakfast, dessert, or a light meal anytime, these four South Indian specialties, intrinsic to South Indian

Chapter Twelve

cuisine, would sustain and satisfy me, and keep the cost of feeding myself ungodly cheap throughout my South Indian journey.

The ancient trading post of Cochin, a strategic harbor on the Arabian Sea and the first European settlement in India, ruled during the colonial era first by the Portuguese, followed by the Dutch, and lastly the British, and for centuries the center of the Indian spice trade, would be my first stop in Kerala state. The port of Cochin is also home to the oldest European church in India, built by the Portuguese circa 1503, and the original burial site of Portuguese explorer Vasco da Gama, who discovered the sea route from Europe to India.

In Cochin one also finds the oldest synagogue in the Commonwealth, built circa 1568. A sizeable Jewish population once existed in Cochin and the market area around the synagogue, where the remaining Jews of Cochin live, is officially named Jew Town, with designated street signs. I will admit, the Jew town street signs gave me more than a few chuckles. India has a long history of unparalleled religious tolerance and for the Jews of Cochin there is no negative connation in the term. To the contrary, having the city fathers name their community Jew Town has always been for them a source of pride.

I stopped by the tiny synagogue, as much a museum as it is a place of worship. Priceless works of art of invaluable artisanship passed down through the ages adorn the historic synagogue's exquisite interior. I spoke with an elderly gentleman. He said only a handful of Jews remained in the once thriving Indian-Jewish community of Cochin. Most of the young people had immigrated to Israel.

I became intrigued and mystified. I wanted to learn all about these people. How had their ancestors arrived in this faraway place, when, and under what circumstances? Pockets of Jews in unusual places have always fascinated me. But the Jews of Cochin also imparted sadness upon me. I imagined how lonely they must be. Their children had all left.

No guide books had yet been written to guide one around these most unknown of parts and far-flung destinations and the internet didn't exist and wouldn't for another twenty years. Backpackers depended solely upon each other for information. And so, through the good old fashioned traveler's grapevine I would learn of the backwaters of Kerala state. Known as the Venice of the East, the Kerala backwaters are a mind-blowing jungle labyrinth of interconnected canals, lakes, rivers, and inlets running hundreds of miles through lush scenery of inexpressible tropical rain forest beauty.

A series of colorful and crowded bus rides, standing room only, packed in like sardines, with people riding on the roof and hanging off the sides, delivered me to one of several locations from where the backwater journeys are launched. I spent the night, and in the early morning hour I boarded a small boat carrying roughly a dozen passengers. Through brackish waters cloaked in lush floating dense clusters of exotic vegetation, we pressed on, our vessel navigating a divine jungle maze of unparalleled verdant splendor, immersed in a heavenly sea of emerald green, embraced by boundless breathtaking landscapes of gorgeous coconut groves interspersed with tiny jungle villages.

I believe the Kerala backwater journey qualifies as a description defying experience. Therefore, I have taken the liberty to finalize my efforts in the most uncomplicated of terms by simply saying: Few earthly locations will leave the voyager as blown away as will the backwaters of Kerala State.

And as an added bonus, to make the trip even more spellbinding, a fellow backpacker rolled a joint and passed it around. I had heard the marijuana grown in Kerala state ranked among the best in the world. I wouldn't disagree.

Coming out of the undreamed of beauty of the Kerala backwaters I continued journeying south along Kerala's Malabar Coast, to the scenic white sands of Kovalam on the shores of the Arabian Sea at the southern tip of India. The beaches of the South Indian town of Kovalam were in the early stages of becoming another popular Western travelers' seashore destination. Many liked Kovalam as much as Goa, and some, I had heard, liked it even better. On the still undeveloped tropical shores of Kovalam, lodging consisted primarily of thatched roof huts spread out amongst the coconut trees.

I had stopped feeling bad over the opportunity I left behind in Goa. To pass up the beauty of Kerala state would have been unforgivable.

One day, while walking the trail through dense tropical palm groves from the beach back to my quarters a pack of small to medium size barking dogs came out of nowhere and began following me. The smallest one lunged at me and nipped my ankle. In India dogs aren't pets as we know them in the West. In India dogs are scavengers and many go unvaccinated.

I hurried back to my hut and took a look, and sure enough the skin had been broken. I was petrified. I had heard the incubation period for rabies is three weeks. Did I have accurate information? I hadn't a clue. But did it matter? Nothing less than initiating the rabies injections mattered now. A fellow traveler told me of a Catholic charity hospital in town where I could get the proper treatment.

I had every intention of going to the hospital. But each morning when I awoke I would eat breakfast first, delicious upma, and after breakfast, rather than head for the hospital, I would walk down to the beach instead and there I would linger, and another day would pass.

And so I went about business as usual, after having been bitten by a wild, angry canine in a third world country. No way am I going to die from rabies. It's too outrageous. It couldn't possibly happen to me, I stupidly tried to convince myself, on one hand, and on the other hand, wondering when the madness would begin, knowing full well rabies is a death sentence. To this day, I shudder when I think about the episode, and there is no doubt in my mind that choosing not to seek treatment was by far the riskiest, dumbest, most brainless, foolish decision anyone could ever make. And I doubt a human being exists who would disagree.

Pensive, I stood on a rock jutting out to sea under a hot noon-day South Indian sun, thinking about how far I had come on this journey and all I had seen. Tides rolled in, striking the rocky shoreline, splattering me with cool and welcoming salt water splashes. I had traveled, by land, not only from London to New Delhi, but all the way down the East Coast of India as well, and now I stood at the end of India in the charming South Indian town of Kanyakumari in the state of Tamil Nadu, the southernmost tip of the sub-continent, where the Indian Ocean, the Arabian Sea, and the Bay of Bengal meet, where the sunrises and the sunsets are of such magnificence pilgrimages are made for the sole purpose of witnessing their happening, and where, at certain times of the year, one can see the sun set and the moon rise over three seas simultaneously.

From Kanyakumari I traveled to the ancient city of Madurai. Madurai is the oldest city in South India and home to the renowned Meenakshi temple, over two thousand years old, around which the city grew and around which life in Madurai still revolves. Deemed among the most important temples in India, the sacred Meenakshi temple is dedicated to Lord Shiva and his celestial consort, Parvati, also known as Meenakshi. As legend has it, the temple sits on the spot where the wedding of Shiva and Parvati took place.

## Chapter Twelve

The South Indian temples are built in the Dravidian style, an ancient architectural design unique to South India, composed of sandstone, soapstone, or granite, sprawling in scope, with pyramid shaped towers hundreds of feet high, covered in countless, intricate, tiny sculpted stucco figures of the Gods, Goddesses, and celestial beings of ancient Vedic lore, each character painstakingly painted in a rainbow of vivid colors. The stucco figures alone present an astounding image. Intrinsic to the South Indian landscape, found nowhere else in the world, the South Indian temples are a phenomenal sight to behold, and standing among the most impressive is the Meenakshi temple in the city of Madurai.

Inner sanctums lined with ancient pillars perfectly positioned in complex geometric patterns; a room with over a thousand oil lamps; a pool where the God Indra washed away his sins in worship to Lord Shiva; walls decorated with precious murals of the Gods and Goddesses; priceless sculptures and statues, each one dedicated to the deities Shiva and Parvati, only touch the surface in describing this most glorious of Eastern wonders. Like so much in India, the temple in Madurai is an invaluable piece of ancient history still active today, allowing one to see life in India the same as it was millenniums ago.

In vibrant eye catching batik design and the finest of silky soft cotton, nowhere have I seen sarongs of such artistic beauty as those worn by the men of South India, adding one more element to the unequaled exoticism of the Southern half of the subcontinent.

The meditation course would soon begin. Traveling by bus through the states of Tamil Nadu, Karnataka, and Maharashtra, I headed back to Bombay, making a few more stops in small South Indian towns to break up the journey.

Upon arrival in Bombay I checked into Krishna's guesthouse and as always after a hard traveling day, I gave myself a good scrubbing, paying no attention to a few dead bugs floating in my bucket bath.

❋

The sole guesthouse in the village of Igatpuri filled up fast. Every train coming from and heading to Bombay seemed to make a stop in this tiny tranquil place, and with each new arrival came more young international adventurers from Australia, New Zealand, Europe, Canada, and America, flooding into the dormitory rooms of the Igatpuri guesthouse. I couldn't believe how many had arrived by day's end. Dozens and dozens, and all had come to take the meditation course. Wow! How did I miss this? All of these India travelers had taking a Vipassana meditation course with S.N. Goenka on their to-do while in India lists. Some were coming back a second and third time, and some even more. And I only found out about it now, halfway through my second journey to India.

In the morning after breakfast the guesthouse emptied out. I followed the crowd as a long line of backpacking travelers hiked up a steep dirt road. The International Vipassana Academy, Dhamma Giri, Hill of Dhamma in English, sat at the summit. The center, only two years old at the time, included a large meditation hall, dining room and kitchen, male and female dormitories, and a scattering of rustic individual huts. Many enhancements would come, including a beautiful pagoda. The hilltop location also offered a magnificent panoramic view far into the distance of rich valleys and meadows, and farmland plowed by oxen. We registered and dormitory beds were assigned us.

In the dispensing of the Buddha's teachings, it is not allowed to earn money or profit in any way. Donations must always cover the costs. In the Igatpuri Vipassana meditation center, the donations collected from the students in the previous course would now pay for our ten day course and the donations collected from us will pay for the next course, and so on and so on, ad infinitum; hence, not only is nothing bought, sold, or earned, but every person involved is provided the opportunity to give.

The teacher's time is given on a one hundred percent voluntary basis. And the students who live on the grounds and work running the center, their time is also given on a one hundred percent voluntary basis. Those who cannot afford the amount of the suggested donation are allowed to give what they can or take the course free of charge. No one who seeks the Dhamma is ever turned away.

Assured of our property's safe storage and return, management instructed us to turn over our cameras, radios, cassette players, journals, and reading material. We were also instructed to suspend any other meditation or yoga practice. These guidelines have been put in place to eliminate distraction. While taking the course the student is expected to focus on nothing else but learning the Vipassana meditation technique.

The day begins at four o'clock in the morning. A gong resonates throughout the meditation center, waking the students up. A two hour sitting follows. Breakfast comes next and dinner at noon, our last full meal of the day. In the evening students are served tea and fruit only. We were now on a Buddhist Monk's schedule. So far, I had gathered a good deal of information, but I still had no idea what I had gotten myself into.

The food was delicious. The curried dishes seasoned perfectly. No mouth on fire here. By far the most excellent Indian cooking I had ever tasted. And the chapattis were the best in all of India.

Everyone piled into the meditation hall in the evening after fruit and tea, leaving rows of flip-flops at the entrance.

Noble silence had now gone into effect. No speaking during the entire ten days. If one has an issue requiring immediate attention, they could speak to management. Ever accommodating, management would try their best to resolve issues. In the attire department, my white baggy draw-string cotton pajama pants and loose fitting Indian shirts, all I ever wore in India anyway, served me well. No changes needed there.

Approximately one hundred students had signed up for the course. Men sat on one side of the huge meditation hall, women on the other. Meditation cushions were provided and in place. I choose one and seated myself in a cross-legged position. On a raised platform in the front of the hall sat a middle-aged Indian man clad in a white shirt tidily tucked into a Burmese sarong. His clean shaven face revealing a smooth complexion of light golden brown. His trimmed silver-gray hair neatly parted and combed to the side. His appearance gave no indication whatsoever of what one had come to expect an Indian guru to look like. His wife sat beside him, clad in a traditional Indian sari. Both sat in cross-legged positions. He sat facing the men's side, she on the women's.

An Indian by ancestry, S.N. Goenka was a successful businessman who grew up in a Hindu family in Burma, where a sizeable Indian presence had developed during the colonial era. In 1955 S.N. Goenka began study under Sayagi U Ba Khin, a well respected government administrator who had worked his way up to becoming the first accountant general of the post colonial independent Burma. Sayagi U Ba Khin had also become a teacher of Vipassana meditation.

Vipassana, meaning: to see things as they really are, had been preserved in secluded Buddhist monasteries in Burma for two and a half millennium. Sayagi U Ba Khin designed a method by which laypersons could also learn this technique. S.N. Goenka became a devoted student.

## Chapter Twelve

In 1969, S.N. Goenka moved his family back to India and as his teacher had requested, he began tirelessly teaching the Vipassana meditation technique to all who wished to learn. As prophesized, after twenty-five hundred years, the Dhamma had returned to the land of its birth.

Radiating a genuine and deep compassion combined with a brilliant ability to teach and explain the Buddha Dhamma in ways everyone could understand, S.N. Goenka would gain high approval in Hindu India and among Buddhist monks as well, the latter rare for a lay person.

In the beginning, Goenka hoped to gain a following of Indian students, but an unforeseen phenomenon coinciding with his own arrival in India would soon set in motion an unexpected turn of events. With the opening up of the overland trail, young people from the Western world had begun arriving in India at a steady pace. And so, surprisingly, or perhaps not so surprisingly, the majority of Goenka's earliest students would come from the counterculture backpackers, and from the ranks of these youthful spiritual seekers Vipassana meditation, known also as insight meditation and also as mindfulness, would be spread to the Western world.

At the end of each day Goenka would give a talk, known as the evening discourses. I looked forward all day to hearing his soothing voice and incomparable style of speaking and teaching. The evening discourses were the highlight of the day for me. In these talks Goenka would teach the Dhamma through stories, parables, and humorous tales, explaining the process as no one else could. What good fortune I had for the opportunity. There will never be another like S.N. Goenka.

The inescapable universal law of impermanence: Everything is temporary and in an endless state of change. This, the Buddha teaches, is the cause of human suffering.

The way out of suffering, the Buddha explains, is to free the mind of the illusion of the ego. To liberate the mind from the endless cycle of longings, cravings, yearnings, passions, desires, and material attachments, an unquenchable thirst, impossible to satisfy, leading only to pain and suffering, because everything, without exception, is subject to impermanence, death, and decay.

The goal then is to develop a purified mind living in the present moment only, wisely observing the ever changing phenomenon of existence, moment by moment, without attachment, but with perfect equanimity, compassion, right understanding, and vigilant awareness of the impermanent nature of all things. The Buddha had discovered the way out of suffering. Satya Narayan Goenka would now show us the path.

We took our monastic vows. Goenka began by chanting from the Buddhist scriptures in Pali, the ancient Indian language in which the Buddha's teachings had been preserved in their original form. I looked forward to hearing the heartfelt sound of Goenka chanting in his deep voice. To hear him chant in the delicate hour of dawn moved me most of all.

We were to begin, Goenka instructed, with mindfulness of the breath. Pure observation of the present moment. And the bare reality of the moment, Goenka explained, when all is still and silent, is the breath, nothing more, nothing less. The mind will wander. This is known as the monkey mind, a continual chatter, the mind's non-stop jumping from one thought to another. We had begun the process of quieting the mind. When thoughts intrude, we were told, observe, without attachment, and let them pass, always bringing the mind back to the breath.

For three full days, sitting a total of ten hours a day, we were to concentrate the mind on nothing but the sensation of the breath as it touches a spot above the upper lip, coming in and going out of the nostrils. Observing the breath is known as Anapana. It would sharpen the mind's

## Chapter Twelve

concentration for the fourth day when Goenka would teach us the Vipassana technique.

The course would span twelve days. The first day, the day of arrival, is a day of registration, acclimation, and introduction, followed by ten full days of sitting, and on the morning of the twelfth day the course would end.

On the third day, as I walked out of the meditation hall on my way to the dining room for the noon meal, a stabbing pain pierced my left foot by my little toe, forcing me to let out a loud involuntary shriek. I had stepped on a scorpion. The agonizing pain began climbing up my leg, moving toward my private area, which had me freaked out. The manager of the center, Graham, an Australian, came to my assistance. Graham told me to sit down and he would be right back.

Within minutes Graham returned with a syringe and injected an antidote into the area of the bite. To my enormous relief, the burning pain stopped heading for my groin. My foot continued throbbing though, and would not completely subside until the end of the following day.

Out of all the people there, a meditation hall packed with over one hundred people, I'm the one to get bitten by a scorpion. It seemed as if the damn thing had been waiting at the door just for me. And right on the heels of having been bitten by a dog on Kovalam Beach. All of a sudden, I'm under attack by beasts and bizarre crawling creatures.

On a positive note, of all the strange things that have happened to me, I can now add bitten by a scorpion to the list. Not everyone can do that.

On the fourth day we were taught Vipassana. We were instructed to focus our attention on the top of the head, applying all of our concentration to whatever sensation we find there. From the top of the head we were to begin moving our attention through the entire body, systematically, slowly scanning from head to foot, applying vigilant awareness to each bodily sensation, allowing neither attachment, aversion, nor craving, whether pleasant or painful, to come into play. Pure observation only of the nature of every sensation, moment by moment, examining it, watching it, accepting the reality of it, and moving on, anchoring the concentration back on the breath when the mind wanders.

For the next six days I would sit in a cross-legged position, a total of ten hours a day with eyes closed, doing nothing but observing the arising and vanishing of bodily sensations, a process which takes one deep within the psyche, quiets the mind, purifies the mind, trains the mind to live in the moment, trains the mind to stay calm and maintain wisdom in all of one's reactions, and when applied correctly and diligently, in combination with right living and high moral conduct, is capable of bringing one to the egoless state, where suffering ceases. Surgery of the mind, Goenka called it. We were being taught the process by which we too could attain the Buddha mind.

Sitting motionless for hours in a cross-legged position completely unnatural to my Western bones proved no easy task. But I was determined, no matter how much pain racked my back and legs. I followed Goenka's instructions. I observed the pain. I made it through. And not only did I make it through, but I signed up for another one.

Metta, Goenkaji's meditation on loving kindness, would bring the course to its conclusion on the morning of the twelfth day.

In India the suffix, ji, is added at the end of a person's name to convey honor and respect. It is never requested, expected, or demanded. It is up to each individual to decide upon addressing someone as such.

As Goenkaji concluded the meditation on loving kindness with a beautiful chant in the Pali language, people began to rise and move toward the front, and when

## Chapter Twelve

reaching close to where Goenkaji and Mataji sat, everyone knelt down on their knees, stretching their arms out with head touching the floor. I followed suit, and I cried like a baby. I don't know why. Many others did the same. It had been such an intense and emotional ten days, sitting in silence, doing nothing but watching your own mind. At the time, I thought we were paying homage to the teacher. But in Buddhist tradition, I would learn, to do so would be considered glorification of the ego; therefore, it is not done. It is to the Dhamma, the Buddha's teachings, we show our veneration.

Over a span of twelve days S.N. Goenka had brought me to a thorough understanding of Buddhism, knowledge I had been attracted to and interested in learning for several years. I simply didn't know where to look. And I had learned a genuine meditation technique at last.

I felt as if the final piece of the puzzle had at long last been found. S.N. Goenka had given me the tools I had been looking for. As he spoke about in his discourses, one must travel the path on the experiential level, not merely on the intellectual level. S.N. Goenka had given me the knowledge to do so. But as I would discover, sticking with a regular meditation practice would prove an undertaking far from easy. It seems the mind will always come up with excuses, if you let it.

I had signed up for the next English language Vipassana meditation course with S.N. Goenka set to begin in six weeks. I would travel north into the Himalayas in the intervening time.

From Igatpuri I traveled first to the former Maharajah Kingdom of Jaipur, capital of the desert state of Rajasthan, the only place in India where camels outnumber cows.

Founded in 1727, Jaipur is renowned for its splendid Maharajah palace and gardens, celebrated for its unique geometric urban design based on astrology and classic ancient Vedic architectural theory, the first planned city in India, but most of all, Jaipur is known as the pink city. During the days of British rule, in honor of the visiting Prince of Wales, later to become King Edward VII, the entire city was painted pink. Much of the city has retained this hue and it is a magical sight to behold.

From Jaipur I traveled to New Delhi. I had lost count how many times I had now been to New Delhi. Surely enough times for the capital of India to feel like home. Delhi would be my jumping off point into the Himalayas, with the Kulu Valley and Dharamsala as my two main destinations. In route I would stop in the former British hill station of Simla, the most popular of the Himalayan mountain resorts established by the British to escape the scorching summer heat of the plains.

Echoes of history followed me, firing up my imagination as I wandered the hilly lanes of Simla. Few places in India have retained as high a level of colonial charm. One could feel them, ghosts of the crown, strolling the promenade in the cool air of twilight at seven thousand feet, she in the latest European fashion, he in polished uniform or in his dandy best.

Many an English girl, during the years of imperial rule, chose setting sail for marriage in faraway colonial outposts, facing sweltering heat, monsoon rains, mosquitoes, malaria, and hard drinking men over a life of monotony in a dismal English town.

In colonial India she would have servants and nannies, a house boy and a cook, at her beck and call, and a husband who, when not engaged in the carrying out of his company's business affairs or his royal obligations as an officer of the crown, spent much of his day getting drunk, as was the favorite pastime of the English, with his compatriots at the British gentleman's club. And she, quite content in his absence, would spend her time sitting under the ceiling fan taking tea and gossiping with her fellow ladies of the Raj.

Imperialism at its best, and yet, I don't know why, but I find the days of British India so intriguing.

From Simla I continued traveling north into the scenic Kulu Valley, to the village of Manali, situated at an altitude of seven thousand feet, on the road to Leh, close to the edge of Kashmir, bounded by magnificent snowcapped Himalayan peaks rising to heights of twenty-two thousand feet.

In the sweet Himalayan village of Manali I sat savoring a bowl of Tibetan noodle soup in a rickety wooden shack with one tiny table and a wood stove, and no room to spare. The proprietors, a Tibetan couple, had no other means of support, and they were so appreciative of what little they had. Every evening of my stay in Manali I would return to their tiny restaurant for a bowl of noodle soup and they were so humbled. And I too was humbled, and I could only wish they knew how much they had taught me.

While hiking the forest surrounding Manali along a gentle mountain river winding through magical Himalayan woodlands, I came across tiny log built hermitages and Hindu shrines hidden deep within the Himalayas. I also encountered a solitary sadhu living in the forest, performing his penances, exposing himself to the elements, sleeping in the cold mountain night. We bowed with hands folded in prayer position and said Namaste.

In the mornings, before embarking upon my mountain hikes, I would go into the village and collect my breakfast. I would make three stops. First, I would buy several bananas from a street vendor. Next, I would buy a disposable clay bowl of yogurt from a shop in the village's small bazaar, and from another shop in the bazaar I would buy several slices of wonderful freshly baked bread, and there, in the shop where I had purchased my bread, I would sit at a wooden table on a wooden bench, take out my camping knife and slice my bananas, a small quantity for my yogurt and a hearty amount to place upon my bread, creating for myself a delicious banana sandwich. But the proprietor became angry with me because I wouldn't buy my yogurt from him. I had good reason. His yogurt was runny. The other guy's yogurt was thick and creamy.

The true source of his anger could have only been the baba who made the better yogurt. Despite his rudeness, I still couldn't stop buying my bread from him. The soft and moist texture of his bread transformed my inventive culinary creation into supreme slices of the tastiest banana bread. No other bread in the village compared. But now I felt uncomfortable sitting in his café, because every morning he would make an annoying comment about the yogurt, so I would take my food into the woods and sit on a rock by the river instead.

This Indian dude could learn a thing or two from the humble Tibetans. I could have continued sitting in his shop, flaunting the delicious thick and creamy yogurt he with so much frustration could not duplicate. Many would have. The entire episode couldn't have been more ridiculous. The guy who made the better yogurt was probably his brother-in-law. And I couldn't help but once again think about how much I loved this land.

In 1950 Communist China invaded and occupied the sovereign Himalayan Kingdom of Tibet, claiming historical rights to the land. Persecution, oppression, and the destruction of an estimated six thousand monasteries, temples, and other religious, cultural, and historic buildings would follow, and many Tibetans would lose their lives. Tibet's ancient Buddhist culture had fallen under threat of extinction.

*Chapter Twelve*

In 1959, followed by an estimated one hundred thousand refugees, the Dalai Lama fled his homeland. They made their way to the Indian border, an arduous and dangerous journey across the vast Himalayan expanse. In a generous overture, the Indian government had extended political refuge, offering the Dalai Lama land in the foothills of the Western Himalayas where he could establish a government in exile.

Led by his Holiness the 14th Dalai Lama, the Tibetan refugees arrived in the former and all but forgotten hill station and British garrison of Dharamsala. The new government in exile would soon find a permanent home in the deserted British settlement of McLeod Ganj, named after a colonial governor, located four kilometers north of Dharamsala at an altitude of six thousand, eight hundred feet.

McLeod Ganj, nicknamed Little Lhasa, after Lhasa, the capital of Tibet, soon developed into an enchanting Tibetan village and would grow into a popular destination for Western travelers. Taking advantage of the opportunities, showing their entrepreneurial talents and willingness to work hard, the Tibetan refugees built guesthouses and hotels to accommodate the steady stream of international backpackers who had begun flowing into their village, while others ran restaurants and quaint cafés serving Tibetan and Indian cuisine, and they learned the preparation of tasty European and American pastries, pies, and cakes, catering to the culinary needs of the wanderers and seekers from the Western world arriving in Little Lhasa to experience the unique charm of the Tibetan people and their precious ancient culture.

Beautiful handcrafted Tibetan garments, exquisite blankets and shawls, decorative Tibetan handicrafts, each piece an instant collector's item in the West, and rare Tibetan art and jewelry, filled the small shops of the

Himalayan hilltop town. Tibetan monks softly strolled the colorful streets. Tibetan prayer wheels graced the village. One could join meditation sittings and spend hours reading books in an extensive Buddhist library, free to the public for all to use. Thanks to the generosity of the Indian Government, preservation of priceless Tibetan culture had been secured.

On occasion, the Dalai Lama welcomes people on the grounds of his residence, a meet and greet, so to speak, and anyone who wishes can shake the Dalai Lama's hand. As I wandered about the town one morning a fellow traveler informed me of one such event taking place as we spoke.

I came upon the Dalai Lama temple complex where his holiness resided. Western travelers stood in line, waiting their turn to shake the Dalai Lama's hand. I joined them, taking my place in the back of the queue. Bodyguards padded people down. Strict security had become an inevitable necessity out of fear the Chinese government wished to assassinate the Dalai Lama.

My turn came. I looked into the Dalai Lama's eyes as he extended his hand, and as he looked into mine, we shook hands, his face aglow with the ever present smile the world has become so accustomed to seeing.

I walked back out to the streets of little Tibet. Wow! I couldn't believe it. I just shook hands with the 14th incarnation of the Tibetan God of compassion, and I did it on his home turf.

Within a short period of time, I found myself in the indisputable presence of two saintly souls, S.N. Goenka and the Dalai Lama, and a third would soon follow.

I couldn't leave India without stopping one last time in Rishikesh, among my all time favorite places in the world. During this stay in Rishikesh I would learn that Anandamayi Ma had taken up residence in her ashram in Hardwar.

## Chapter Twelve

Anandamayi Ma, a contemporary of Paramahansa Yogananda, came into this world in 1896 in East Bengal. I would have the honor of seeing her in 1978. She would leave her body four years later.

Anandamayi Ma began showing uncanny yogic and mystical abilities at a young age. As a little girl, Anandamayi Ma would go into deep meditative trances; dance in spiritual ecstasy; perform yoga poses; chant mantras, and with no formal education she would speak in the words of a fully realized soul. Many considered her an avatar.

I decided to pay the ashram in Hardwar a visit.

I would arrive at the ashram with a few mild dirt stains on my white baggy draw string cotton pajama pants after a dusty train ride from Rishikesh. One of Anandamayi Ma's Indian disciples approached and commented on the condition of my pants.

"You shouldn't come to see the Holy Mother looking this way," he said.

I knew he meant well, disciples are always protective of their gurus, although I doubted the enlightened being I came to see would care one bit.

This wouldn't have happened if your countrymen did a better job of keeping the trains in your country clean, I felt like saying to the bothersome baba, but I held my tongue and apologized instead before slipping out of my flip-flops and entering the ashram.

Anandamayi Ma sat on an elevated platform. Roughly two dozen people, both Indians and Westerners, sat on the floor around her, accepting the holy gift of darshan, the definition of which is as follows: "The beholding of a holy person which bestows spiritual merit upon the beholder."

A deep silence permeated the room. Anandamayi Ma looked at us and we looked at her. She had a kind and gentle smile on her face, as if she were watching children at play. Her eyes were fixed upon us, and yet, at the same time, one could feel she was somewhere else. I almost felt as if she wasn't there at all. Where she was I couldn't say, nor do I think there are or have been too many others who could either. Our group of unevolved mortals sat in silence, absorbing her transcendental energy.

The new season at the beach loomed large over my head. I knew they would fill my spot if I didn't make it back to work by Memorial Day weekend. But I couldn't bear the thought of returning to the Western world just yet, so immersed in the East had I become.

Uncertain thoughts flooded my mind. What would happen if I missed the season? My job at the beach had been my anchor for the past six years. My livelihood and lifestyle had been built around it, in stone. Everything would change if I gave up my waiter job in the summer resort. How else could I make money so fast and still have over half of the year free to travel? But I also knew it would have to end sometime. Truth be told, I had grown weary of waiting tables. But one thought troubled me above all others. What will my life be like when I come off the road for good? I worried I may never feel at one with myself again.

I completed another ten day Vipassana meditation course. Once again I sat at the feet of S.N. Goenka, whom I now considered a living Buddha. And if not, then certainly the closest I've ever come to one. After the meditation course I returned to Bombay. My fourth stay in Krishna's guesthouse. And as did New Delhi, Rishikesh, and Varanasi, Bombay had also begun feeling like home. Nowhere else in all of my travels would I experience such complete feelings of familiarity and home as I would in India.

From Bombay I would embark upon yet another marathon train ride, forty hours, clear across India once again,

## Chapter Twelve

only sideways this time, from the West Coast to the East Coast, instead of from top to bottom, taking me to the city of Madras, India's fourth largest city.

Sri Lanka, known as "the jewel of the Orient," is a small island nation sitting in the Indian Ocean off the Southeastern Coast of India. I had made my decision. I would sail to the island of Sri Lanka and stay there as long as I could. In other words, I would stretch out my stay in the Eastern world until I had only enough money left to get home. I had reached the crossroads. The summer season in the bustling beach resort on Maryland's Eastern Shore would have to carry on without me. I had cast my fate to the wind.

I would spend one night in Madras, now known as Chennai. The British had taken it upon themselves to change the names of a number of Indian cities. In the post colonial era, India had changed them back, including Bombay, now known as Mumbai.

The colorful South Indian city situated on the Bay of Bengal in the state of Tamil Nadu certainly merited a longer stay, but I needed to get myself down to the docks from where the boat to Sri Lanka sets sail before my six month Indian visa expired. One can't see everything. This I learned long ago. But when all is said and done, I believe the record will clearly show I damn well gave it my best.

From Madras I traveled to the small South Indian town of Rameswaram, not quite to the end of India again, but close. From Rameswaram I would board the boat to Sri Lanka. Rameswaram is a holy city, playing a prominent role in the Ramayana, the classic story of Lord Rama's incarnation on Earth.

In the epic ancient tale, the demon Ravana is holding Rama's wife Sita prisoner on the island of Lanka. To rescue her, Lord Rama builds a bridge across the sea from Rameswaram to Lanka, aided by his faithful servant

Hanuman, the monkey God. Among the most beloved of the deities in the Hindu pantheon, Hanuman symbolizes the perfection of loyalty and selflessness. Hanuman's devotion to Lord Rama has no bounds.

Rameswaram is located on Pamban Island. A railroad bridge built over a narrow channel connects Pamban Island to the mainland. This railroad bridge is recognized as an engineering marvel. It is also considered one of the most dangerous railroad bridges in the world. The narrow bridge spans two kilometers, which isn't long at all, but when one is sitting on a moving Indian train in a place that already seems like the outer edges of reality and all one sees front, back, both sides, and below is the Indian Ocean, two kilometers seems like infinity, eternity, and insanity all rolled into one.

Known during the colonial era as Ceylon, the island of Sri Lanka is a short boat ride, about five hours, from Rameswaram. Sri Lanka's population at the time of my visit numbered in the neighborhood of fifteen million. Theravada Buddhists comprise seventy percent of the population. The remaining are Hindu, Muslim, and Christian.

●

When I was a young boy I had a hobby collecting stamps. I would mail order them through advertisements on the backs of comic books. A dollar would buy hundreds of stamps from all over the world. I had several stamps from Ceylon and I remember how enthralled I was by these stamps. No other stamps gave me such feelings of enchantment as did my stamps from Ceylon. Perhaps I felt a magical resonance in the sound of the name. Or perhaps the vibrant images on the face of the stamps, sunny, mystical, and unknown, filled my mind with wonder and caused me to dream. This memory, as if a premonition, has remained vivid in my mind throughout the years, and now I find myself on a boat crossing the Indian Ocean, sailing toward the Island of Ceylon.

I would arrive in the capital city of Colombo after an all night train ride from our ship's point of entry. Upon first impression Sri Lanka looks and feels much the same as India. The differences soon become apparent. Absent were the bearded sadhus and loincloth clad holy men. In their place one saw Buddhist monks in saffron robes strolling about. Absent too were the free wandering sacred cows, and barely visible were the colorful pictures of the Hindu Gods and Goddesses and the celestial abodes in which they reside found covering the walls of almost every home and place of business in India. A remarkable level of cleanliness, order, calmness, and quietude I found noteworthy as well. An enchanting Buddhist version of India, in miniature, is how I can best describe Sri Lanka. And the island's excellent cuisine also included my favorite South Indian specialties, adding to my delight. Sri Lanka would quickly shoot high up on the list of my all time favorite countries.

I gathered information fast along the traveler's grapevine and soon set out for my first destination, the historic hill station town of Kandy, Sri Lanka's last royal capital before surrendering to British rule, tucked away in the island nation's impossibly gorgeous mountainous interior.

Endless heart stopping vistas of lush rolling hills looping, twirling, and tumbling into undreamed of emerald blue valleys and wistful misty meadows aglow in ethereal auras of lavender and lilac will pass before one's eyes, taking the traveler on a spellbinding journey deep into the heart of Sri Lanka's tropical tea plantation country. Deemed among the most picturesque passages on the planet, every moment of the legendary train ride from Colombo to the ancient Kingdom of Kandy will take the voyager's breath away.

Among the many points of interest in Kandy is the renowned Temple of the Tooth. A tooth believed to have belonged to the Buddha is housed within the confines of this most sacred Buddhist shrine.

From the exotic hilltop tea plantation town I headed for Sri Lanka's Eastern seaboard, and there I would plant myself, upon the "jewel of the Orient's" pristine golden sands, in a tiny thatched roof beach front hut, surrounded by welcoming villagers and dozens of adventurous international low budget travelers, spending my final two and a half months on the road in a majestic untouched palm fringed island paradise.

Sri Lankan men would hide amidst the coconut groves watching Western women sun bathing nude on the beach. How excited they must have been when the girls would walk into the ocean, the tropical sun shining down upon their lovely European behinds. And I will not deny I gave a good look too.

On one occasion, after a swim in crystalline island waters glistening in blissful turquoise hue, I came back to my spot on the beach where I had left my South Indian sarong. I ran into a problem. My sarong had gone missing. The beautiful sarongs of South India held high value to a Sri Lankan man, and one of them had obviously run out from the palm groves where he was hiding and stolen mine. I now stood stark naked on the beach. Despite their traditional Eastern values, the locals tolerated the Western travelers sun bathing and swimming in the nude, but I couldn't walk back to the village in the shape I was in, the villagers would be appalled and my fellow travelers would laugh me off the face of the Earth.

I panicked. What am I going to do? This is a nightmare. In a fright, I cast my gaze along the shoreline. Luckily, I spotted a sunbathing European couple within reasonable proximity. I began walking toward them. The Westerners would swim and sun bathe naked, but bodies were covered at all other times, so when they saw me walking toward them full frontal, they were shocked. I told them what had happened. They couldn't stop laughing. I asked the guy if he would lend me his sarong for a few minutes while I went back to my hut. Mercifully, he agreed.

I had been on the road for ten months and what a fitting end to what would not only be my longest journey, but, unbeknownst to me at the time, my last. The little boy with his stamp collection and his dreams of an exotic faraway place called Ceylon.

The month of August moved along and I hadn't returned to my job in the summer resort. Living in paradise upon the heavenly shores of Sri Lanka without a care allowed me to live in the moment more than I ever had, but now, as I prepared to head back to America, the worries over my uncertain future began coming around again.

But first, a more pressing issue faced me. How do I get back to the Western world? I wasn't even sure if my remaining money would get me back to Europe by air. I had four hundred dollars left and I would still need money for the flight from Europe to New York, and from the Big Apple I would still need to purchase a bus ticket back to Baltimore.

The possibility I may be forced to travel back to Europe by land now entered my mind. I began mentally preparing myself to travel clear across India one more time, cross the border into Pakistan and begin the overland journey a second time, in reverse, the thought of which was a bit more than my road weary mind could bear. Thank God the Russians came to my rescue.

Could I fly to London for under three hundred dollars? To my amazement, and it amazes me to this day, but yes, I could. Aeroflot, the Russian airline, offered a two hundred dollar flight, half way around the world, from Sri Lanka to London.

## An Extraordinary Tale of Travel

The Aeroflot flight from Colombo to London was the strangest flight I have ever taken. The stewardesses were shaped like boxes and looked like bull dogs. The meals were white bread sandwiches with some kind of unrecognizable paste on them. And the way they served us, they practically threw the sandwiches at us.

We made a stop to change planes in the Moscow airport; a drab square shaped cheerless building permeating with a dismal aura of bleak, cold war era depressing Communist gray. Food and refreshment were nearly nonexistent and the bathrooms smelled. And these are the people we're so damn worried about? A maddening six hours would pass waiting to board my flight to London.

Upon invitation, I spent another week in London in the home of an English couple I met in Sri Lanka. This time I had my own room. I didn't have to sleep at the foot of their conjugal bed.

I thought about the French girl. I wondered if she was still in London. I hadn't a clue how to get back to her place and I didn't have a phone number. When I arrived home I would find a letter from the French girl among a pile of mail my father had been holding for me. She was still in London and she wanted to see me. Damn! Just my luck. As my return to America drew near, I had stopped having my father forward my mail to me.

It had been six years, pretty much to the day, since I first hitchhiked across America, and I had no thoughts of seeing my traveling days come to an end. But destiny had a different plan for me now, one that would plant my feet firmly to the ground for a long time to come.

The years would pass. From time to time I would talk about the wandering life I once lived, before my children were born. You should write a book, people would say. No easy task, and many years would slip by before I decided to give it a try, and many more would sail past as I sat

*Chapter Twelve*

infinite hours fingers to the keyboard in solitary pursuit of the elusive written word and how to best tell the tale of a little travelin' I done, a long time ago.

www.ingramcontent.com/pod-product-compliance
Lightning Source LLC
Chambersburg PA
CBHW021933290426
44108CB00012B/850